HUMAN DEVELOPMENT AND

Human Development and Political Violence presents an innovative approach to research and practice with young people growing up in the context of political violence. Based on developmental theory, this book explains and illustrates how children and youth interact with environments defined by war, armed conflict, and the aftermath of displacement, poverty, political instability, and personal loss. The case study for this inquiry is a research workshop in three countries and a refugee community of the former Yugoslavia, where youth aged 12 to 27 participated in activities designed to promote their development. The theory-based *Dynamic Story-Telling by Youth* workshop engaged participants as social historians and critics sharing their experiences via narratives, evaluations of society, letters to public officials, debates, and collaborative inquiries. Analyses of these youth perspectives augment archival materials and researcher field notes to offer insights about developmental strategies for dealing with the threats and opportunities of war and major political change. Findings indicate that young people interact with such situations in normative ways.

Colette Daiute is Professor of Psychology and Head of the Ph.D. Program in Developmental Psychology at the Graduate Center, City University of New York. She has published widely on social development, international issues in child and youth development, uses of literacy and technology, and qualitative research methods. Her previous publications include the books *Writing and Computers* (1985), *The Development of Literacy through Social Interaction* (1993), *Narrative Analysis: Studying the Development of Individuals in Society* (2004, co-editor Cynthia Lightfoot), and *International Perspectives on Youth Conflict and Development* (2006, co-editors Zeynep Beykont, Craig Higson-Smith, and Larry Nucci). Professor Daiute has received numerous research grant awards from organizations including the United States Institute of Peace, the Spencer Foundation, the William T. Grant Foundation, the Rockefeller Foundation, the National Council of Teachers of English, Harvard University, and the U.S. government. In addition to teaching in the United States, Colette Daiute has also lectured and organized research workshops internationally, most recently at the University of Warwick (United Kingdom), Pontifícia Universidade Católica do Rio de Janeiro (Brazil), the University of Zagreb (Croatia), the University of Belgrade (Serbia), and the University of Manizales (Colombia).

Human Development and Political Violence

Colette Daiute

The Graduate Center, City University of New York

CAMBRIDGE
UNIVERSITY PRESS

CAMBRIDGE UNIVERSITY PRESS
Cambridge, New York, Melbourne, Madrid, Cape Town, Singapore,
São Paulo, Delhi, Dubai, Tokyo

Cambridge University Press
32 Avenue of the Americas, New York, NY 10013-2473, USA

www.cambridge.org
Information on this title: www.cambridge.org/9780521734387

First published 2010

Printed in the United States of America

A catalog record for this publication is available from the British Library.

Library of Congress Cataloging in Publication data

Daiute, Colette.
Human development and political violence / Colette Daiute.
    p.   cm.
Includes bibliographical references and index.
ISBN 978-0-521-76780-4
1. Youth and violence.   2. Developmental psychology.   3. Life cycle,
Human.   I. Title.
HQ799.2.V56D35   2010
303.60835 – dc22   2009036863

ISBN 978-0-521-76780-4 Hardback
ISBN 978-0-521-73438-7 Paperback

For Jack

CONTENTS

LIST OF FIGURES

LIST OF TABLES

PREFACE

When writing a letter to a public official, Visnja,[1] a young woman whose life has been defined by war, echoes sentiments expressed by many other young people growing up during and after political violence across the world.

> *Hmmm, hmmm, who should I write to? I am 24 years old, and for 10 years already I have problems, I live in them. Who should I talk to, and who would be open to listening to the "complaints of the youth" and take them seriously? Everyone is shaking their head for 10 years already, the old guard politicians are still shaking their heads, and they tell us 'it will be better.' . . . Yeah, right!*[2]

Comments like Visnja's implore those of us who work with young people to learn more about how they perceive environments of armed conflict and its aftermath. Toward that end, the goal of the research discussed in this book was to interact with young people involved in practical activities to gain insights about the development of individuals and society. With an innovative theoretical approach, we ask, "How do young people growing up in political violence understand their plight?"

In spite of our advances, civilization at the beginning of the 21st century continues to be characterized by political violence, which is experienced by increasing numbers of young people (Barber, 2009;

---

[1] All young people's names are pseudonyms.
[2] Texts and talk by youth are translations when not originally in English.

Boyden, 2009). Like many of her peers aged 12 to 27 years across a region fractured by wars during the 1990s, Visnja notices that the views of youth are not taken seriously amidst the din of political conflict and inertia. That Visnja's frustration verges on sarcasm is all the more understandable given the recent international recognition of children's rights, support for youth civic engagement, and child-oriented projects like the Millenium Development Goals, 2015 (www.unicef.org/mdg).

With more than 40 nations at war and many others struggling with insurgencies, the effects on children and youth are an urgent concern. Nevertheless, research and practice have focused quite narrowly on psychopathology and social reproduction, especially among young people directly involved in and exposed to acute phases of violence, such as child soldiers, witnesses to death and assaults, and refugee orphans in camps. Because the effects of war persist long after fighting has officially ended – on average, at least seven years (Collier, 2003), an entire generation if not more is subject to myriad consequences, including displacement, poverty, homelessness, exploitation, political instability, interrupted education, unhealthy living conditions, discrimination, and a lack of resources for "youthful pleasures," as one teenager in our study lamented. To account for the broad reach of political violence across space and time, a developmental approach is long overdue.

Although millions of children's lives are defined by political violence, we know little about what young people notice, what matters to them, what challenges and opportunities they perceive, or how they draw on resources to deal with those circumstances in their everyday lives. How do bombing, death of loved ones, interruption of schooling, and loss of friends who had to flee figure into their attention, explanations, and goals? Although most youth are concerned about unemployment, for example, they also appreciate free time for spontaneous and caring relationships, even if they have that freedom because "there's nothing else to focus on but hedonism," as one youth commented. Defining development as the mutual interaction of individuals in society, we can usefully focus on the perspectives of children and youth whose ideas elders have marginalized. Marginalization sometimes occurs to protect young people, such as from learning about the horrors committed by neighbors during war; sometimes to protect society, such as from facing responsibility for recruiting children to fight; or to serve other ends, such as excluding minorities from participation.

"Human development" and "political violence" do not seem to belong together. It is, for example, difficult to believe that humans as advanced as we are in some ways still resort to violence as a political strategy. When we think about young lives, it is, moreover, difficult to believe that children could possibly develop well in the context of armed conflict and the consequences that follow. At the same time, we know that development turns on the uniquely human capacities of language, thought, and creativity, which children learn early to use for their benefit, and thus could apply to chaotic and impoverished situations. The potential of considering such cultural development (Vygotsky, 1978) to explain the consequences of political violence in children's everyday lives is enormous, albeit untapped. The former Yugoslavia is an appropriate case study for such inquiry not only because of the recent, tragic nature of its dissolution but also because a generation born in one country is now growing up in separate countries and experiencing very different environmental, political, economic, and social circumstances. With this case study, we consider adolescents making transitions to adulthood in nations making political transitions from war to peace and from communist dictatorships to capitalist democracies.

Given the tensions and dangers in contexts of political violence, taking young people seriously, as Visnja urges, is not simply a matter of interviewing them. Human development involves participation in purposeful activities, so it makes sense to elicit youth perspectives in realistic contexts. Participation is, for example, subject to requirements such as the preferred story to tell about the war, tensions such as conflicts between honoring parents' sacrifices, orienting toward one's own goals for a better future, and dealing with public pressures to avoid stories that could represent a country in a negative light internationally. Taking young people seriously requires employing research tools that address such realities in their everyday lives, the realities of interacting with other people, institutions, the environment, and their own thoughts. Developmental inquiry must, therefore, occur within the context of meaningful practical activities.

I wrote this book to integrate theory, research, and practice relevant to child and youth development in extremely challenging circumstances, so I imagine audiences working with diverse goals from diverse disciplinary perspectives. A primary audience is researchers and students who are interested in whether and how diverse challenges affect human development. Educators and program developers are a major audience, as they consider issues of context and developmental processes for designing and implementing programs in extremely challenging situations. My hope is that adults and young people working with youth in schools, community centers, and clinical practice also find a perspective and information that are useful to their activities. This practice-based approach, moreover, offers a new way to design research in situations requiring intervention. When I argue that we consider the normative nature of growing up in crisis situations, I do not imply that political crisis is optimal or acceptable as a developmental context, but that we must understand the full range of interactions to design research, practice, and policy.

The research for this book involved immersion in interdisciplinary studies of the effects of war on children and youth, accounts of the 1990s' wars in the former Yugoslavia, and ethnographic work with nongovernmental organizations (NGOs), educational institutions, independent scholars, and young people. Some of the archival research, for example, focused on the organizers, goals, and activities of programs devoted to youth development across the region, in particular peace education programs sponsored by numerous institutions including the European Union; the Council of Europe; Ministries of Education, Science, and Sport; Human Rights Centers; academic and outreach programs at universities; school systems; and NGOs working closely with children and families. The empirical phase of the study involved creating a workshop curriculum consistent with programs I had observed, implementing this *Dynamic Story-Telling by Youth* research workshop with young people, and analyzing young people's work to learn about their views.

ORGANIZATION OF THE BOOK

Chapter 1 reviews previous approaches to studying the effects of human-made crises, concluding that what is missing is a developmental approach. Chapter 2 offers a theoretical and methodological rationale for this developmental approach based on principles of cultural–historical activity theory, bringing these theoretical premises to life with practices in the *Dynamic Story-Telling by Youth* workshop, which serves as a context for the basic research about development in violence.

Chapters 3 through 6 present young people's perspectives on conflict as it has affected various aspects of their lives and goals for the future. We learn from those chapters how young people use cultural tools, such as narrating, to manage (mediate) personal and societal relations, as would their peers in more mundane contexts. Chapter 3 explains that young people can echo their specific national scripts but also that these scripts are living history evolving in relation to current circumstances rather than the frozen narratives of war. Chapter 4 reveals the particularly contentious local knowledge that emerges as young participants shift positions of social–relational discourse. Chapter 5 focuses on youth participation in their communities as an important site of self and societal development. Chapter 6 focuses on "sociobiographies," individual variations within and across the diverse national psyches identified in Chapters 3 and 4. Chapter 7 zooms out from our illustrative case study to suggest implications for human development research, practice, and policy in other regions plagued by political conflict and transition.

ACKNOWLEDGMENTS

Because the project discussed in this book builds on my previous research, I feel as though I have been nurturing it along for a long time, in a most focused way since 2001, when I broadened my focus on social development in conflict from United States to international contexts in which children are experiencing major challenges to their well-being and development. This current research reaching from Serbia in the East to New York in the West has, of course, involved the support of generous foundations, organizations, and individuals. Support for the journey to the former Yugoslavia came first from the Rockefeller Foundation Bellagio Center, which supported my transitional research for an international conference to shift the study of child and youth conflict from a primarily biological one to a more integrated bio-socio-behavioral analysis. That project resulted in the volume *International Perspectives on Youth Conflict and Development* (Oxford University Press, 2006) involving coeditors Larry Nucci, Craig Higson-Smith, and Zeynep Beykont and chapter authors from across seven continents, to whom I am indebted for their insights and collaboration. More recently, I am grateful to the United States Institute of Peace, the National Council of Teachers of English, the PSC-CUNY Research Fund, and the Graduate Center of the City University of New York for grants that made this transnational research possible. The ideas, conclusions, and suggested implications herein are mine and not those of these supporting organizations, but I hope these organizations find the work useful, persuasive, and indicative for future agendas.

Several scholarly institutes made it possible for me to engage in the interdisciplinary conversations required for this approach to transnational child and youth development in armed conflict. During my work on this project, colleagues at seminars at several gathering places involved me in their activities and patiently listened to a developmental psychologist, not typically at their table: The Harriman Institute at the Columbia University School for International Affairs, where I spent my sabbatical as a Visiting Scholar analyzing data and writing drafts; The Institute of Advanced Study at the University of Warwick, where I was a Visiting Fellow discussing material from several chapters; and the Center for Place, Culture, and Politics and the Center for the Humanities, both at the Graduate Center of the City University of New York, where participation in seminars on war, violence and political change introduced me to literature and debates in political science, philosophy, history, geography, and English. Opportunities to present preliminary analyses at the University of Zagreb and the University of Belgrade were also essential to my being able to progress from analyzing the rich reflections by young people to writing about them in a way that communicates across contexts.

Administrators, youth advocates, and young people at several NGOs participated in the project in a range of ways by inviting me to observe their activities or participating in the research. Among many other activities, these colleagues discussed the ongoing needs of youth across the region, commented on and translated materials, recruited participants, led workshops, and hosted me and my research assistants. NGOs involved in various phases along the way include RACOON in the United States, Suncokret and Globus in Croatia, Group Most in Serbia, Prism Research and Krila Nade in Bosnia and Herzegovina, and the Bosnian Bakery in the United States. Individuals in these organizations who deserve my sincere gratitude include Maja Turniski, Mei Eldorazdi, Dragan Popodic, Rada Gosovic, Dino Djepa, Snjeziana Kojic Hasanajic, Lejla Kadic, and Indira Kajosevic, among others. I am also extremely grateful to research assistants, especially Luka Lucic, for relevant conversations, data-analysis contributions, helping with the workshops translations, and coauthorship on related studies; to Danielle Delpriore and Vicky Barrios for their assistance in coding; and to Nikolina Knezivic, Dean Valutec, and Maja Turniski for translations. Very special thanks to Maja Turniski, who first invited me to Croatia, where I observed her important work with Predrag Mraovic and an amazing group of young people who were hopeful, creative, and loving while growing up in difficult circumstances.

Many thanks to Sarah W. Freedman, Alexander Motyl, Merry Bullock, and Jerome Bruner for their time, wisdom, and critical and encouraging comments on the draft of this manuscript. Their close readings provided an invaluable sense of audience for the final manuscript and the basis for ongoing conversations. I am also grateful to Simina Calin for her astute editorial guidance. Thanks to Jack Wright for his assistance with the manuscript. The encouragement of Doris and Joseph Daiute forever has been essential to staying with this large and long-term project.

Finally, but not least, to Visnja and the other young people who participated so generously in this study and activities leading up to it, I offer my thanks and respect not only for your plights but also for the dignity with which you have weathered them. My sincere hope is that if you read this book, you think that I listened to you, took you seriously, and got it right.

FIGURE 1.1. Caught between decay and future.

1

Beyond the *Youth Gap* in Understanding
Political Violence

Youth are never taken seriously, and we sometimes have ideas that would be good for all people.
                    Alex, Croatia

...Some things do depend on us; war, consequences of the war, poverty; the influence of the church interfering with the state affairs, which must not be so.
                    Ljubicia, Serbia

As we hear in these comments by two teenagers who have grown up in the shadow of political violence, their generation is aware of the past and its legacies. These brief quotes mention many details that young people in easier situations may not notice: "consequences of the war," "the influence of the church interfering with the state affairs," youth responsibility for the future ("some things do depend on us"), and their capacity to contribute to the benefit of society ("we sometimes have ideas that would be good for all people"). These reflections echo the letter we read by Visnja in the Preface, pointing out, ironically, that youth perspectives are usually ignored: "Who would be open to listening to the 'complaints of youth' and take them seriously?" On the other hand, those in power are stymied about how to create a future: "The old guard politicians are still shaking their heads, and they tell us 'it will be better'. . . . Yeah, right!" Scholars have contributed information about children and youth as the objects of study in situations of political violence, but the literature has offered little from the perspectives of young people themselves.

Previous research and practice have focused, in particular, on two types of responses by young people growing up during or after armed conflict: pathology and risk. After a brief review of these approaches, I discuss the need for inquiry into youth perspectives on political violence to fill the remaining gap in research and practice.

HOW DO YOUNG PEOPLE RESPOND TO POLITICAL VIOLENCE?

Research and practice on the human effects of political violence have increased in the past decade. Young people, especially in developing countries, are the major group affected by violence (www.unhcr.org), so assessing the costs to them is important. Children are, after all, vulnerable to and inheritors of situations created by others. Consistent with such reasoning, representations of *child* and *youth* in scholarly and practical discourse evoke images of victims, potential villains, or both. To examine the prevalence of those representations, I did a computer search of the phrases "child/youth armed conflict" and "child/youth political violence" in a social science database of articles from 1983 through 2008, and I noted how the young person was

described. The search indicated that 65 percent of the relevant cita-
tions portrayed the figure of the young person in terms of war-related
damage and concerns about cycles of violence.

The Damage Response

The following e-mail message from a male teenager in Bosnia and
Herzegovina (BiH) suggests the overwhelming focus on psychopathology as a response to war. Once an esoteric medical diagno-
sis, post-traumatic stress disorder (commonly referred to as "ptsd")
is available for war-related humor.

> *Dear Friends, I'm sorry for not coming to the meeting. can't get
> out of bed, that old ptsd acting up again!!!!!!!! Ha ha ha ha ha!!!!!!
> From D.*

In this e-mail to his supervisor and peers at a community center, D.
uses "ptsd acting up again" as an excuse for not being able to "get out
of bed," obviously playing, "!!!!, Ha ha ha ha ha," with the overuse of
what is sometimes a result of exposure to violence. Along with similar
examples in my field notes, this message hints at the overuse of medical
explanations for responses to war, in particular war-related damage
to the young. Suggested by D.'s humorous approach, such terms have
become commonplace in lay discourse.

More than 41 percent of the articles in the database of relevant
scholarly literature on political violence represents children as victims. Terms like *ptsd, depression,* and *anxiety* are common, with or
without scientific measures designed to assess those disorders. Medical language, including *suffering, vulnerability, helplessness, behavior
problems,* and the need for *healing,* appears widely in research and program reports. Terms for antisocial personal traits, like *aggressiveness,
victims, internalizers,* and *externalizers,* are also prevalent. Research
has identified damage to functional systems, including moral deficits,

such as to child soldiers who have been forced to kill (Posada & Wainryb, 2008), and lack of perspective-taking abilities among those who may be repressing traumatic memories as perpetrators or victims. Because imagining, considering, and empathizing with the perspectives of others are major sociocognitive capacities (Damon, Lerner, & Eisenberg, 2006), assessments of these processes are relevant to development in situations of violence. This figure of the child as victim is, furthermore, consistent with the consideration of interpersonal effects such as *abuse, bullying, forced migration, sexual exploitation, abduction,* and *child labor.*

Researchers have explained that psychopathological responses like ptsd occur but are overdetermined (Bonanno, 2004). Although the medical definition of ptsd includes thoughts and behaviors that disrupt normal activity and social relations for up to 6 months, researchers and practitioners apply it across much longer time spans. Even when applying concepts like ptsd correctly, research indicates that the disorder occurs less than once reported (Bonanno, 2004; Inter-Agency Standing Committee [IASC], 2007; Summerfield, 1999), suggesting a need to study resilience (Barber, 2009; Boyden, 2003). Those citing the overattribution of psychosocial damage have urged researchers to broaden their inquiry beyond acute phases of violence to the devastating residual effects across time and space (Boyden & Mann, 2005; Daiute & Turniski, 2005; IASC, 2007).

Representations of vulnerability and psychopathology have practical implications. Knowledge about the nature and course of violence-related trauma and developmental deficits is useful to clinicians (Apfel & Simon, 1996). At the same time, explanations emphasizing vulnerability could promote passivity, in part because such responses garner financial and political support (McMahon, 2009). Scholars have also proposed that focusing on youth victimization and risk may be consistent with government efforts to negate political activism by children involved in violence, such as when they participate on the frontlines of battle (Boyden, 2009) or when they protest against violence and injustice (Daiute, 2009a). Although contributing insights for therapy, focusing on damage to individuals reduces the analysis of political violence to the relatively narrow scope of *intra*personal processes. Political violence is, however, an activity that occurs over a broad range of actors, spaces, and time. Broadening inquiry to address this complex nature of violence can complement prior research.

Cycles of Violence

The other major representation of the young person in situations of armed conflict is one of potential villain, either directly or as a result of having been a victim. Twenty-four percent of the articles about effects of political violence on children and youth represent children and especially youth as potential villains (9%) or victims at risk for becoming villains (15%). Mentions of *risk, prevention, perpetrator, child soldier, rehabilitation, neo-Nazi,* and *ethnic hatred* express this view.

An implicit idea behind this view is that children internalize the beliefs, values, and practices of their societies, families, and like-minded peers. In situations of political violence, older people exhibit actions and subjectivities that socialize young people to their ways. Often referred to as *social reproduction,* this phenomenon is mentioned in sociological research, some anthropological research, and psychological research emphasizing the enculturation of a child into society via collective memories of violence and the practices of ethnic cultures.

At the same time that such deficits are imposed on children and youth, adults in their societies express the need to protect young people from the horrors of the past, which, in turn, results in reducing conversations about history. Explanations based on views about social reproduction focus on causes and effects of violence as inevitable sequences of events, such as a history of animosity among people of different ethnic groups sharing the same spaces and resources. When we assume a broader political perspective, we realize, however, that such views reduce the analysis, such as to ethnic hatred in the former Yugoslavia. Most simply stated, even children growing up during the 1990s wars point out that if their parents and grandparents had lived with Serbs, Croats, Bosnians, Catholics, Muslims, and others peacefully for nearly a half century, why, all of a sudden, did they have to fight and kill one another? Resonant with that question, numerous detailed political analyses document the exploitation of ethnic differences and tensions by leaders who were economically motivated to fracture the loosely integrated republics of Yugoslavia (Gagnon, 2004; MacDonald, 2002; Silber & Little, 1995; Woodward, 1995).

An assumption related to concern about cycles of violence is that children grow by internalizing past history. Implying this view are comments by parents who are reluctant to answer their children's questions about the past for fear that stories about the war will harm the children and, perhaps, their own image as parents (Freedman & Abazovic, 2006). Also, despite arguments for reconciliation after inter-group conflict, there are fears that narrating violent events could easily ignite emotions, fueling ongoing cycles of violence. Such formulations imply that learning is a one-way process from adults to children rather than *inter*-action in everyday activities. Assumptions that young people internalize the views of the previous generation are consistent with an emphasis on the passing along of master narratives or dominant discourses (Salomon, 2004). In accordance with such logic, research and practice have explored interventions designed to overcome or prevent past animosities, for example, by promoting positive social–relational understandings and perspective taking.

The social-reproduction explanation, like the focus on damage, defines the problem within the individual. Analyses that focus on an

individual life course, for example, tend to consider a child's exposure to violence, protections from such exposure, antidotes to it, and
a child's own inclination to become violent. Evidence for such cycles
of violence exists, but researchers continue to debate the nature and
extent of the explanation that violence begets violence in any predictable way (Boyden, 2003; Widom, 1989). Research has broadened
from examining cause-and-effect cycles within families, neighborhoods (Earls & Carlson, 1999), and cultures (Ware, 2006). Within
this latter line of research, the focus is on individual young people's
behavior measured in outcomes like fighting, school delinquency,
expulsions, criminal offenses, intergroup conflicts, group identity,
self-esteem, and other factors related to living in low-income, ethnically diverse neighborhoods. Similar studies contribute information
about ecologies of violence, but explanations could also focus on
young people's reasoning about the circumstances of violence surrounding them or their goals. Cultures develop systems of meaning, which may include rationales for violence (Barber, 2009), so the
dynamic nature of meaning systems warrants further inquiry in the
increasingly volatile global situation. In political–economic revolu-
tions, in particular, young people cannot simply follow in their elders'
footsteps because so much has changed since parents, teachers, and
older siblings interacted with former regimes in education, the media,
and public life.

Political changes, such as holding fair elections and allowing
media independence in former dictatorships, are imposed without
precedents or role models, a situation that is especially acute in the
postwar Western Balkan nations gradually entering the European
Union (EU). Although EU economic standards for candidate nations
present incentives and hope, political requirements, such as turning over war criminals, affect young people who are aware of being
associated with violence in their country. Diverse pressures apply to
youth interacting internationally (such as on the Internet) and during migration or other travel. For example, Serbians face prejudice

for the crimes of Slobodan Milosevic, Croatians face ties with the Third Reich in World War II, and refugees face double threats from Americans who resent their immigrant status and from Bosnians at home who may resent their having abandoned the homeland in crisis.

Along with important information about the damaging effects of war, postwar transitions, and related consequences, we need to know how young people make sense of circumstances like displacement, political–economic instability, and lack of infrastructure, especially as those circumstances impact adolescent transitions to adulthood. To learn about the developmental nature of growing up in environments defined by political violence, we can usefully shift the perspective away from assumptions about damage and fear to inquire with young people about how they perceive their situations. In other words, we can take young people "seriously" to learn about the legacies of war that matter in their lives, the factors that "depend on them," and their "ideas that could help all people."

THE NEED FOR YOUTH PERSPECTIVES

As suggested in the quotations at the beginning of this chapter, young people feel the need to express their knowledge about society and the need to be heard by those in power. This need is supported by other academic and practical sources.

Of the articles about the effects of armed conflict on the young, 19 percent point to a broadening away from the damage and reproduction models. Approximately 13 percent of the reports define children's roles in terms of broader sociopolitical issues, and 5.9 percent analyze conflict in terms of young people's understandings about effects. Survey research has, for example, offered information about young people's attitudes and activities (Kovac-Cerovic, Popadic, Knezevic, & Matkovic, 2006; Popadic, 2000; Srna, 2005), providing foundations for in-depth inquiry into the complexities of these views. This shift to

more active representations of young people is clearly worth explo-
ration, but it requires new theory and methods.

Research on the useful employment of young people in contexts
of armed conflict has begun to show, for example, that serving in the
field as medics and cooks offers stable institutions, education, and
opportunities for productive and, in some ways, protective activity to
children who are bereft of their parents (Honwana & De Boeck, 2005;
Sta. Maria, 2006). Although the powerful in society create and allow
seeds of violence to grow, young people caught up in those situations
become the focus of blame as members of *youth gangs* exacerbating
violence. Ethnographic research in the oil-rich delta region of Nigeria
shows, in contrast, that some of those same youth labeled *gang members* develop strategies for dealing in socially conscious ways with
the competing motivations of local leaders to comply with multinational corporations and the need for local control over precious
natural resources (Akinwumi, 2006; Ukeje, 2006). Such observations
have led to interest in learning about how children and youth engage
developmentally in conflict.

Shifting the focus from youth subject to subjectivity is imperative
for creating analyses of violence that integrate individual and societal
development. Young people's interpretations of their environments
can provide a foundation for education, community development,
and international relations, because those views not only provide a
way for educators and leaders to connect with young people but also
contribute insights about orientations and goals that could influence public sentiment in the future. Other rationales include young
people's desire to speak, their awareness of self-determination rights,
and their capacity to understand the challenges and opportunities in
contemporary realities. Such youth perspectives are not completely
separate from those of their elders or the goals of the state but are
likely to be unique in how they link the past and the future from the
perspective of present experiences.

Studying young people's perspectives requires a different paradigm for considering the effects of political violence. Both damage and social-reproduction models assume that political violence is an interruption in some natural course of events. Instead, as we see in the situation of the former Yugoslavia and other contemporary societal transformations, war changes society dramatically and, consequently, the circumstances of development with which the postwar generation interacts. In the former Yugoslavia, for example, adults and older youth once lived within a communist dictatorship now separated into distinct, emerging capitalist democracies. Even though the "old guard politicians" are still in power, as Visnja stated, many postwar institutions like education, civil society, and government are creating democratic practices, like voting, if not complete democratic philosophies. Young people have firsthand knowledge of the new practices and probably experience contemporary circumstances more openly than adults who speak for them based on knowledge and ideology from the previous system. Although it is clear that war can cause psychological as well as physical damage, the idea that individuals or states heal after a war may not be what actually happens with the passing of time. Similarly, fears about the passing along of hatreds that fueled the war and, for some, that justified committing atrocities, may be exaggerated because the prewar mentalities have changed.

Given political, economic, and social changes, the postwar generation is also likely to develop unique goals based, in part, on the fact that they cannot rely on realities of the communist past, such as guaranteed access to health care and, in part, on the fact that their future is tied to participation in Europe and the wider world. The transformed political system, rituals of daily life, and goals for the future across ex-Yugoslavia, as in other dramatically changing societies, warrant eliciting young people's perspectives about the state of the society and the effects of the war.

A major innovation for young people growing up at the beginning of the 21st century, especially in newly formed and developing states, is children's rights. Although the design and implementation of children's-rights treaties are not perfect, there is growing consensus that young people's views must be sought and considered, at least in matters affecting them. The frustration expressed in the quotations about adults not taking young people seriously occurs in light of the stalled promise of Article 12 of the United Nations Convention on the Rights of the Child (UNCRC) and attests to the ongoing youth gap in scholars' understandings of political violence. Especially relevant to young people's critiques, the UNCRC was ratified at a time of major geopolitical reorganization related to the demise of the Soviet Union in 1989 and the rise of new forms of globalization. In addition to numerous other rights, including those protecting children from participation in war, the UNCRC underscores children's right to self-determination (albeit qualified) as one among 53 other rights declared in the UNCRC, as follows:

Article 12
1. States Parties shall assure to the child who is capable of forming his or her own views the right to express those views freely in all matters affecting the child, the views of the child being given due weight in accordance with the age and maturity of the child.

2. For this purpose, the child shall in particular be provided the opportunity to be heard in any judicial and administrative proceedings affecting the child, either directly, or through a representative or an appropriate body, in a manner consistent with the procedural rules of national law. (UNCRC, 1989; www.un.org)

The UNCRC has led to some successful interventions in extreme cases of child abuse, such as programs to demobilize child soldiers (www.crin.org). The treaty has also spawned numerous initiatives for children's participation in community development programs (Hart, 1999). More research is required, however, to learn about the issues, institutions, and individuals that young people perceive as limiting their right to self-expression and development. A poignant example of the wisdom of young people in war-affected areas is their resistance to certain impositions by the EU related to education reform in the newly formed Western Balkan states. Numerous comments by young people acknowledge that adults in charge of education reforms rely, for example, on outdated standards of the socialist education system, resulting in abstract applications of democracy rather than practical ones (Spajic-Vrkas, 2003a; & b). Many of these young people raised during the war have fresh ideas as witnesses to violence and as participants in international relief organizations and popular culture. Although they are not without skepticism about democracy, contemporary generations are well aware of the contrast between the old and the new in their rapidly transforming societies.

A DEVELOPMENTAL ANALYSIS TO FILL THE *YOUTH GAP* IN RESEARCH AND PRACTICE

An alternative view to the figure of child as victim or potential villain is a developmental view. A developing child is not only subject to surrounding forces but is also actively weighing various options. As suggested in the following quote by a scholar making sense of political change at the beginning of the 20th century, human development also involves persuasion.

> *Persuasive discourse – as opposed to one that is externally authoritarian – is, as it is affirmed through assimilation, tightly interwoven with "one's own word." In the everyday rounds of our consciousness, the internally persuasive word is half ours and half someone else's.... It is not so much interpreted by us as it is further, that is, freely, developed, applied to new material....* (Bakhtin, 1935/1981, p. 345)

In this view, societal change depends on what is "persuasive" to people, including to young people. Rather than repeating past "authoritarian" discourse completely, young people "interweave" their perceptions and needs as they interact with others in the circumstances where they find themselves in their everyday realities, where they develop "new material" from unique perspectives in history. Such living history can complement responses like trauma and repetition of a violent past. Although not directly applied to explain development in political violence, this dynamic view of an individual in society is one that we can usefully apply to understand the normative realities for many young people at the beginning of the 21st century.

Filling the gap in scholarly knowledge requires redefining the problem in terms of social–relational complexity. Societies positioned differently around conflicts interact with one another in complex ways, as do individuals in those diverse contexts who must engage with the multiple diverse meanings circulating in times of change. Rather than reducing the analysis to cause and effect, we consider relations within and among groups and individuals relative to a broader political system, as suggested in cultural–historical activity theory (also referred to as sociohistorical theory and sociocultural theory). This developmental analysis asks, "How do youth growing up in environments experiencing political violence and transition interact with the circumstances where they find themselves? On what do they focus? What sense do they make of events? Toward what goals do young people direct their energies?" Addressing these questions requires defining youth perspectives as context-sensitive, that is, organized in terms of goals and obstacles. While more purely maturational theories explain children's abilities as gradually turning toward society (Piaget, 1968), the theory guiding this inquiry assumes goal-based orientations from the earliest interactions, when human babies and their caregivers attend jointly to relevant animate and inanimate objects in the world (Nelson, 2003; Tomasello, 2005; Vygotsky, 1978). As children venture out to the playground, school, and broader community, their involvement with sociopolitical issues increases. For this reason, educators and civil-society activists should involve young people with history, which rarely happens: "after widespread violent conflict, some societies suspend the teaching of history because they cannot achieve consensus on how and what to teach" (Cole & Barsalou, 2006, p. 1). Human development research likewise must inquire into young people's participation in the complex systems required to understand past, present, and future events.

WHAT IS DEVELOPMENTAL ABOUT POLITICAL VIOLENCE AND TRANSITION?

Organizations like the United Nations (UN), United Nations High Commission on Refugees (UNHCR), the World Health Organization (WHO), human rights groups, and others that monitor violence imply that violence is a system. This insight from the policy world is the analysis of issues related to armed conflict in terms of institutions like "countries" and "staff" rather than only in terms of individuals. The following posting by the UNHCR, for example, reports on displacement (a major effect of political violence) as a unit of analysis beyond the individual, country, and region: "Today, a staff of around 6,300 people in more than 110 countries continues to help 3.9 million persons" (www.unhcr.org/basics.html, February 9, 2009). Although it may seem obvious to policy makers and political scientists, analyzing conflict beyond the individual is new for many who focus on human development in conflict. The concept "political-violence system" is useful for considering conflict in relation to social change.

Building on this view, we define the effects of political conflict as distributed across relatively broad space–time relationships. That is, our definition of *psychosocial activity* locates the dynamics of knowing, feeling, and goal making as interactions among people, groups, and institutions in specific places. Drawing on cultural–historical activity theory, this analysis integrates the orientation of political scientists, sociologists, and anthropologists who analyze political violence in relation to broad causes and effects among institutions and political elites (Honwana & De Boeck, 2005). The orientation could usefully become more typical of psychologists, educators, and community organizers who focus on children.

This cultural–historical analysis considers the development of youth in society as mutually persuasive discourses (Bakhtin, 1935/ 1981). Everyone works, to some extent, with authoritarian discourses promoted by the state and cultural mores as applied to everyday realities that individuals perceive as important. If an authoritarian discourse persuades a 40-year-old man to deliver a death threat to a neighbor of a different religion who was reluctant to leave town during the war, that man is likely to perceive with animosity the expelled neighbor's family returning to claim their house after the war. By contrast, the man's teenage daughter and son are persuaded by a postwar authoritarian discourse of social inclusion promoted at school and in the community center. From that perspective, children and teenagers are curious, if not enthusiastic, about new young neighbors, even those from a different ethnic group or religion. While for adults, the returning neighbor's family dredges up bad memories, perhaps guilt and other negative emotions, for the children there is a sense of excitement about an expanded social scene and signs of life to render less creepy a house that lay broken down and vacant for as long as they can remember.

Building on this idea that multiple, sometimes conflicting discourses interact in differing persuasive ways, we have the basis for a developmental analysis that is interactive rather than predetermined. Applying these ideas to a case study of a political-violence system involves a new analytic perspective to address new questions about human development during and after armed conflict. Complementing the prior focus on individual units of analysis based on the figure of victim, potential villain, or cycles of both, we broaden to sociopolitical analyses that integrate old, new, authoritarian, and persuasive discourses across changing societies. An alternative approach to focusing on individuals' damage requires broadening to a political system.

CASE STUDY ACROSS A POLITICAL-VIOLENCE SYSTEM

For a century now, scholars building on the sociohistorical theories of Vygotsky, Leont'ev, and Luria have worked to explain how individuals' minds, personalities, and identities are social rather than self-contained and naturally unfolding. "Activity theory is an integrated approach to the human sciences that . . . takes the object-oriented, artifact mediated collective activity system as the unit of analysis, thus bridging the gulf between the individual subject and the societal structure" (Engestrom, Miettinen, & Punamaki, 1999). "If a collective activity system is taken as the unit, history may become less manageable, and yet it steps beyond the confines of individual biography" (Engestrom, 2009, p. 26). This means that when we study individuals, their lives, their understandings of their lives, and the connection of individual lives to one another, we must consider them in interaction. For this reason, we design research so we can examine how activities embody relationships.

In a situation of political violence, an activity system involves meaning-making about the causes, manifestations, and consequences of a crisis affecting the social and physical environmental system and individuals within it. Beginning with the premise that children interact with the environments where they grow up, a research design must account for people, events, and meanings that are persuasive in the contemporary situation. This means focusing on what matters to young people growing up in different positions across time (born before, during, or after a war), geopolitical location (different postwar countries), and goals (analyzing problems in society, expressing one's personal experience, and engaging in other purposeful activities).

The former Yugoslavia is fascinating as a developmental system because the youth generation was born in the country of Yugoslavia, experienced wars that broke it apart, and now lives across numerous countries, some oriented toward Western Europe, others eastward toward Mecca, and still others positioned between alliances to Russia and the EU. Unlike other political separations in the region, such as the Czech and Slovak Republics, violence characterized the breakup of Yugoslavia, which exacerbates developmental problems and possibilities for the transitional generation orienting toward adulthood. Tensions within this system organize people's everyday lives. By extending beyond individual sites, groups, and countries, we seek to identify the tensions not only in terms of individual subjectivities but also in terms of salient goals and opportunities in each context. Working with youth organizations across the system, we ask young people what is on their minds rather than assume that they are damaged, dangerous, or holding onto collective memories of the past. The government and other elite actors must create political systems for democracy and stability, but their work depends in large part on knowledge of the generation growing up with the new systems.

The political system of the former Yugoslavia is neither naturally occurring nor necessarily functioning as a political unit, in part because migration and displacement continue to occur across the region. Tensions defining distinctions across the system include, for example, that the 1990s wars occurred but that the origins, causes, stakes, and consequences differ depending on where one is currently standing. Disagreements about what happened, who was right, who is suffering most, and so forth are played out in local and national public spaces: in the International Criminal Tribunal for the former Yugoslavia (ICTY), in neighborhoods, in the media, in places of worship, and in private conversations among family and friends. In addition, societies and individuals across the former Yugoslavia have different material and psychosocial positions within their local contexts.

A detailed account of the wars is beyond the scope of this book, but the timeline in Figure 1.2 provides information related to inquiry about the effects of war as a developmental process. Events, places, and actors involved in the geopolitical project of Yugoslavia and the resulting states are integrated as a developmental system.

Figure 1.2 presents a timeline with dimensions of the political-violence system of the former Yugoslavia that are likely to affect young people growing up in this system. This figure depicts major settings and events across time and space. Those listed in the first four columns become meaningful, as discussed by 137 case-study participants during several years of activities across four countries of this system. After the rationale and description of the political-violence system presented in this chapter, subsequent chapters focus, first, on young people's participation to create living history from their perspectives during the second half of 2007 then on various psychosocial activities and orientations of youth across this system.

The 1990s breakup of the former Yugoslavia and the resulting political transitions create the context for human development at the beginning of the 21st century. A brief review of events acknowledged by many scholarly accounts serves to chart the territory, but I ask readers to keep in mind that it is the youth perspectives presented in subsequent chapters that are the histories of primary interest.

Tensions in Yugoslavia mounting since the death in 1980 of the longtime dictator, Josep Broz Tito, were exacerbated with the breakup of the Soviet Union and the fall of the Berlin Wall in 1989. From 1945 to 1991, Yugoslavia existed as a socialist federation of six republics with inhabitants claiming a wide range of ethnicities and religious persuasions. Several moves for independence began a sequence of events that led to the catastrophe of geopolitical fragmentation (Silber & Little, 1995). As a result of political–economic shifts in the region, Slovenia and Croatia, the two Yugoslavian republics with potentially independent resources, such as proximity to Western Europe in the case of Slovenia and geographic position on the Adriatic coast in the

Phase in a political-violence system	Time	Space	Events	Case-study participants
Relatively Peaceful Dictatorship	1945–1980	Yugoslavia	Socialist dictatorship	Parents, teachers of our participants born, educated, grow
Tensions Build	1980–1989	Yugoslavia	Turbulence	Generation experiences war as children, born 1980–1988
Violence in Region	1989	Eurasian Region	Breakup of the Soviet Union	Generation born during or after war, 1989–1995
			Affects entire region, world	
Provocations of Violence	1991	Slovenia and Croatia	Declare independence	
Extreme Political Violence	1991–1999	former Yugoslavian region	Wars fracturing Yugoslavia into numerous countries; bombing; killing; raping; "ethnic cleansing" – massive displacements	Study participants interact in society
		Europe and the world observe, get involved		
Major Violent Events	1996–1999		Bosnian wars (1992–1995)	
		NATO	NATO bombing of Belgrade (1999)	
Ongoing Tensions Violent Events and Threats Aftermath Political Instability	post-2000 2000–2008	Serbia former Yugoslavian region now Western Balkan states	Assassination of President Dinjic Sovereign states formed, constitutions created Formal peace agreements continued	
Related Confusion about Identity	2007		Displacement, returning to prewar homes	137 youth aged 12–27 share their views in a research workshop discussed in this book
Economic Instability, Unemployment Uncertain Future			Migration because of economic difficulties Tribunals; pressure to turn in/capture war criminals Provinces break from Serbia (Montenegro, Kosovo)	
Pressures Related to EU Membership		European region	Accession process creates tensions in name of progress, peace, stability	

FIGURE 1.2. Dimensions of a political-violence system for child and youth development across the former Yugoslavia.

case of Croatia, declared independence in 1991. These moves were followed by Serbia's aggressive response, such as declaring an independent Serbian state within Croatia. Violent conflicts followed in that area from 1992 to 1995, and the siege of Sarajevo heightened attacks on Bosnian territory in 1994, reportedly as an attempt to stave off independence movements in that area. Violence across the region led to hundreds of thousands of deaths and as many forced migrations from 1991 through 2000, with related events through each successive independence move.

Numerous accounts of these wars mention, in one way or another, the fact that people of different ethnic and religious origins had lived together peacefully as neighbors, families, and participants in public life during Yugoslav times. The rapid shift from "brotherhood and unity" to "ethnic cleansing" is characterized by a range of extreme psychosocial orientations like "ethnic hatreds," "protection," and "defense" that justified violent acts.

The resulting expulsions, ethnic cleansing, bombings, and physical violence left between two hundred fifty and four hundred thousand people dead across the area (depending on the source), hundreds of thousands physically and/or emotionally wounded, and approximately 3 million people displaced within the region or beyond, many emigrating several times, and many eventually returning to their prewar homes (www.unhcr). Violence that increasingly accompanied regional secessions included armed conflict, mass killings, rapes, seizures of property, and massive displacements across the region and to other continents. In addition to death, displacement, and injury, there was extensive destruction to the built environment, political–economic infrastructure, and civil society (Gagnon, 2004; Johnstone, 2002; MacDonald, 2002; Silber & Little, 1995; Tanner, 1997; Woodward, 1995). Such landscapes set the scene for the development of mistrust, bitterness, revenge, and retribution with which the children and youth of today interact.

As shown in Figure 1.2, violent events occurred at different times across the region. Violence was, for example, most acute in Croatia from 1991 through 1995, whereas in Bosnia it occurred from the mid- to late 1990s, and the bombing of Belgrade took place in 1999. Amnesty International reported that as recently as August 2005, two hundred thousand people remained displaced in the Western Balkans. Investigators continue to identify unmarked graves from that period. It may take years to determine the exact number of casualties that occurred in the now-separate countries and to forge definitive agreements about the perpetrators and the victims. There is, however, agreement that the generation growing up since the early 1990s is experiencing difficulties, including the loss of family members, either through death, disability, or displacement; scant resources; and exposure to gruesome evidence of past events continuing to emerge in neighborhoods, the media, and local stories. At the same time, an ongoing dilemma is the tension between the possibilities of a new political–economic system and troubles sustaining its growth.

This necessarily simplified history became associated with different broad narratives about causes and effects of the wars of the 1990s. To account for events and actors interacting with the war-affected generation, we consider development beginning with the birth of Yugoslavia, which was organized as a socialist dictatorship under Josep Broz Tito. Although many scholars point to contradictions involved in creating a national identity among the myriad ethnic, religious, and local groups across a region of some 47 million people, Yugoslavia was peaceful, prosperous, and relatively outside the Cold War tensions.

As a result of the 1990s wars, the postwar generation, whose parents grew up and were educated in Yugoslavia, now lives in different locations across the region (as shown in Figure 1.3) and the world, including the United States. Examining youth perceptions of these diverse circumstances offers insights about how age, cultural origin,

Former Yugoslavia

FIGURE 1.3. Map of the former Yugoslavia and resulting Western Balkan region.

and national affiliation may matter less than interaction with the circumstances of daily life (Daiute & Lucic, 2008). Given the violent breakup of Yugoslavia, the contentious nature of recent history depends on the persuasiveness of national and generational positions. Rather than the weight of history, which was shattered with the secessions and wars, factors determining persuasive discourses among youth in each nation could be quite dynamic. Despite agreement about some of the major events of the wars, current national positions toward the past differ dramatically in how they narrate events, causes, consequences, perpetrators, and victims. Resulting political–economic circumstances also differ, as do opportunities for youth and societal development.

As outlined in Figure 1.2, conflict builds and resolves over long periods and is, therefore, a developmental process spanning generations rather than an aberration affecting only those directly involved. Although the acute phase of war may have ended, tensions continue over situations like Kosovo's recent declaration of independence from Serbia, tribunals, the status of refugees and returnees, as well as a range of effects including poverty, instability of legal institutions, lack of health and social services, opportunities for new ways of knowing, potential for involvement in societal reorganization, and critical thinking. As we will see in subsequent chapters of this book, these factors frustrate a postwar generation motivated to enjoy a positive future and distinguish itself from the generation that waged war.

INSIGHTS ABOUT YOUTH PERSPECTIVES IN CONTEXT

The 1990s was a turbulent decade defined by transitions from the Cold War that affected children and youth growing up in very different areas of the world. At the same time the wars were fragmenting Yugoslavia, public schools serving children from diverse ethnic backgrounds in the United States reported increased incidents of intergroup conflict (Elliot, Hamburg & Williams, 1998). A relatively protracted history of tensions over hard-won civil-rights legislation for African Americans in the 1950s, 1960s, and 1970s, culminated in educational practices designed to address the tensions. Responding to an increasing number of violent events toward the end of the twentieth century, educators developed myriad violence prevention programs based in theories of social development and risk management, among other foundations (Elliot et al., 1998; Lelutiu-Weinberger, 2007; Selman, Watts, & Schultz, 1997). The line of research that sought children's understandings of interethnic-group relations and conflict offers insights for our present concern of state violence internationally. Before illustrating how adolescents use social–relational activities in the context of political violence, I briefly review an "aha moment" when I observed how younger children expressed their understanding and action around ethnic-group conflicts in a violence-prevention program in U.S. public schools.

An "Aha" Example of Child–Society Interaction

To learn about the understandings and actions of seven- to ten-year-old children in the third and fifth grades in U.S. urban public schools, I designed a sequence of oral and written discourse activities within a violence-prevention curriculum focusing on conflict among children from different ethnic groups. Grounded in cultural–historical activity theory, the series of individual and collaborative assignments to write about personal experiences of conflict and to write endings to fictional children's stories about ethnic conflict gave children a range of expressive contexts reflecting on conflict. These writing activities also provided the research team with data for considering theoretical questions about how children worked with principles from the violence-prevention curriculum to change their views about ethnic conflict over the course of one or more school years. We hoped that children would gradually adopt curriculum ideas like "use words, not fists, when you have a strong disagreement with someone," but children's uses of the narrative writing activities revealed a profound, even cunning, manifestation of the interdependence of social and individual psychosocial activity.

Analyses of the curriculum, classroom interactions, and hundreds of autobiographical and fictional narratives indicated that the seven- to ten-year-olds in the study increasingly shaped narratives about their personal experiences of conflict to conform to the values promoted in the curriculum, such as using words instead of fists to resolve interpersonal problems. In a parallel series of narratives about conflicts involving fictional characters, the same children increasingly expressed counter-curriculum values, such as fighting and expressing intense emotions (Daiute, 2004; Daiute, Buteau, & Rawlins, 2001). Such flexibility indicated the social–relational nature of different narrating activities, in particular, mediating the narrator's presentation of self in relation to the values of audiences. These children not only expressed and transformed understandings about conflict in their narrative writings over time but also used the activities to engage with the social context in sophisticated ways.

The following excerpt from a teacher-led classroom discussion about children's autobiographical stories offers a glimpse into how values about the correct way to think about and manage conflicts are formed. As is common practice in U.S. classrooms (Graves, 2003), a fifth-grade teacher asked students to share stories about personal experiences, in this case, focusing on conflict issues like those in literature the class had read and analyzed. This interaction occurred after one child, John, shared his story about a conflict with people of an ethnic background differing from most in the class. The teacher launched a discussion about how conflicts escalate by connecting the student's experience to the literary selection *Felita,* a book the class had read about discrimination against Puerto Rican immigrants in New York City during the 1960s:

> 1 TEACHER: ... *Is there anybody else who is making a little connection between* Felita *when I tell you that kids in our class attacked the Lebanese kids down the block with water balloons?*
> 2 STUDENT: *What was the reason* [for the conflict]*?*
> 3 TEACHER: *It doesn't sound like there was really a serious reason. We're not getting on you guys. We're not getting on you guys.*

After referring anonymously to "kids in our class attacked the Lebanese kids down the block with water balloons," the teacher turned to several students who had been involved and said, "We're not getting on you guys," apparently to reduce the sense of blame implicit in her selection of this real-life event to connect to an ethnic conflict in literature and, ultimately, to the role of racism in the conflict process. After John interjected the following explanation about his perception of the sequence of events, the teacher guided her students to consider the perspective of their adversaries:

> 4 JOHN: *Because they tried to lock us in the park because of the door, right. Whenever you close it real hard, it gets stuck and you have to try and . . .*
>
> 5 TEACHER: *And they were purposely trying to lock you in?*
>
> 6 JOHN: *Yeah, that's what happened.*
>
> 7 TEACHER: *. . . They started, but you continued. I hear constant escalation. Do you, Emily, or do you hear any de-escalation yet?*

Voicing what may have been the point of view of the Lebanese children, the teacher responded to John, "And they were purposely trying to lock you in? . . . They started, but you continued." In this excerpt as in many others among numerous instances of discussion, the teacher transformed this account of events near school into a lesson about "escalation," asking another student, Emily, to make the connection for her classmates.

> 8 EMILY: *Escalation.*
>
> 9 TEACHER: *Escalating, all right. What's your connection to Felita here?*
>
> 10 EMILY: *When they beat Felita up.*
>
> 11 TEACHER: *When they beat Felita up.*
>
> 12 EMILY: *Because . . . she was a different color . . .*
>
> 13 TEACHER: *A different, a darker complexion, and the fact that she was Latin and that her mother was really dark. You know what, kids, I worry very, very often, the difference between black and white is extremely obvious, and sometimes we forget when the difference is not so obvious, that the things we're doing may be tinged with a little racism there. In the fact that we're treating children who are different than us in a way that we might not treat each other, just a point for you to think about a little. Just a point for you to think about a little bit.*

The teacher extended beyond the children's reported experiences further by comparing details about skin color and discrimination in the book *Felita* and "that the things we're doing may be tinged with a little racism there." She then attempted to make the definition of racism real for her nine- and ten-year-old students by saying, " . . . we're treating children who are different than us in a way that we might not treat each other. Just a point for you to think about a little."

Given this and many other such discussions, it is not surprising that children would learn to avoid narrating events in their lives that may appear to escalate conflicts, especially if they could be interpreted to be racist (Daiute, Stern, & Lelutiu-Weinberger, 2003). The effects of this conversation are visible across several stories by John, a ten-year-old boy identifying as African American, in response to the request, "Write about a time when you or someone you know had an argument or disagreement with someone your age."

> *My conflict is when me and my best friend Robert and I was fight because i didn't want to be on his team so and we solved it later that day nobody got herti and that is when we became best friends.**

As suggested in the curriculum to teach children effective strategies for dealing with interpersonal conflicts (Walker, 1998), John, like several hundred of his peers, ended the year by narrating personal experiences with strategies like explaining differences of opinion ("because i didn't want to be on his team"), trying to include an adversary's point of view ("we"), resolving conflicts without physical aggression ("we solved it later that day nobody got herti"), and maintaining friendships above all else ("we became best friends").

During the course of the same school year, as John's autobiographical stories became more peaceful, his responses to an assignment to complete a fictional story, like other students' responses, became increasingly full of conflict details. The activity asked the

---

* Texts appear as written by the child.

seven- through ten-year-old participants to complete a story based on the following starter:

> *Jama and Max were best friends. Pat moved in next to Max, and they began to spend lots of time together. One day, Jama saw Pat and Max walking together and laughing. Write a story about what happened next. What happened? How did the people involved think and feel about the events? How did it all turn out?*

Hundreds of children completed the story, most introducing some type of conflict, which the research team analyzed for the nature of the conflict and resolution. Most children used this fictional story in different ways than they used the autobiographical-narrative activity (Daiute, 2004, 2006). Children who identified with minority backgrounds like John, used the fictional context to express values very different from those promoted in the curriculum and in their own autobiographical narratives (Daiute, et al., 2003). In the following fictional narrative, for example, John includes descriptions of violence, such as references to punching, fighting, and laughing with a negative twist.

> *Jama saw Max and Pat and she said what are you laughing about. Max said about you pat stared to laughing. And then Jama punnch pat in the face and then Max stared to laughing. Then pat and Max, jama stared to fight. Then jama punched maxs and pat in the face Then jama got punch in the face when jama got home her mother said what then.*

Various elements illustrate the less-than-friendly nature of this story. The first-person protagonist engages in forbidden fighting and veers into negative emotional terrain, with laughing as mocking rather than as joy. Also different from the autobiographical accounts at the end of the school year, this story has a suspended ending: "her mother said what then."

We learned from children's strategic uses of narrating in this study just how much social values become part of an individual's psychosocial orientation, as shared, for example, in a personal experience story. In that process, we learned how important an individual's motivations to be perceived positively in the social group shape autobiographical writing while the need to release tensions that would clearly be perceived less favorably emerges in fictional writing that is not necessarily true. In that study, we learned how even young school-aged children adjust their self-presentations to social messages. Building on that work, this study offers insights about how knowledge, identity, and orientation to the world are distributed across individuals and social groups in discourse and not only through it.

The previous study is particularly relevant to the theoretical issue of individual and societal interdependence from a period when discourse – histories, myths, and rationalizations – led to violence. The period of transition beyond violence is preoccupied with the appropriate narratives for positive futures. Prosocial class discussions and children's abilities to factor them into their narrations and their perceptions of life experiences are clearly important, if not profound. These findings suggested that in education and research, as in society more broadly, discourse is the mediation of social and individual consciousness rather than a window into individual minds and hearts.

Based on those findings, I extended the practice-based research design with a generation growing up during political violence and transition. The interaction of self and society exhibited dramatically on a smaller scale in U.S. urban classrooms could, I hypothesized, be operating in the sociopolitical realm of development toward the future among postwar youth across the former Yugoslavia.

A pilot study showed how children and adolescents engage with different narrative activities to express a range of knowledge, self-presentations, and goals. Adolescents in Croatia expressed diverse knowledge about the past, present, and future when they had the opportunity to narrate conflict from diverse generational perspectives (Daiute & Turniski, 2005). Participants offered different knowledge about and interpretations of conflict in narratives with older protago- nists (the generation directly involved in the 1990s wars) and younger protagonists (postwar peer generation). The finding about the dis- tributed nature of narrating is consistent with results of the study of younger children's strategic use of narrating in the school-based violence-prevention program in a U.S. city (Daiute, 2006) discussed above.

As one cultural–historical theorist explained, personality "orig- inally arises in society ... and [one] becomes a personality only as a subject of social relations. ... The method of ... dialectics requires that we go further and investigate the development as a process of 'self-movement,' that is, investigate its internal moving relations, con- tradictions, and mutual transitions" (Leont'ev, 1978, p. 105).

This comment about the dialectic nature of personality moti- vates question, including: What are the dynamic relations at the forefront of life among a postwar generation? What are the rele- vant diversities in those contexts that set those "moving relations" meaningfully in place to create contradictions and mutual transi- tion? How can we usefully characterize the political-violence system of the former Yugoslavia in terms of the moving relations, contradic- tions, and mutual transitions in play among the postwar generation across those societies? With such clear distinctions among the con- temporary youth generation (up to their mid-20s) and their elders in terms of war experience, current environment, and future prospects, the nature of the psychosocial dynamic is intensely contested and in need of analysis to inform practice and theory. In addition to living with the consequences of war, the contemporary youth genera- tion is participating in schools, community centers, media, and pub- lic institutions undergoing reform in varying degrees and speeding toward capitalist democracies, most specifically with the influence of the EU. Thus, although the generation that experienced the war and grew up in the prewar socialist society shares knowledge and ways of knowing with their children, the postwar generation is living among diverse new influences and the attendant need to express the motivations, fears, and other subjectivities in material and symbolic circumstances of daily life. What, then, is persuasive to these young people?

From the challenges of a classroom serving children of diverse ethnic backgrounds in a large U.S. city, we consider this interaction of individual and societal story-telling as a dynamic developmental space in contexts of war and transition. Tensions between societal stories, such as the correct way to think about people who are different and to approach conflicts with others, may in the present be more subtle than they are in the immediate aftermath of war. The processes of creating one's autobiography in relation to societal imperatives and the corresponding changing societal narratives are worthy of examination across a range of contentious contexts. Although many designs for practice and research in crisis settings entail drawing or other art-related performances, it is in focused verbal interactions that meaning, dissention, and progress take the most dynamic shape. Certainly it is time for inquiry about the use of such cultural tools.

ADOLESCENCE AND POLITICAL TRANSITION

Positioned precariously between childhood and adulthood, adolescents may be especially qualified to use a range of expressive activities for sharing experiences from third- or first-person stances, in fictional or autobiographical contexts, and in relation to the expectations of diverse audiences, including those who maintain a "last-century mentality;" those who want to create new ways of organizing life; and those from afar whose ill-informed, critical, pitying, or other perceptions are conveyed in stereotypical narratives readily available in the media. To examine mediational processes, I present a case study that analyzes various activities by young people living in four countries positioned differently in the aftermath of the war in the former Yugoslavia. Effects and causes of conflicts are also ideological and symbolic and thereby shared in the stories of individuals, groups, and nations. This developmental approach to studying conflict occurs in the context of activities including story-telling, social interaction, and community participation, which offer a test of practice-based research methods.

As part of a workshop with youth surviving the Yugoslavian conflict, one hundred and thirty-seven 12- to 27-year-olds in Bosnia & Herzegovina (BiH), Croatia, Serbia, and a refugee community in the United States reflected on social conflict (Daiute, 2007). Compared with scale-based measures designed to assess traumatic reactions like internalizing and externalizing symptoms, the discursive practices in this study invited participants to express a range of knowledge about and orientations to conflict. The study was designed to address questions of whether and how young people living across four countries during the 1990s, when half of our cohort were preadolescents and adolescents during the war (currently aged 19 and older) and half were children or babies (currently aged 18 and younger) are experiencing diverse effects of violence. Chapter 2 describes the workshop in terms of several principles of cultural–historical activity theory, which I propose as tools to increase our understanding of human development in the context of political violence.

Along with many other expressions, the drawing in Figure 1.1 at the beginning of this chapter suggests the need to fill the gap in our understanding about youth perspectives on political violence. It is those perspectives – knowledge, understanding, and goals in practical activities – that constitute history. Young people's perspectives, grounded in real time and space, comprise a living history of political violence. Together, the various expressions that young people shared create a story, in terms eloquently defined by Jerome Bruner:

> *The fabula of story – its timeless underlying theme – seems to be unity that incorporates at least three constituents. It contains a <u>plight</u> into which <u>characters</u> have fallen.... And it requires the uneven distribution of underlying <u>consciousness</u> among characters with respect to the plight.... Whether it is sufficient to characterize this unified structure [of meaning] as <u>steady state</u>, <u>breach</u>, <u>crisis</u>, <u>redress</u> is diffi-cult to know. It is certainly not <u>necessary</u> to do so, for what one seeks in story structure is precisely how plight, character, and consciousness are integrated* (Bruner, 1986, p. 21).

Chapter 2 describes the context of story-telling for youth perspec-tives to complement the various other types of responses about polit-ical violence. Accounting for youth consciousness about the plights into which the characters of their nations have fallen will evolve as youth history.

The drawing in Figure 1.1 depicts a youth caught ambivalently between "decay" and "future." A young man living in a country frac-tured by war and continuing to suffer the consequences poignantly rendered the dilemma of his generation: being caught between what is problematic ("decay") and a future that is, at best, uncertain ("?"). By presenting a youth caught in an historical dilemma, the draw-ing expresses a critical perspective not yet offered in research or practice.

SUMMARY

The argument in this book is that a sociohistorical analysis of young people's engagement in conflict and its aftermath provides new insights about the effects of political violence and human devel-opment more generally. This argument is consistent with the idea that human development in war-affected environments is normative. Normative-developmental contexts are "good enough" (Winnicott,

1971), providing that at least some relationships are close, loving, friendly, supportive or stable, thereby allowing children to muster intellectual and emotional resources for exploring and, eventually, mastering their surrounding environment. Young people's uses of story-telling and other discursive activities can be such resources. The purpose is not to replace bad effects with good but to consider human development, in particular during the second decade of life, in ways that do not assume vulnerability or risk. When I argue that we consider the normative nature of growing up in crisis situations, I do not imply that political violence is optimal or acceptable as a developmental context but rather that we must understand the full range of interactions to design research, practice, and policy. These ideas raise several questions, including: What are the theoretical bases for a normative analysis of conflict? How do we explore those ideas? What results do we find from such systematic analysis?

FIGURE 2.1. Youth and society work together.

2

Youth and Society Work Together

This chapter presents a practical research design to learn about young people's experiences of political violence and transition. The *Dynamic Story-Telling by Youth* (DSTY) research workshop involves young people aged 12 to 27 across four countries resulting from the recent wars to learn about how they interact with the circumstances where they find themselves. Before discussing this theory-based research design, I present vignettes based on fieldnotes, project archives, and reports to offer insights about the workshop settings. These vignettes focus on the workshops, which occurred in the context of community participation, like that pictured in Figure 2.1 and as appropriate to urban as well as rural settings.

SERBIA, AUGUST

It's a Saturday in August when 31 young people could have been picnicking near the river, sitting with their friends at a café, or helping out at home. Instead, these young people came looking curious, if not enthusiastic, to former government buildings to participate in a workshop eliciting youth voices and to communicate with other youth across the region. Recruited through an NGO active since the war in positive social change, the youth gathered in now-underused buildings in what was the capital of Yugoslavia when the participants were young children. The research workshop is led in their language by a young Serbian man now studying for a Ph.D. in the United States and a local educator, with assistance from two other young adults living in Belgrade. On summer break from high school, college, or job-hunting in the context of nearly 30 percent unemployment, these young people have volunteered to share their knowledge and experience about growing up in dramatically changing times. Contradictions in the setting include the drab concrete buildings contrasting with the intense engagement of the young people's story-telling, their cautious hope for a future contrasting with graffiti showing "EU" crossed out on a concrete wall outside, the paucity of technological resources like computers contrasting with beautiful writing and drawing created with markers and paper. These contradictions embody the tensions we will learn about from these generous young people.

BOSNIA AND HERZEGOVINA, SEPTEMBER

In the capital of BiH, 37 youth, one group of students in a computer lab at the high school and another at the university, share their experiences in a city that was under siege for three years by the Yugoslavian army still holding on to control in the mid 1990s as the country was ripped apart. In the midst of their beautiful city of mixed cultural and religious symbols on nearly every street, these young people cherish their diversity, not even needing to look up to see the minaret next to the dome of the Christian orthodox church and the Hebrew letters on the synagogue against the backdrop of crowded graveyard on a distant hill. It is early fall when these youth have gathered to participate in the same workshop design as their contemporaries in Serbia, Croatia, and the United States. Scurrying through the busy, chaotic streets, youth in BiH count on education as a unique stabilizing factor in the midst of a government with a multi-member, ethnically divided presidency designed to ensure power to each group. Impatient and sentimental, these youth are ever aware that they embody the city's survival, having been infants and young children when bombings damaged their homes and filled the city with smoke, death, destruction, and ingenious attempts for survival. As we learn from their writings and conversations, this place, its people, its traffic, and its pain organize the experiences that the generation growing up with war expresses to the local research group who translate and bring the workshop activities to life.

NEW YORK, SEPTEMBER

Across the world, 25 young people who were born in what is now BiH gather in the wood-panelled café of a Bosnian bakery in a small, northeastern United States city. The children and their families were deemed the lucky ones, having been rescued in United Nations–sponsored convoys, having escaped by private means, or having been expelled from their homeland during acute stages of violence. A college student from the community runs the workshop with me, following the same practice-based research design as in Serbia, Croatia and BiH. As they gather, these young people acknowledge one another, many quite familiar and others merely acquaintances in the local network of Bosnian refugees and immigrants. The older participants are speaking to one other in Bosnian, most of the younger ones whispering and laughing in pairs or small groups. As I introduce myself to each one, I tell them we will start in a few minutes with an overview of the workshop and time for them to ask questions. I tell them that I hope the aroma of the bakery will not distract them, and that because it is Ramadan, we will wait until the end of the day to give them pastries to take home and share with their families when the time for fasting ends. Several giggled at this and thanked me. One girl mentioned that she comes to the bakery with her mother; another boy said that he often comes here on errands for his family. Seeming nervously eager, they are ready to participate on this day when they had chosen to interrupt their normal routines and rituals.

CROATIA, APRIL AND JUNE

"Eager" characterizes the approach across two workshop locales in Croatia. One is a small village near a border that was contested in the war, and the other, less than a 2-hour drive along country roads to the north, is a city of Austro-Hungarian architecture, some of it partially destroyed by bombings during the war. I notice many different sights, sounds, and sensations in the Croatian locales: one now a city with a lively street life, the other a quiet town with only a person or two passing me on a 1-mile walk from where I'm staying to the community center, except for during market time when there's actually a crowd. Although the city is host to international entrepreneurs, which some of the young people describe as "buying up our country," the small town is the site of encounters among people whose experience no one can assume to know for sure: people returning to claim land taken from them during the war, refugees from a neighboring country, and students from farther west and east in Europe and beyond, volunteering to help the children rebuild their town. Space in the small town is ample, these youth having full access to the former movie theater in the town center when they participate in community activities, while in the city, workshop

organizers borrow space in a local school where participants can use computers.

> *Back to "eager," there's a sense of purpose that seems to unify these young people in Croatia who have had very different experiences. The differences become clear when I ask one young man from the small town to help out with the workshop in the city because of his understanding of the research goals, his leadership skills, and easy manner. Although he probably could have used the financial payment for helping out with the other workshop, he declined because he had never been to the city, was reluctant to go, and thought he never would. Nevertheless, this young man, like his national peers, participates locally, albeit sometimes cautious about venturing beyond (whether to the capital of his country or other capitals of Europe). To a one, the 39 young participants in Croatia seem focused on future prospects but are knowingly skeptical about the costs to their family relationships, friendships, romances, joys, and annoyances of local life.*

Inviting young people growing up in different positions of a political-violence system to create a social history is an approach based on several principles of cultural–historical theory. As I explain in this chapter, practice-based research builds on the understanding that young people's perceptions, knowledge, and goals develop in the context of meaningful social activity, and that youth, like all of us, share experiences in relation to actual and imagined audiences. For these reasons, young people across the settings described briefly at the beginning of this chapter echo the national and local circumstances as well as their own personal positions in those settings.

In this context, we explore, without assuming damage or deficit, how young people interact with diverse circumstances, even though these contexts are defined, at least in part, by political violence and instability. To elicit this complexity, the DSTY workshop invited young people to reflect on their societies and their roles in those societies in a variety of ways. Nations and communities across what was once a country have, for example, different points of view about the war and different goals in the postwar period (Gagnon, 2004; MacDonald, 2002; Silber & Little, 1995). Young people growing up in those contexts develop understandings related to the specific situation (Daiute & Lucic, 2008; Daiute & Turniski, 2005). Because change during and after periods of political violence is fraught with conflicting knowledge, values, and goals, research should allow for surprises based on young people's lived experiences, not only stereotypes based on past events.

Grounded in the idea that "there's nothing as practical as a good theory" (Lewin, 1951), we draw on principles of cultural–historical theory. Scholars building on the cultural–historical theory of Vygotsky, Leont'ev, Luria, and Bakhtin have explained how individuals' minds, personalities, and identities are social rather than self-contained and naturally unfolding. According to various versions of this theory, the psychological life of an individual is inextricably entwined with public life in public space. Uniquely human processes like consciousness and intention occur among individuals and groups in real-life contexts. Compared with other developmental theories positing that children eventually gain the ability to interact socially, cultural–historical activity theory defines humans as profoundly social from the start, as expressed in this translated excerpt by a major founder of the theory:

> *Every function in . . . cultural development appears twice: first, on the social level, and later, on the individual level; first between people (interpsychological), and then inside the child/person (intrapsychological). This applies equally to voluntary attention, to logical memory, and to the formation of concepts. All higher functions originate as actual relations between human individuals.* (Vygotsky, 1978, p. 57)

Four major principles of cultural–historical theory are evident in this excerpt, which continues to intrigue scholars, educators, and clinicians since it was first published in revolutionary Russia. According to this view, human development is an interactive process of individuals and societies in everyday life. History is thus not an abstract story from the past but a meaning-making process in which individuals and groups contend with perceptions and interpretations of events as they participate in public and private life. Young people's perspectives are important in this view because they are not only *about* problems but also *merged* with them in contemporary life. Among the many symbol systems that create meaning is language, the quintessential human activity.

The past is relevant in this process as young people interact with their elders, traditional institutions, and objects in the world. The more abruptly and dramatically the environment changes, the less young people can rely on interpretations from the past. From this perspective, we consider how a young person raises questions about contradictory knowledge, as stated by one 15-year-old girl who has lived in various places across the region: "How is it that different ethnic groups lived peacefully in Yugoslavia for so many years, then one day began killing their neighbors they didn't even think of as different the day before?" Because of the shared consciousness and mutual influence of individuals in society, this girl, like her peers, can reproduce the commonly accepted narrative of war in her homeland ("different ethnic groups lived peacefully in Yugoslavia"), a motto of brotherhood and unity that some say is a myth, while also critiquing that myth ("How is it that . . . then one day began killing their neighbors"). In the absence of adult explanations for such unexpected and, for some, inexplicable events, young people create their own interpretations as "active, responsive, transformative orientation" (Bakhtin, 1986, p. 68). For example, many are quick to mention the incompetence of the war generation played out in daily life as drunkenness, pettiness, and reluctance to talk about war events that everyone knows occurred (Daiute & Turniski, 2005; Freedman & Abazovic, 2006).

These and other ideas about the developmental nature of growing up in troubled times are the foundation of the DSTY research workshop, a unique set of activities for creating a contemporary history from young people's perspectives about both their problems and opportunities.

DYNAMIC STORY-TELLING BY YOUTH

I animate principles of cultural-historical activity theory with a practical research design. The design considers human development in a political system lasting 52 years, from inception to dissolution and the aftermath, from the perspective of young people whose childhoods span different periods of that system. The older youth, aged 19 to 27 during the study, had been directly exposed to violence and attendant consequences as children and teenagers, whereas the younger group of adolescents, aged 12 to 18 during the study, were infants or preschoolers and thus more protected from public violence. In this way, we consider the intersecting bio-psycho-social developments from birth to young adulthood in relation to the dramatic, violent destruction of Yugoslavia in four of the resulting countries. Research in the context of practice is supporting postwar development as well as studying it. For this reason, I created a workshop that, after fieldwork and pilots, is consistent with goals for positive development of youth and communities across the region.

The heart of this practice-based research is a 5- to 6-hour workshop (on a single day or during several) as one among other similar activities in community centers organized by NGOs. In research workshops from the spring to the fall of 2007, young people, their mentors, their teachers, and our research team wrote, discussed, and shared stories, reflections, letters, and surveys to reflect on the circumstances and development possibilities in their societies, in brief to create a social history. The workshop was designed around socially significant activities to elicit participants' engagement with social structures, obstacles, and opportunities. As illustrated in the vignettes at the beginning of this chapter, the workshop occurred in a community or school-based context.

All activities are "socially significant" so that they can "address structure, motives, and units of measurement" (Veresov, 2006) relevant to these circumstances. In practice, this means that the workshop design evolved from observing activities across the region, reading reports about youth concerns and activities, assessing young people's interests during pilot studies, and drawing from theory-based studies with conflict-related activities in the United States (see Chapter 1).

The DSTY activities occur within the broader system of societal change and, more specifically, are related to community-development activities. NGOs across the Western Balkans, like other regions in conflict and transition, create community centers, often with international funding, leaders, and volunteers, and ideally working with local people. The community centers tend to attract young people because of their updated resources, including space for social activities, interactive technologies, instruction, and opportunities to impact society. Although NGOs have come under increasing critique as being self-interested (McMahon, 2009), they provide contexts for actual and imagined developments of new ways of thinking and acting. Many community centers foster youth leadership with activities like creating agendas for rebuilding bridges destroyed in the war, reclaiming abandoned lakes, creating day-care centers, and entrepreneurial activities using local resources, such as making and selling local crafts or foods. As shown in Figure 2.1, for example, young people devoted some of their time off from school in the summer to clear a local lake of overgrown brush and trash left from a nearby refugee camp. In addition to providing gathering spaces, such physical activities are opportunities for developing skills for democratic participation and social inclusion. Although not all the young people who volunteered for the workshop were equally active participants in such organizations, the participation of familiar organizations makes the concept of meaningful collaboration explicit.[1]

---

[1] Recruitment for participants in BiH, Croatia, and Serbia occurred through NGOs, which spread the word among other groups and, in some cases, similar local organizations and educators. The reasons for recruiting through NGOs

Make Your Voice Heard

Communicate with Other Young People,

Create Ideas for Youth Curriculum

This is an invitation to participate in a research workshop:

Purpose:

• To raise the voices of young people in dramatically changing situations,

• To communicate with youth in other communities across the world,

• To write stories of everyday life in your community; to tell current history from youth perspectives

• To gather youth suggestions for curriculum about development in changing societies

Benefits to you?

• Meet new people, do something important with friends

• Learn some new computer & communication skills,

• Earn a gift certificate or movie tickets,

When?

Saturday xxx from 12:00 pm to 6:00 pm, including breaks & snacks

How do I sign up or find out more? Send an email message to (local organizer) or call.

FIGURE 2.2. Flyer to call for participation in the *Dynamic Story-Telling by Youth* research workshop.

As shown in the flyer used to recruit participants for the DSTY workshop (Figure 2.2), activities involve various types of

were their involvement with young people, mentoring of community activists, access to local sites for a research workshop, interest in the DSTY, and willingness to offer feedback and to cooperate in general. Most important was the belief that participants would be comfortable with local people and contexts. My research offered contributions to the NGOs for their assistance in recruiting, hosting, translating, and other aspects of the data collection. I and/or my research team were present at most of the sessions.

collaboration. In the introduction to the workshop, I or another member of the research team explains the purpose of the research as a way to learn more about how a generation growing up during extremely difficult times like war and its aftermath share those views not only with researchers, educators, and community leaders but also with young people across the geographic and political landscape involved in similar situations. In this sense, we highlight the interactions within and across contexts.

If "all higher functions originate as actual relations between human individuals" (Vygotsky, 1978), we must understand contexts to understand people. Young people interact with the circumstances in their environments, including the problems, not only by observing but also by organizing their perceptions, interpretations, and actions in relation to those circumstances. Thus Aida, one participant in the United States, positions herself as an observer of discrimination, from which she and her peers suffer daily as Bosnian Muslim immigrants. From the cross-site analysis, we learn of the sense of responsibility that Ljubicia and her peers feel in Serbia, associated with the hundreds of thousands of deaths resulting from a shrinking former political entity fighting to keep its power base. Such positions are not static but crafted in terms of speaker–audience relations. For example, the young immigrant in the United States may have been reaching out to researchers for sympathy, and the youth from Serbia trying to show that her generation is sensitive to crimes of the past done in their name.

As indicated in Figure 2.3, the workshop is also collaborative because of the dynamic nature of the activities, which include explicit interactions in discussion groups, such as during the guided review of research results, discussion of the public story, and small-group work to design an original youth survey. More implicit collaboration occurs when participants read survey results by youth in other contexts, imagine peers who would fill out their original survey, imagine the public officials to whom they wrote letters, or narrate their experience to show their best face to potential audiences.

Workshop Activities (adaptable by context)	Chapter Focusing on Results
Introduction to the workshop	
Overview of purpose and scope; time for participant questions and comments; Participant consent to participate.	Chapter 2
Completion of "Youth Perspectives on Society" Survey	Chapters 3 & 5
Youth Participation in Community Activities	Chapter 5
Discussion of Problems in Society &	Chapter 3
Discussion of Positive Qualities of Society Depending on local resources, participants complete survey in on-line survey tool, with pen and paper, or orally, in their native language or language of choice.	Chapter 3
Write narratives about conflicts in daily life from diverse perspectives, about actual and hypothetical experiences.	Chapters 3, 4, 6, 7
Complete and Discuss Survey Responses by Youth in Other Countries	Chapter 5
Read and Discuss a Public Story, about a local event where young people were actively involved	Chapter 5
Create an Original Youth Survey	Chapter 5
Participants Evaluate the Workshop	Chapter 2

FIGURE 2.3. Activities in *Dynamic Story-Telling by Youth* research workshop and placement of results.

Communication is culture in action. Because meaning-making occurs in discourse, the workshop design involves communication other than primarily drawing and nonverbal activities typically used with young people in crisis or recovery situations. When trying to understand the plight of war-affected children and youth, we heed a second theoretical principle to consider history as alive, with reference to the future and the present as well as the past. A major implication of this principle is that research findings impinge on the participation of children and institutions, like the research enterprise itself. This participation must be meaningful, goal directed, and evocative of important social relations. To ensure that youth growing up in extremely challenging contexts have ample opportunity to engage substantively in individual and collective reflection, we include a full range of discursive activities not only to learn from young people but also to encourage their development.

Consistent with the focus on trauma and social reproduction, previous research involves checking items on surveys, drawing, role-playing, or, less frequently, clinical interviewing. Whether explicitly or implicitly, such practices promote emotional release, serve to assess individual capacities, or treat psychopathologies. Also consistent with those approaches is the view that verbal and nonverbal expressions rather than complex interactions in sociopolitical situations offer a window into a young person's mind and heart. Typically, clinicians, youth workers, and researchers emphasize drawing because it allows for the release of unspeakable horrors (Apfel & Simon, 1996). Some programs use role-playing, poetry, or music to connect with youth cultures. Sometimes, more nonverbal means are used with youth whose lack of education may render oral and written expression difficult, if not impossible. Because all but the most isolated young people learn language, however, activities with explicitly social purposes are also possible in supported contexts. The DSTY workshops build on research about the sociopolitical nature of written and oral language, as well as on previous evidence that, beginning in childhood, young people can use collaborative and individual writing as a means of development because it is social communication (Lee & Smagorinsky 2000; Smagorinsky, 2006). Dictation can be the first step to literacy, and in most cases, meaningful expression provides a context for becoming literate in surprisingly brief periods of time. Children who are not yet fully literate can, for example, dictate their stories that become the basis for ongoing literacy instruction.

In politically contentious contexts, researchers and practitioners should consider assumptions in the silences between words in oral language and between the lines in written language. Issues of societal conflict, for example, become embedded in national and international ideologies, expressed as "frozen narratives" and "myths" (MacDonald, 2002). For this reason, activities must offer participants opportunities to engage with social issues, relationships, and intentions in diverse stances. The idea that language is embedded in sociopolitical messages then invites young people to express different perspectives, including those of the generation who fought the war, their own generation, and future generations of their transformed communities. Because discourse is social in these ways, different speaker and writer perspectives imply different goals and audiences. When we assume that each expression carries with it contexts and purposes from diverse points of view, we know to design activities that allow for individual and group diversity.

MANAGING PUBLIC AND PERSONAL LIFE

Another principle relates to *mediation*, the use of language and other symbol systems to perceive, manage, and develop self–society relations. Mediation involves connecting one's own consciousness to others'. Mediation is, stated simply, human genius at work, the "conductor[s] of human influence on the object of activity" (Vygotsky, 1978, p. 55). On this view, discourse and other symbol systems do not simply transmit meanings or reveal individual character and intentions. Instead, beginning at an early age, children use cultural tools, at first with gestures and sounds, then single words, and eventually complex genres like narratives in ways that are "externally oriented...aimed at mastering and triumphing over nature" (*ibid.*) *and* as "a means of internal activity aimed at mastering oneself" (*ibid.*). Understanding discourse in this way provides a bridge among researchers, educators, and community leaders working with young people. When we define language as a cultural tool that mediates individual–society relationships, rather than as a mere transmitter of information, we inquire into the dynamics of social relations and social change.

For young people in dramatically changing societies, in this case the former Yugoslavia, mediation is a social–relational process that creates a shared world in transitions from war to peace. Depending on how it is told, a story with the ending "We are all refugees" could be used to highlight connections between children of adversaries or to explain the impossibility of forging a connection; as one young woman said, "We are all refugees, so we Bosnians could never be friends with the enemy."

Previous developmentalists focused on mechanisms within individuals, such as the maturing of cognitive processes like equilibration between a child's accommodation to forces in the environment and, in a very different direction, assimilation of the environment to his or her own way of thinking (Piaget, 1968). From the psychodynamic perspective, developments occur within the individual in terms of conflicts, such as those related to sexual maturation (Freud, 1909) and the mastery of the self in context (Erikson, 1980). The cultural–historical approach, somewhat like object relations theory (Winnicott, 1971), offers a proposal for units of analysis that integrate a person in relation to specific issues, often contentious ones, in the environment. As human beings create meanings with shared symbol systems like language, their intersubjective worlds become ever more available for use and development. This process is still greatly underexplored in the social sciences and especially lacking in studies of children growing up in extreme circumstances.

SOCIAL RELATIONS AND SOCIAL CHANGE

Cultural–historical principles also imply a notion of development that is not a linear unfolding of predictable capacities but a complex interplay of processes emerging in diverse, goal-oriented social relationships. Activities that are collaborative, participatory, and mediated with cultural tools should, in principle, allow for diversity and flexibility not only by people across settings but also, and even more importantly, by an individual engaging in different ways with events, other people, and institutions. A high school or university student focused on demonstrating motivation and skill for employment will, for example, try to perform relevant skills. In a letter to a president, this motivated youth will highlight what he or she perceives as societal problems requiring solutions. Assuming the social–relational nature of all activity – in this case, focusing on discourse within and about dramatically changing societies – a workshop has to allow for dynamic relations and positioning for each participant and for groups across the four contexts.

The concept of *genre* is useful in the DSTY workshop because it connotes a collaborative process in several senses. First, the notion of genre implies that discourse is language in context. Genres are thus not just formats or frameworks but meaningful situations enacted in culturally shared ways. Second, genres are dynamic, occurring in real-world activity. For this reason, genres, like sentences of human language, conform to accepted patterns but are free to differ for each speaking situation. Third, genres are cultural tools, in that they are used by people to *do* things in more or less culturally acceptable ways.

This social nature of genre evolved from decades of research with children organizing experience in terms of rituals in their lives (Nelson, 2003). These rituals may be shared and developed in two broad ways of thinking, described as "narrative" and "paradigmatic" (Bruner, 1986, pp. 12–13). The paradigmatic mode "deals in general causes, and in their establishments, and makes use of procedures to assure verifiable references and to test for empirical truth" (Bruner, 1986, p. 13), but the narrative mode "deals in human or human-like intention and action and to the vicissitudes and consequences that mark their course" (*ibid.*, p. 13). Narrative and paradigmatic ways of thinking are, moreover, not only in people's heads. The idea presented here is that thought is integrated with activity in the world, not only as abstract representations but also as "social relations in goal-directed activity" (Engestrom, 2009). Genres are thus culturally developed, that is, meaningful, shared, and repeated discursive routines. Genres are oral, written, or nonverbal symbolic expressions that function as "links in a chain of communication" in which "no utterance is the first to break the silence of the universe" (Bakhtin, 1986, p. 69).

The concept of genre implies that discourse is not contained in any text; rather, it is an event involving people with actual and potential audiences in terms of shared values and expectations. Because children are socialized with genres organized for typical events and roles, they learn the explicit and implicit features of various local situations. Genres serve to organize perception, experience, action, and interpretation (Bruner, 1990). In this way, genres are cultural tools, akin to the lenses that guide a wearer's interaction in the world. Because we wanted to engage participants' knowledge and intentions within social–relational contexts, the DSTY workshop design includes a range of genres so that each person in each context has diverse relational possibilities.

The analysis of discourse genres shown in Table 2.1 illustrates a systematic approach to fostering communicative complexity in activities related to young people's social histories in contentious contexts. To allow for different social–relational expressions, the research workshop involves three genres: inquiry, narrative, and advisory. Inquiry activities elicit and share information, focusing in this case on how people perceive their societies. Narrative activities emphasize youth experiences, relationships, and self-determination. Advisory genres emphasize youth determination of society. Although these genres may differ generally as described herein, each activity involves diverse social configurations of the speaker/writer–audience–goal, allowing for diverse youth stances. In particular, as outlined in Table 2.1, youth stances across the activities in the research workshop vary for explicit and implicit relational qualities of connection, interpretation, and power.

Table 2.1 lists several dimensions of youth–society relations enacted in the workshop activity designs. The first column lists activities in terms of the three genres: inquiry, narrative, and advisory. For each genre activity, the second column indicates the nature of the youth participant's stance, that is, the extent of each genre to allow for youth connection, interpretation, and/or power. Defining *stance* as the social–relational quality of the activity for these three major

TABLE 2.1. *Discourse Genres by Youth in the Context of Political Violence and Transition*

Participation activity	Youth stances			
More (+) to Less (−) continuum	Connection +/−	Interpretation +/−	Power +/−	Emphasis of youth participation
Inquiry Genres				Emphasis on connection to issues in society
Respond to Survey	+	−	−	
Guided Review of Survey Results	+	−	+	
Create Original Youth Survey	+	+	+/−	
Interpret Results of Youth Survey	+	+	−	
Narrative Genres				Emphasis on youth perspectives, performance, and self-determination
Narrate Peer Conflict	−	+	−	
Narrate Adult Conflict	−	+	−	
Narrate Hypothetical Community Event	+	+	+	
Public Story	+	−	+	
Advisory Genres				Emphasis on youth determination of society
Write Letter to Leader	+/−	−	+	
Evaluate Workshop	−	−	+	

aspects of communication (connection, interpretation, and power relations), some activities are designed to enhance one particular relation, such as youth power or connection, whereas another activity enhances interpretation. The column to the far right of the matrix in Table 2.1 states the emphasis of youth participation across the genres, with inquiry activities overall emphasizing connections with society (social structures and interpersonal relationships), narrative genres emphasizing youth perspectives, and advisory genres emphasizing youth power.

Inquiry Genres

Inquiry activities serve to ask and answer questions. This mode of discourse, described in earlier research as paradigmatic, emphasizes statements of knowledge and truth (Bruner, 1986). Profoundly social, knowledge and truth in inquiry activities depend on relational elements: Who is asking questions of whom, and to what end? To move beyond assumptions that youth in postwar contexts are at risk for reproducing ethnic hatreds, we asked young people to respond to *and* create inquiry questions. On the one hand, we created a survey with open as well as focused questions about how they view society; on the other hand, we invited them to ask questions of the research team and of youth across the broader political-violence system. Three inquiry activities offered opportunities for participants to interact with others in different ways: *to connect* with the workshop and varied audiences, *to interpret* primarily with attention to their own personal perspectives, and *to assert authority* (*power*) in the activity. By responding to questions in a researcher-designed survey, participants evaluated the qualities of their societies.

Questions on the researcher-designed survey include, "What is the biggest difficulty for young people in your city or town? What other problems are there? Please explain." "What are the positive or best qualities of life in your city/town? What other positive qualities are there? Please explain." Each of these questions is followed by closed-ended survey items asking participants to indicate the importance of specific problems and positive qualities one would assume to be of relevance to youth across these settings. With these questions, we asked participants to focus on issues of society as a step toward the ultimate goal of their considering and possibly transforming their views about local and national circumstances. Asking about positive as well as problematic issues in society was important for identifying diverse ways that children may have been using the physical and symbolic remnants of war as transported into obstacles they face in their daily lives.

A second inquiry activity designed to increase participant connection and power was the *Guided Review of Survey Results.* As shown in the instructions for this activity in Figure 2.4, participants become involved in the research process by reviewing results of the previous *problems/positives in society survey* by peers who had also taken the survey.

Because it involves group discussion, this activity increases participants' connection with one another as well as with others whose

---

Guided Review of Results of the Dynamic Story-Telling by Youth Survey Completed in Other Settings

Read the attached qualitative results of the survey you took just a few minutes ago. The purpose of this activity is to engage your thinking and discussion of your views compared to those of your peers – near and far. Please make notes as you read and think about the results, then share with your group of 4 people, deciding on a recorder who will present the summary of your discussion to the full workshop group.

1. What do you think about responses to question # 16?

    a. What surprises you?

    b. Do you have questions about the results?

    c. How would you change these questions?

    d. Discuss the results.

    Question # 16. What is the biggest problem for youth in your city (town or country)?

Sample responses

    1. The biggest problem is disinterest and inactivity of youth in any kind of after school activity. They complain about the lack of activities, at the same time they would not do anything for their own benefit. They also easily allow themselves to become lethargic and lazy. Outside negative factors would be ignorable if they themselves were more active.

    2. docility (being easily led), fear of unemployment, pessimistic views about the future of the country and society.

    3. Youth are never taken seriously, and we sometimes have ideas that would be good for all people. In my town there are not enough places for youth to go out with friends. And sometimes youth simply do not have normal friends. And there are many more problems but if I wrote all that now I would not have enough time.

    7 more representative responses offered . . .

FIGURE 2.4. Instructions for the *Dynamic Story-Telling by Youth* workshop activity to review results by participants in other countries.

2. Read the attached quantitative results of the survey you took just a few minutes ago. The purpose of this activity is to engage your thinking and discussion of your views compared to those of your peers – near and far.
1. What do you think about responses to question # 17?
    a. What surprises you?
    b. Do you have questions about the results?
    c. How would you change these questions?
    d. Discuss the results.

17. Please indicate how important the following problems are for the development of young people.

	Very	Important	Somewhat Important	Not Important
Crime	**52.9%**	35.3%	8.8%	2.9%
	(36)	(24)	(6)	(2)
Unemployment	**69.6%**	24.6%	5.8%	0
	(48)	(17)	(4)	
Lack of future prospects	**66.7%**	29.9%	2.9%	1.4%
	(46)	(20)	(2)	(1)
Tensions between people	**40.6%**	39.1%	17.4%	2.9%
	(28)	(27)	(12)	(2)
Lack of entertainment & recreations	**43.5%**	40.6%	15.9%	0
	(30)	(28)	(11)	

FIGURE 2.4 (continued)

responses are included in the results (albeit implicitly). Having the opportunity to review and interpret the survey also increases youths' authority over data evaluating society. As stated in the workshop manual, "Young people are often the subject of research but not typically involved in it, other than as consumers." This activity gives participants the opportunity not only to view results of the survey completed earlier but also to interpret and evaluate the survey. Because they do not have previous research experience, the guided interpretation of survey results builds on young people's developing problem-solving skills by asking them to summarize what they see in the results, to notice any patterns, to comment on results that surprise them, to be attentive to any contradictions, and to consider what they would have asked differently. In addition to these critical-thinking activities, the research review offers young people a glimpse into what youth from the other areas of the study are thinking and thus could be a step along the pathway to transcultural understanding. In terms of the pathway in the workshop, this activity offers preparation for the highlight of creating an original youth survey. In addition to increasing participants' connection and power over information, this activity is a meaningful use of computer software and the Internet.

When in the position to view results by peers, participants can reconsider their responses, compare them, and learn about how their generation views the issues. This activity offers the opportunity to consider contradictions resulting from different youth stances, which is easier to do, not only for young people but also for adults, when considering others' statements. When responding to questions about positive qualities in society, young people involved in the guided review of results with peers observed, for example, that others' statements seemed like slight exaggerations, which then provoked lively conversation about whether their own responses would seem that way to participants in another country.

A third inquiry activity to promote a different connection, interpretation, and power is the workshop highlight to create an original youth survey. Instructions for the activity appear in Figure 2.5. This activity is introduced with the question, "What do we want to know from young people in the other areas about important issues in their lives as they move from being children to being adults?" Instructions also suggest that the young survey makers consider asking about broader issues, such as whether and how their societies prepare youth for this transition. A major research interest was what these youth would want to know, if anything, about the nature of educational, social, or other supports their former adversary countries were offering. Other purposes include making social connections explicit (among the small, face-to-face working groups and with the

Dynamic Story-Telling by Youth, Make your own survey
1. Write the first draft of the survey.
    a. What would you like to know?
    b. What types of answers would you like? There are three types offered:
        One Answer – Allows the participant to give a single line answer to the question.
        Choice – Participant can chose from a few (multiple) given answers.
        Open Ended – Allows your participant to express ideas and opinions.
2. Discuss the area and questions you would like to ask young people in other areas of the ex-Yugoslavia and the U.S.
3. Create a title.
4. Write your questions in the format you think will be most appropriate.
5. Preview your survey and make any necessary changes.
6. Write an invitation for others to take your survey.
    a. A few engaging sentences
    b. If you like, create an attractive image or logo
        If you select or create an image, please do the following to make sure it's in a format we can use in Survey Monkey:
        Save your image as a .jpg or .gif file on your computer or flash drive, write the exact name of the file. Be sure to tell one of the workshop leaders that you have saved an image.
7. After the workshop, we will add your survey to the larger survey By and For Youth.
8. We will send this survey to you for you to take and then you can get results as well.

FIGURE 2.5. Guidelines for activity to create an original youth survey, "By and For Youth."

international peers for whom the surveys are designed) and gathering information from youth leaders and educators about what young people feel are important issues, needs, and learning goals. The activity also adds to the inquiry tool kit an opportunity to use computer application tools and the Internet to create surveys and view responses.

Having themselves taken the survey in the first activity, participants were especially engaged working in small groups to create different types of survey questions. This activity contributes to the overall research/practice purpose by involving participants in the inquiry process as question askers and as members of a broader transnational community of youth (albeit virtually). The research team compiled the surveys by all the groups of youth participants into a survey titled

"By and for youth," posted on Surveymonkey.com, and sent the link to all participants for their voluntary completion and review.

Analyses of these youth surveys show that the participants created a fascinating set of questions for their transnational and local peers (see Chapter 5). Although we had hoped that all the activities would be interesting, this was a highlight because it allows young people to express their views about the stories and other information they feel they need to move themselves and their societies forward to a peaceful and productive future.

Participants were especially enthusiastic about this activity, exerting a lot of energy to write questions and create illustrated advertisements enticing others to respond to their questions. The research analysis could then determine whether and how these reflections conform to past or new national concerns.

Narrative Genres

We ask whether and how adolescents in this case study echo the now-frozen narratives of war and postwar consequences or employ their narrative abilities not only to share stories but also to use them to mediate self–society relations. More specifically, we addressed questions including: How do adolescents across diverse postwar contexts narrate conflict? How do those adolescents use systematically varied opportunities to narrate conflict? What do we learn about adolescents' use of communicative complexity to integrate and transform societal narratives?

The written narrative mode is relevant for several reasons. Previous research in the United States and internationally indicates that adolescents have the encoding and decoding skills necessary for writing narratives. In addition, the use of computers for many of the workshop activities, including narrative writing, appealed to potential participants and the directors of organizations who recruited them. Moreover, writing narratives provides a relatively individual context for comparison to the more explicitly interactive ones in the workshop.

Narrators work not only with plot structures but also with affordances of the narrating context, such as expectations of present and imagined audiences, power relations among the narrator and the diverse audiences, and features of the physical and social settings. In this way, we become aware that discourse is performance. In terms of the qualities of youth stances guiding the workshop design, the narrating activities most prominently involved interpretation, with less explicit connection than in the inquiry or advisory activities. Because autobiographical narrating is expected to represent actual events, activities to narrate conflicts among peers and adults would thus involve less power or, in this case, poetic license, than a fictional narrative. As shown in Figure 2.6, the DSTY narrating activities allow for this range of options.

Peer Conflict Narrative: *Write about a time when you or someone you know had a conflict or disagreement with someone your age... Who was involved? What happened? Where was it? When was it? How did those involved think and feel about the conflict? How did you handle it? How did it all turn out?*

Adult Conflict Narrative: *Write about a time when adults you know (or the "community") had a conflict or disagreement... Who was involved? What happened? Where was it? When was it? How did those involved think and feel about the conflict? How did they(you?) handle it? How did it all turn out?*

Fictional Community Narrative:

Using the following story starter, complete your own version of the story.

"_____ and _____ (from two groups) met at a ground-breaking of the new town center building. Everyone at the event had the opportunity to break the earth for the foundation and to place a brick for the building. It was an exciting community event and everyone was pleased that the new building would mark a new future. As they were working to begin the foundation, _____ and _____ had a conversation about how they would like to make a difference in their town so their children could live happily together. All of a sudden, someone came with news that changed everything! What was the news? How did everyone involved think and feel? How did it all turn out?

FIGURE 2.6. Invitation to narrate conflict from diverse perspectives.

As explained previously and in earlier research, power in a fictional narrating activity likely results from the fact that its author is protected (at least somewhat) from conforming to societal requirements and expectations, which may actually fictionalize the more explicitly autobiographical activities. The collaborative narrating activity to discuss a public story allows for the most explicit social connecting and power because it also involves evaluating the story and the related events. At the same time, the social requirements of collaboration limit interpretive force compared to the other narrative activities because collaboration tends to involve consensus. To provide for an explicitly collaborative narrating activity, the DSTY workshop includes reading and responding to a story about a public event involving youth activism relative to a major local issue in context, as shown in Figure 2.7, the Appendix, and the discussion below.

Recent psycholinguistic analyses implore us to consider narrative diversity in terms of narrator stance (first- versus third-person focus), audience, narrating context, cultural organizations of meaning (scripts), and significance (evaluative devices). Narrators use these features, intentionally or spontaneously, as tools for perceiving

---

1. Gather in groups of 3 or 4 to read and discuss the public story, then gather everyone in the workshop, where each small group can summarize the major points of their discussion.

2. Read the story.

3. Write a few sentences saying more to agree or disagree with what at least three of the people mentioned in the article.

For each story, 4 or so characters in the story expressing different points in the story are listed, with room for participants' comments about that person's role and/or views in the event.

4. What questions do you have about the background that led to this story?

(See Appendix I for Summaries of Public Stories Discussed by Youth across Positions in the DSTY Workshop)

FIGURE 2.7. Guidelines for discussing the public story.

situations, organizing meaning, and gaining insights from the narrative experience itself. Narrative structure and significance are thus not static but are a collection of affordances that can be combined in flexible ways (Heft, 2007). Asking adolescents to narrate from diverse character perspectives encourages them to broaden beyond their subjective understandings and to focus, for example, on how people with whom they might not otherwise empathize spontaneously (parents, teachers, leaders) are coping with challenges in their lives. Such flexible narrating activities extend basic perspective-taking processes to awaken communicative complexity and, perhaps, critical reflection.

This use of narrating as a mediational tool operates on a large scale, such as in Croatia's explaining the need to expel non-Croats from their "homeland" and Serbia's complaining about hundreds of years of aggression by outsiders and the effects of recent political–economic isolation (Gagnon, 2004). At the same time that such narratives circulate in public and private discourse, alternatives are created by those devoted to postwar development, including NGOs, educators, and youth motivated to create a peaceful and productive future. Considered in this way, narrating integrates individual and societal activity. I propose that narrating from diverse perspectives, especially in highly contentious sociopolitical contexts, might engage a broader range of adolescents' knowledge than narrative tellings or writings from first-person perspectives.

This practice-based research considers how young people positioned differently around a war make sense of their own experiences, connect to others' experiences, and relate those experiences to societal issues and their own goals. In the context of research workshops from the spring to the fall of 2007 (Daiute, 2007), young people, their mentors, their teachers, and the research team created, shared, discussed, and inquired about stories of conflict in the present and future as a positive way to reflect on the past. By building on the goals of community centers in the region and expressing the need for a social history from the youth perspective, we establish a collaborative orientation to research workshop activities. Workshop activities involve young people in the development of social history from the perspective of their transition to adulthood. In addition to this motivational and practical purpose, workshop activities are designed to engage within – as well as across – participant/context diversity, specifically about issues of conflict and development salient in the postwar period. To allow for such complexity, the affordances of narrative activities are varied systematically so adolescent narrators can use their developmental capacities for communicative flexibility.

As shown in Figures 2.6 and 2.7, these activities systematically vary elements of narrator stance by shifting the character perspective from the social world of peers to that of adults and to a hypothetical but realistic community, thereby changing the explicit exposure of the narrator self to actual and potential audiences. The young authors are most personally exposed in the peer-focused narratives and less exposed in the adult-focused narratives, where most, in this study, assumed the stance of observers (see Chapter 4). The hypothetical-community narrative activity offers the most opportunity because fictional characters have more leeway to express knowledge and issues considered less than ideal or taboo. In this way, we invited adolescents to tell others' stories as well as their own and to narrate openly in autobiography and indirectly in fiction.

Although the first-person stance allows for a wide range of possible stories, it also exposes narrators to judgment by the immediate audience (researchers, community-center directors, and peers) and distant audiences (reflections on the family and society). Recounting first-person narrative may, of course, be easier and more interesting, self-focused, heartfelt, or authentic, but it also requires special consideration about how the author will be perceived. In this postwar context, for example, all youth who are exposed to the media, attend public school, and engage in public life know that the Balkan countries are being judged for their war-related past, including ethnic cleansing. Youth in Serbia, moreover, know that their former president,

Slobodan Milosevic and their society by extension is often character-ized as the major aggressor of the war, whereas youth in Bosnia know that their society is perceived as a major victim of ethnic cleansing. Young people's awareness of such distant audiences, as well as the more present ones who could directly censor war-talk, for example, or exert pressure for resilient narratives, may make them especially cautious in first-person accounts where their thoughts and actions are on display as authors, protagonists, antagonists, or bystanders.

In contrast, narrating conflicts among adults invites adolescents to focus on the generation who experienced the war and to express information that someone might withhold if it were to portray him or her negatively. The narrator is thus freed to express knowledge or subjectivity, such as the bitterness of those who experienced the war, without feeling they might be perceived as personally expressing an unpopular "mentality of the past." The hypothetical-community nar-rative shifts the narrator stance again with a more subtle invitation to narrate conflict by asking a participant to establish two charac-ters "from different groups," albeit leaving open the nature of the group and asking for completion after the turning point "someone came with the news that changed everything." This activity uniquely mentions the option to express relationships among characters of dif-ferent genders, generations, cultures, and so forth without requiring that they be in conflict.

Because adolescents and young adults across a wide range of lin-guistic cultures have developed abilities to use the basic structural conventions and evaluative devices of narrating (Berman & Slobin, 1994), they are likely to be increasingly in control of the social-relational dimensions, such as using fictional narratives to express knowledge and experience that audiences may perceive as negative. Such communicative complexity is, I argue, a developmental process that emerges with these diverse narrating experiences. This design, in brief, allows young people to distribute their knowledge and subjec-tivity about conflict across narrative perspectives, thereby providing

opportunities to demonstrate communicative flexibility. The resulting narratives then provide data we can use to analyze variations of
meaning within and across these activities and to learn about adolescents' abilities to use discourse as a mediator of experience. This
new knowledge about narrating, in turn, is central to a developmental
approach to studying effects of political violence. Participants in the
research workshops did indeed use a range of narrative elements, not
only interacting with the diverse circumstances where they lived but
also engaging with different aspects of their own personal knowledge,
experience, emotion, and intention. As shown in the three narratives
by 15-year-old Rudy in BiH, similar yet systematically varied narrative
activities involved interaction with different aspects of "human-like
intention and action and to the vicissitudes and consequences that
mark their course" (Bruner, 1986, p. 13).

Rudy uses three narrative contexts to interact with different dimensions of social life: his community, the workshop setting, and an
imagined world. In the story about a conflict with a peer, Rudy progresses from being an unsuspecting participant to someone attacked,
frightened, and isolated.

Conflict among Peers

> *During the break at school, while I was waiting in the line for
> sandwiches, a boy from another class put a firecracker in my rucksack
> which was on my back. I didn't even notice that until other students
> started to laugh and move away from me. Then I realized that my
> books were burning, so I threw the rucksack onto the ground, and
> ran away because I was scared. I was very angry and scared because
> I didn't find it to be funny, but rather dangerous. The worst thing
> was that the other students either ran away or laughed; none of them
> defended me, nobody said anything to that boy.*

At the end of the story, Rudy masters the situation for himself
and for the reader by commenting negatively about the people who
hurt, isolated, and failed to defend him: "The worst thing was that

the other students either ran away or laughed; none of them defended me, nobody said anything to that boy." Although offering little insight about others in the conflict with peers, Rudy opens the subjective realm of others in a story about a conflict among adults.

Conflict among Adults

It happened at the crossroads when two drivers got out of their cars and, for some reason, started an argument (probably one of them violated traffic regulations). They stopped the traffic and nearly started to fight physically. The other drivers were yelling and cursing from their cars. A young man interfered and made the two men stop arguing. Personally, I was appalled by the incident and I was particularly irritated because they prevented the others from moving.

Although he also ends this story with a negative judgment, Rudy conveys the emotional tension of the participants: " . . . nearly started to fight physically," " . . . other drivers were yelling and cursing," and so forth. Rudy enters the story in two ways: first, apparently siding with the "young man [who] interfered and made the two men stop arguing," and then with his closing, "Personally, I was appalled. . . . " With these two brief narratives, Rudy demonstrates his own abilities to feel, project, and judge the morality of a situation. He also astutely observes how adults "prevented others from moving," which resonates with the local political situation. Lest we think him too serious, negative, depressed, or defensive, Rudy crafts another stance in a fictional story.

Fictional Community Narrative

The news was that the mayor appeared and told the people who were present that the city administration donated a certain amount of money to the Center so it could obtain necessary equipment such as computers, video recorders, and other technical devices. Everybody was extremely excited and happy. Eventually, they threw a big party attended by the mayor himself.

This story performs positive intentions and actions. After distancing himself from the powerful mob of the schoolyard and voicing the heroism of a bystander in the chaos of a city street, Rudy uses this fictional story to foreground the generosity of the most powerful man in town, the mayor, to make people happy. Thus, although not explicitly about power, these three stories mediate such relations across a broader system than is evident in any single narrative. As discussed in subsequent chapters, when we consider the range of workshop activities as mediators of living history, we gain insights about young people's understandings of the environments where they find themselves.

OVERVIEW OF THE PUBLIC STORY ACTIVITY

An important stance for youth reflection on public life and their role in it is to reflect on youth participation as it has occurred in society. While one major public story across these contexts could be a national version of the 1990s wars, a relevant developmental approach is to provide a context where young people can reflect on youth activism in relation to a major current event. A local event of youth activism would provide a context for participants' reflection on a major national issue relevant to young people in their context to create a spontaneous demonstration or other active engagement with current history. Beyond that, such events would also most likely involve a range of youth perspectives, thereby articulating increasing maturity about young people's reflection on political issues. In addition, having the opportunity to discuss such events and different perspectives about them in small and large groups during the workshop activities would provide a unique stance for considering one's own participation in public life not only in terms of personal philosophy (which may model on family members' or other adults with personal influence) but also in relation to one's own generation. As shown in Figure 2.7 (above), the public story activity involves practice discussing youth activism around current events but also insights for research, education, and community development activities about the range of positions among participants' and the nature of their debates about these issues. For adolescents and young adults such civic engagement is a developmental process deserving support and warranting inquiry.

In a political violence system, such events would, most likely, be related somehow to the politics of war and transition. Archival review of youth activism during the participants' childhood and adolescent years revealed several major events. Several criteria evolved in transforming related news stories and books into a template for public story discussion and a specific story for each context. Criteria for our public story design included: 1) identify an event within the past few years that is of national or local political importance, 2) that elicited public response by young people, such as a demonstration, teach-in, etc., 3) with reports in the news offering information about the event, in particular a range of youth perspectives, 4) allowing for a story that could be condensed into a few pages of summary with enough detail, potentially interesting, enlightening, and worthy for discussion in the DSTY research workshop.

Advisory Genres

Advisory activities, including writing a letter to a community leader and evaluating the workshop, make the most consistent shift to an authoritative youth stance.

You are the author:
How can your city/town/country prepare young people for a better future? Explain by writing a letter to the head of your school, the

mayor, president, or other leader you think can help make this change.

Dear:

Youth letters to officials potentially offer different information than young people might reveal in less authoritative activities or in those with less important interlocutors. As discussed in Chapter 3, young people wrote letters with authority, knowledge, and sometimes even humor and panache. (Analyses of the letters appear in Chapter 5.)

The final advisory act was to evaluate the workshop using the form shown in Figure 2.8 below (p. 73).

The social stances of connection, interpretation, and power vary across these activities as illustrated in Table 2.1. *Social power* is defined as the explicit positioning of an author/speaker in relation to the others in the context and in discursive products, offering experience-based advice to a community leader and asking questions and interpreting responses of other youth. In contrast, writing a narrative or responding to an adult-created survey positions youth in a relatively weaker relational stance, albeit with more freedom to interpret situations than in openly collective activities that require negotiation, as in the collaborative review of other youths' survey responses.

In summary, the location of an audience, whether explicit or implicit, near or far, defines the social-relational dynamics of an oral or written communication activity. For example, the presence of an explicit audience, whether a community leader, a peer, a researcher, or all three, shapes (opens or limits an author's and speaker's interpretive power, if that author or speaker wants to appear knowledgeable, reliable, or appealing in some other way to that audience). Implicit audiences introduce other potential interlocutors who may judge or praise, including local and national institutions; leaders and participants in the former Yugoslavia, such as those who provoked war; the EU, with which the destiny of the youth is entwined; international institutions and individuals, whose financial support has helped youth activities and national recovery; international audiences, whose opinions are expressed in the media (e.g., documentaries and Internet blogs); and those serving as models for characters in narratives. Such factors combine in a little-acknowledged dimension of communicative complexity and its role in development, perhaps especially in contentious situations (see Chapter 7 for further discussion of this process).

PARTICIPANTS

Because foundational theoretical principles focus on development in context, the actual implementation of the research workshop had to be consistent with the local context. For this reason, as stated in the field note excerpts at the beginning of this chapter, the actual numbers of participants, workshop contexts, and workshop leaders varied somewhat. Participant recruitment materials were the same but were translated into each local dialect of Serbo-Croatian (now referred to as the different languages of Bosnian, Croatian, and Serbian), and procedures ensured that young people did not feel pressured to volunteer in order to maintain any connection with an organization. Also important was the meaning of the workshop place, making sense for the local context, as described in the chapter-opening vignettes.

Participants were 137 young people, aged 12 to 27; half were actively involved in a local community center and half were not. Of the 132 participants who completed several activities, 37 were in BiH, 39 in Croatia, 31 in Serbia, and 25 in the United States; 63 were younger (12 to 18 years) and 69 were older (19 to 27 years), with more participants 18 and younger in BiH, Croatia, and the United States and an over-representation of older participants in Serbia. These male and female youth represented the majority in their country. In Croatia, this is a mix of returnees (voluntary emigrees or expelled ethnic groups coming home to claim property or to remain for other reasons) and refugees (from other areas who now feel unwelcome in the face of political changes). In Serbia, most participants identified as Serbian, having grown up in Serbia; some were refugees from other birthplaces, and quite a few were of mixed-ethnic parentage. Most participants in BiH and in the United States identified as Bosniaks (Bosnian Muslims).

WHY US?

As discussed previously when explaining the social nature of discourse genres, the research theory and design assumes that young participants interact with a variety of present and imagined audiences. The present audiences include workshop leaders, which, in all contexts, included adults and young adults in local organizations, a representative of the international research team, and other workshop peers. Of course, appeal to and issues with specific audiences is a task for research to interpret, ideally by using knowledge of the context, consultation with participants, and a systematic design. For that reason, I mention my own position, which is clearly represented throughout this inquiry.

As the project director, I was an audience member as well as a participant. The systematic design of the research workshop and, as presented in subsequent chapters, the analysis allow for multiple audiences, including me. As a participant observer, I communicated with participants in person via workshop materials and/or via the Internet before, during, and after the workshops. In two countries, I was a workshop co-leader, as my speaking ability in Bosnian, Croatian, and Serbian is more rudimentary than my reading ability in those languages. In the other two countries, another research team member led the workshops. In all of the interactions, I stated that the goal of the research was to learn about "young people's perspectives on their society, in particular for their development" and "such development in rapidly changing societies like theirs." Although I did not focus on war or the past, I said that we would ask about conflict because it is relevant to our everyday lives. I reiterated my interest in the participants' perspectives in relation to specific audiences that would be introduced in the activities and in relation to those that might be evoked in the activities. In this way, I tried to be open as an audience via clearly stated goals, requests, and responsiveness to youth questions. My status as an international researcher certainly, however, influenced interactions in ways that I mention with the findings when possible.

When introducing the project and workshop to young people across the contexts, I told them about my professional history and relevant personal information. I explained, for example, what I do on a typical day as a developmental psychologist, university teacher, and researcher. I described some of my previous research, mentioning the questions I asked, where I did the research, and the surprising findings, such as those that emerged during my work with children and teachers in the United States. I then explained how those findings led to questions about the related nature of development during adolescence in societies that are also changing. After a flurry of comments, I recognized, with my then-rudimentary understanding of the native language, that those present acknowledged that changes were indeed afoot. One teenager, Susana, asked me, "Why here? Why us? People have many ideas about us." Realizing I needed to offer more detail, I explained my reading of previous research with young people growing up from the early 1990s to the present and that I had not read very much about what "you think." I also explained that I came to this specific place in part because of some personal connections and that, based on previous visits, I thought the work my colleagues were doing in this place took young people seriously.

At one point, Susana said, "I always thought research was like with animals? It's about people too?" I assured her and the others present that my reason for coming was far from the type of research about automatic processes, like in animals, but is instead about thinking and development. I added that the entire project was designed to learn from young people in ways that *they* control, in their language and in their interactions with one another, their mentors, and the researchers. I also emphasized the importance of sharing the findings to increase knowledge about young people without exposing their identities. Susana nodded but persisted, "So you will listen to what we say?" I assured her that I would and offered examples from my previous research reports. I am not sure I sufficiently answered Susana's questions to erase all doubt, but she decided to participate, did so energetically, and occasionally commented about the process to her peers and to me. My point in this account is that I tried to make my interests and myself explicit in the process so that participants could speak directly to me as well as to the other more important people in their lives. That I was from the United States and a psychologist whose interest in children, education, and societies are facts that were always present in some way. With that as a given, I stated my presence as one among a myriad listeners.

PARTICIPANT EVALUATIONS

Before discussing how young people brought the theory-based activities to life and what we learn from those enactments, a review of participants' evaluations offers information about whether they describe the activities as meaningful. Their active engagement during this relatively lengthy workshop is supported by their evaluations indicating that they found it interesting, if not perfect.

The participants evaluated the DSTY workshop by responding to five Likert Scale questions (i.e., 5-point scale) and writing open-ended responses to "explain" their response to each item. As shown in Figure 2.8, scale items asked participants to evaluate each major workshop activity: the DSTY Survey, including narratives of conflict, reflections on societal conditions, and letters to officials; the Guided Review of Results of the DSTY Survey; the group discussion of the Public Story (based on local conflict-related current events); and the group work to

---

EVALUATION

Please rate your interests in different parts of the workshop on scale from
1 = very bad, 5= very good

1. Dynamic Story-Telling by Youth Survey
        1   2   3   4   5
   Please explain?
2. *What do you think about reviewing results of the Dynamic Story-Telling Survey?*
        1   2   3   4   5
   Please explain?
3. *What do you think about the Public Story activity?*
        1   2   3   4   5
   Please explain?
4. *How was it to create your own survey and survey invitation in Survey Monkey?*
        1   2   3   4   5
   Please explain?
5. *What was the best part of the workshop?*
6. *What was the worst part of the workshop?*

*Adapted from a workshop survey designed by M. Turniski

FIGURE 2.8. Participant evaluation for the *Dynamic Story-Telling by Youth* research workshop.

create an original youth survey; as well as an evaluation of the overall workshop. Analyses of responses indicate that participants enjoyed the workshop, learned from it, and "felt powerful" (in the words of a participant in Croatia) after being involved in the international effort. Qualitative comments include that the workshop was "interesting" and/or "fun." Participants in other settings were "surprised to get results from other responders to the same survey" and summarized some specific results they found intriguing.

The most highly rated activity in the workshop across all sites was the DTSY Survey: 58.6 percent of the participants rated it as "very good" and 24.3 percent rated it as "good." Another highly rated activity was what we envisioned as the high point of the workshop: creating an original youth survey, which participants knew would be compiled and distributed as part of our ongoing dissemination (52 percent rated it as "very good" and 20 percent as "good"). The activities of reviewing results by other groups and the public story were rated only slightly lower, as indicated by a few more percentage points in the "OK" or "bad" category. Although many enjoyed the process of discussing youth participation in current events, several explained why the story itself was problematic. Reasons offered include, for example, that the Serbian public story had become boring, even though it was historically important as a protest against the past regime, because of so much previous press about the event. Complaints about the Croatian public story centered around the confusing nature of the story itself. The U.S. public story, in contrast, elicited heated and committed debate because of the nature of the event (a protest against a "catch an immigrant game" at a local university) and its resonance with issues in the Bosnian community.

SUMMARY

Symbolic thought is the genius of all people, albeit a capacity that is not typically the focus of research with young people growing up in political violence. Likened to creating tools like fire and the wheel but far surpassing even those, language is a tool that allows thought to travel across time and space. Language can also, however, undermine communication and development if it reifies stereotypes. Although more focused on context and diversity than on the maturation of abstract-thinking capacities, sociohistorical theories concur that discourse fosters "a theoretical attitude to reality" (Elkonin, 1971/2000). Nevertheless, "with regard to adolescence, there is still no description of the ideal action that 'opens up' at the close of elementary school age and is 'attained' in the course of development during the next age-related stage" (*ibid.*).

An increasing number of scholars agree on the importance of the "motivational-needs sphere" of "child–social adult" systems (Polivanova, 2006), especially as adolescents make sense of ecologies of political violence (Barber, 2009). This transformation " ... must be understood as reproducing some aspects of human culture, and it must ensure the formation (or emergence) of a special "subjecthood" (similar to the subjecthood of play activity) (Polivanova, 2006, p. 81). The seriously undercharacterized dimension of human development in extreme conditions like political violence is the use of those capacities flourishing especially during adolescence. People may tell stories to release tension or convey a firmly held belief, but perhaps more obvious, given the theory discussed herein, is the role of discourse to connect with others in goal-directed ways, in particular, for mutual development beyond violence.

People craft stories not to report or merely interpret events. Instead, they interact with the societal and personal "motivational-needs sphere," hence, our focus on the purpose of those stories at the time of telling and within the broader developmental project of the teller at the time. We should consider adolescents (and others) in extreme sociopolitical contexts as not only being influenced by contexts, but more importantly, as using stories as tools to inquire about the world and their place in it. My goal in this book is to illustrate the complex uses of discourse as the intersection of individual and social change.

FIGURE 3.1. Growing up with bullet holes at the swimming hole.

3

Living History

The conflict was about the Homeland war. My opinion is that we shouldn't forget the past but that we must look forward to the future. Adults find it difficult to forget certain things from the past. This problem can never be solved because it exists subconsciously.

Feniks, 20, Croatia

I found myself in a very unpleasant situation: I was coming back from school, and two guys on the school bus were fighting. The reason was the unsolved situation from the past. We all got scared, especially when one of them took out a knife.

Aska, 20, BiH

These narratives by 20-year-olds growing up in very different circumstances of a political-violence system are living histories. What these narratives have in common is that they bring the past into present circumstances, in the one case as "the Homeland war" intrudes on the present because "adults find it difficult to forget the past" and in the other as a fight in public erupts because of "the unsolved situation from the past." The young authors go beyond mere description to explain the effects of such intrusions. According to Feniks, "we shouldn't forget the past," but focusing on it too much is a problem that "can never be solved." In the second narrative, Aska connects emotionally: "[W]e all got scared," as "the unsolved situation from the past" continues to present dangers like fighting and someone brandishing a knife on public transportation. In both narratives, the past is a presence, unwanted yet lurking, unpleasantly, in relation to the present time and space.

These narratives develop in specific contexts, one projecting into the future ("we must look forward to the future"), and the other suspended in reaction to an event ("we all got scared, especially when one of them took out a knife"). Such dynamic interaction of past events with present concerns in specific circumstances is living history. These young people may not be able to define subconscious processes or other people's reasons for fighting, but they recognize the interaction of an individual's psychological life with their everyday environments, a recognition that requires articulation by those of us interested in the plights of youth growing up during and after political violence.

These and myriad other narratives and commentaries by young people living in postwar BiH, Croatia, Serbia, and an immigrant community in the United States offer insights about the interdependence of powerful societal narratives as transformed in youth experiences. Rather than merely an influence or adopted value, the past intermingles with young people's experiences as shared when writing about "a conflict among adults in society" (see Figure 2.6).

As societal changes increase in frequency and speed, so does the need to understand the context-sensitive nature of human development, especially as young people become aware of the challenges and opportunities in their environment. As noted in relation to political–economic inequalities in the United States, children use public symbols as foils for identity development:

> ... *because a child's mind, like that of a grown-up, seizes symbols, craves a general explanation for a particular set of experiences, a nation's name, its flag, its music, its currency, its slogans, its history, its political life all give boys and girls everywhere a handle as they shape and assert their personalities.* (Coles, 1986, p. 61)

Although overshadowed by the recent emphasis on youthful risk, this observation is relevant to our inquiry into living history in political violence and transition. In situations characterized by negative events indelibly etched in the physical and symbolic landscapes, such as destroyed buildings, images of missing parents, changing names of nations, and a paucity of material resources, to name a few effects, we ask how adolescents, having achieved physical independence, use their cognitive, social, and other resources to interact critically and creatively with their environment. Because individuals can change well into adulthood (Arnett, 2004), this process could begin at any time in childhood or adolescence, most likely when those symbols relate to highly salient events like conflict.

This chapter focuses on how young people growing up in the context of political violence and transition integrate the past with contemporary challenges and opportunities. I argue that young people's motivations to integrate the past, present, and future in terms of threats and opportunities to development are common across contexts while the specific environmental circumstances attracting youth attention and interaction differ. I present this argument first by comparing different notions of history relative to human development.

Building on the idea of living history as a dynamic and motivating force, I then summarize analyses of narratives and commentaries by young people observing their societies, which emerge as different across the positions of the former Yugoslavia. Comparing those youth histories to social science reports of political–economic circumstances then underscores the influence of the locally salient circumstances. The chapter concludes by urging others to pay attention to young people's interactions with their environments, including those experiencing political violence, as developmental leading activities.

FROM OPPRESSIVE HISTORY TO LIVING HISTORY

History is typically written by powerful agents in a system, nation-states (via government leaders and laws), multinational organizations, local public officials, teachers, youth organizers, family members, and others who express or withhold stories of the past. Across the former Yugoslavia, like other transitional contexts, young people have been virtually excluded from story-telling processes related to the wars of the 1990s. History is especially oppressive during and after armed conflict as well as through periods of political–economic transition, when nations forge new policies and identities and thus hold tight reins on their representations. In addition to the consequences of violence, there are pressures on everyone to justify or silence past events as they imagine a "bright future" (Srna, 2005). NGOs and schools socialize youth to the values of social inclusion, human rights, democracy, practices of the market economy, and activism, but curricula related to the recent wars are still lacking or designed for ethnically segregated schools in many municipalities. National versions of history tend to be skewed toward justifications for local acts (MacDonald, 2002) and tribunals seek absolute truths about blame and victimhood, resolutions that continue to be elusive (Gordy, 2005). The lack of a contemporary history curriculum means that young people have no specific context for discussing, contesting, and transforming static histories.

Many parents try to protect their children from learning about the horrors they experienced in the war to prevent the next generation from being poisoned with pain, shame, or hatred (Freedman & Abazovic, 2006). Although children are likely to hear stories about the past despite their parents' efforts, such repression leaves gaps in family histories, deprives young people of knowledge they could use to avoid repeating past mistakes, and angers some who feel they have a right to know the bad and the good. Scholars studying effects of violent wars of the early to mid-20th century explain that such repression caused harm surfacing as nightmares or physical symptoms several generations later (Abraham & Torok, 1994; Caruth, 1996).

Despite major efforts by humanitarian workers, international organizations, and individuals who believe that reconciliation requires acknowledging responsibility and serving justice, a "common narrative" required to create a lasting peace in the Western Balkan region remains elusive (Bajraktari & Serwer, 2006). With the official end of the wars in 1999, consequences across the resulting countries differ in political stability, economic development, reconstruction of infrastructure, media independence, and relationships with the EU, among other factors (Goehring, 2007). The diversity of the political–economic aftermath of the 1990s wars is not surprising, in part because local claims over resources, such as potential benefits from tourism on the Adriatic coast, were at least one cause, but also because the region is one of considerable geographic variety. Although education, civil society, media, and other public institutions explain that the young generation *is* the future, few investigators have focused thoroughly on how young people interpret the ongoing challenges to their development.

The notion of collective memory, which some scholars apply to study responses to the past, implies that people adopt the histories they inherit to explain their situation. By loosening assumptions about the power of specific historical memories, that is, by questioning oppressive history as an organizing principle, we consider how young people make sense of their daily lives. If oppressive history is a focus on the past by those who lived it or dwell on it, living history is the integration of understandings, questions, and goals of people engaging with circumstances that challenge and enable them to thrive in the present.

Oppressive histories are distributed via scripts depicting the characters, events, causes, and consequences commonly accepted for circulation in society. Although alternatives may coexist, ideological scripts embed societal mantras that become frozen. A frozen script in Croatia, for example, identifies Serbia as the aggressor, leaving the homeland with no recourse but to defend itself, which required expelling Serbs. By contrast, a script in Serbia begins with Croatian secession and aggression, requiring Serbia to defend the region in the name of brotherhood and unity (Gagnon, 2004). Building on this insight, we consider how, in rapidly changing societies, young people resist and transform societal scripts when given the chance. Even when the recent past is oppressive, we find that young people transform its echoes by narrating present circumstances and motivations for the future. In this sense, history is a cultural tool, a strategy used in creative ways to account for what is decidedly not past. The perspectives of a generation growing up in the midst of dramatic changes are relevant to understanding the tension between oppressive history and living history.

Living history is the set of factors salient to young people as they pay attention to circumstances where they live, like the fights that bother Aska and her peers when they "all got scared, especially when one of them took out a knife" and the subconscious memories that Feniks fears will stall progress. In this view, war-related issues like intergroup tensions may have little explicit impact on youth, may be receding in light of new challenges, like the high unemployment in many transitional post-communist economies, or may be suppressed for a variety of reasons including pressures to move beyond the past.

Since the breakup of the Soviet Union in 1989 and in the current era of globalization and conflict, increasing numbers of children (like those in postwar Yugoslavia) live in contexts where symbols of identity, like flags, sports teams, and religious practices, are highly contentious. Embedded in their own names, the name of their towns, the colors of their flags, the lyrics of popular songs, and the tales people recount in cafés, kitchens, and playgrounds are complexities that stymie experienced political scientists. For example, in a small Croatian town, although discussing recent history is discouraged to avoid conflicts, children know that the name of their town recently changed from a Serbian to a Croatian word because of the war. Young people there have learned allegiance to a country that did not exist when their parents and older siblings grew up, but they also know to be cautious or even scornful about nationalistic claims to a flag, country, or sports team. They are well aware that such claims can excite animosities threatening the fragile peace and, more importantly, their cross-group friendships made possible by the return of families once expelled in ethnic-cleansing campaigns. Likewise, young people know that the unspoken identities as "Serb," "Croat," "Bosnian Croat," or "Muslim" of the peers with whom they have friendly interactions were at the root of war, even though all those people had once managed to live together relatively peacefully as "Yugoslavs."

To learn about sociopolitical development, we pay attention to how the workshop participants use such relevant symbols in interpersonal and public discourse in the community, media, and school. Rather than asking young people, "What happened in the war?" as some do to assess collective memory, we ask them to share their impressions and experiences. As described in Chapter 2, the DSTY research workshop is an intervention designed to engage youth perspectives so they could use social discourses in a range of relevant ways. Questions guiding this inquiry include, What do young people find salient in their social and physical environments? Are young people preoccupied by remnants of past events, such as buildings destroyed in recent bombings, images of war crimes on television, war stories by family members, curiosity about who did what to whom, hatred or mistrust of those identifying with ethnic groups, longing to return to a birthplace, missing a parent or other family member? Or do they focus on present issues that challenge their futures, such as fights that compromise daily life, the lack of education reform, or jobs? How do youth interact with the circumstances that matter to them? Addressing these questions provides information about the insights of people growing up in situations of political violence and instability, as well as the sociopolitical nature of human development more generally.

NARRATING LIVING HISTORY

Story-telling shapes public life, *and* individuals transform public life in their own personal stories (Miller, Hoogstra, Mintz, Fung, & Williams, 1993). It is, for example, through story-telling that leaders justify war and peace, as their political arguments are based on certain sequences of causes and effects, motivations, and involvements of individuals and groups. The beliefs that fuel conflict are, thus, embedded not only in national stories but also in citizens' stories. Story-telling has been used in testimony, community projects for reconciliation, and treaties designed to forge peace. National stories can also, however, suppress power relations and the voices of those left out of any official story (Amsterdam & Bruner, 2000; Scott, 1990). According to Berman, "Language and its control are powerful and recurring themes within this sociopolitical stage where one very quickly learns what can and what cannot be publicly discussed" (1999, p. 139).

Scholars argue that beyond mere reporting, story-telling fosters the development of individuals and society (Bamberg, 2006; Hermans & Hermans-Jansen, 2001; Polkinghorne, 1991). Children become members of their cultures as they learn to think of the world and themselves within the scripts of every day practices (Nelson, 2003). Because story-telling is, moreover, a means of social positioning addressed to audiences and to oneself, children, like adults, use it to perform identities and reflect on them (Bamberg, 2006; Daiute, 2004). Physical events – a salient word, glance, movement, or physical arrangement – are embodied in these interactions among narrator, audiences, and self-subject (Bakhtin, 1986). In this way, story-telling embeds institutional values, power relations, circumstances of the physical environment, and individual motivations (Harre & van Langenhove, 1999). Social scripts organize perception and action (Bruner, 1990).

Different social scripts may co-occur; they may be integrated, like plots and subplots, and they may clash, resulting in a story that seems incoherent. Social scripts have also been referred to as dominant ideologies (Foucault, 2001), ways of knowing (Gilligan, 1993), cultural scripts (Nelson, 2003), master narratives (Solis, 2004), and collective memories (Wertsch, 2002). Narrative theorists have also explained that development occurs via processes such as *valuation*, which is defined as "anything people identify as a relevant meaning unit when telling their life story . . . including . . . a precious memory, a difficult problem, a beloved person, an unreachable goal, an unanticipated death of a significant other, and so forth" (Hermans & Hermans-Jansen, 2001, p. 15). In this way, individual motivations bring social scripts to life as personal stories.

With experience, narrators use diverse social scripts appropriately and cleverly to remember, to guide their actions, to persuade others, or to fit in (Daiute & Nelson, 1997). Recent developmental research indicates processes involving the absorption, resistance, and transformation of such scripts (Bruner, 1986; Nelson, 2003). Because research on war-related discourse and action in political science, history, and sociology tends to focus on motivations and practices of elites (governments, leaders, and journalists), this extension to youth is a unique application of script theory to interdependent adolescent–societal understandings and development in the aftermath of war. Narratives of events and settings comprise the "landscape of action," and the dimension that expresses the significance of those events is the "landscape of consciousness" (Bruner, 1986). These two dimensions of narrating are useful in our inquiry about living history among a generation of youth struggling with the aftermath of war.

In response to an invitation to "write a story about a conflict you observed among adults in society," youth across ex-Yugoslavia narrated conflicts about different issues and resolved those conflicts in different ways. Young people observe the adult social world to learn how it is organized. Those growing up in crisis situations may be especially astute observers and raconteurs of the troubles in public life. It is thus not surprising that most participants in the DSTY research workshop responded to the request for a narrative describing adult conflict (79 to 95 percent across contexts), although some deferred with comments like "older people in my community don't speak English so they can't get into conflicts with other adults" or "I have never observed conflicts among adults." Youth in BiH were most likely to write that no conflicts occurred in their society (21 percent), followed by youth in Croatia (11 percent), the United States (5 percent), and none in Serbia. Claims that adults do not have conflicts are interesting, partly because denial suggests ambivalent ongoing circumstances.

LANDSCAPES OF CONFLICT

Interacting with their environments, young people across four positions of the former Yugoslavia portrayed very different landscapes in narratives of conflicts among adults. The differences emerged via analyses of the images at the center of the narratives (icons), plots (conflict issue and resolution strategy), and conflict scripts (the implicit organizing structure of the narrative).

Settings

Narratives depict events with characters interacting, usually around some "trouble" in the setting (Bruner, 2002). Although lifelike, narratives mediate the narrator's relation to life rather than reflect it cinematically. For this reason, the lifelike center of a narrative – an object, person, action, or emotion – embodies the narrator's selective perception, the reason for telling this story at this time. Settings are, thus, not mere backdrops for conflicts or simple sequences of events. To capture the symbolic nature of this narrative focal point, we proposed the concept of "icon" (Daiute & Lucic, 2008). As focal points of the trouble motivating a narrative, icons are setting-like but symbolic in accord with cultural–historical realities (*ibid.*). Because icons are so pivotal, I present them to set the scene for inquiry into what young participants across the former Yugoslavia find salient in their environments.[1]

The icon in Aska's narrative at the beginning of this chapter, for example, is "guys fighting on the school bus." This is more than a content analysis because icons are symbols in the following senses: central in the plot conflict and important as a junction among the narrator, narrative, and cultural–historical context surrounding them (Daiute & Lucic, 2008). Icons are, thus, interactive person-in-environment meanings. Fighting, for example, exists in the physical world, but that it is worthy of attention and fear relative to the past is a symbolic interaction. Although there are many objects in the world and possible tensions in public life, the choice of fighting with

[1] When identifying icons, we assumed that the narrator is building the story around a socioculturally relevant object. The first step of icon analysis was to identify the specific social or physical object or activity around which a conflict revolves.

a knife on public transportation embodies Aska's living history. Other narratives, including fighting that is peripheral to the plot, are not iconic.

Very different icons are at the center of narratives of adult-focused conflicts by young people across positions in the former Yugoslavia. Icons in adult-focused narratives of conflict in BiH tend to be tensions in public life, such as in public transportation with "arguments on public transportation," "on the bus," and "drivers at a crossroad;" community events like the dedication of "a monument for children killed during the war;" sporting events; or in clubs. Although sometimes depicting acts of violence, the icons in narratives by youth in the United States, in contrast, revolve around activities in the more intimate context of family and friends, as in the examples "my cousin's parents' house," "a fight with my parents," "inviting my uncle to move to America," and "two of my neighbors got in a fight."

Icons in narratives by youth in Serbia highlight public settings in neighborhoods, apartment buildings, backyards in close proximity, offices, grocery stores, and other public places: a neighbor "appropriate[d] half the street with his cars," "husband and wife arguing," "neighbor showed up drunk," "someone painted the graffiti on our building," and "teachers responsible for bad organization . . . during a trip." Youth in Croatia uniquely narrate around icons depicting rituals and seemingly petty disturbances: "new rules of writing in Croatian," "misunderstandings with my English teacher in high school," "wandering chickens," "fighting over a piece of land," "damage they had made to someone's tombstone," and "friends who come to sing and drink each evening."

Across these contexts, we observe that young people focus on different aspects of their landscapes where conflicts occur. Rural settings afford contexts where people argue about chickens roving across property boundaries, compared to urban settings where altercations occur about graffiti on an apartment building walls. Nevertheless, similarities and differences across rural and urban settings have to do with relatively public versus private scenes, the issues, and resolutions of those conflicts, whether chickens or concrete buildings are most prominently in view. What this comparison of icons shows is that social relations revolve around prominent objects and activities of everyday life. Next, we focus on the issues worthy of conflict.

TABLE 3.1. *Percentages of Adult-Conflict Narratives with Different Plot Structures*

	BiH	Croatia	Serbia	United States
Adult-Conflict Narratives				
Conflict Issues				
Social Relationships	0	16.7	26.3	10.5
Differences of Opinion	13.3	22.2	21.1	15.8
Political Issues	3.3	8.3	15.8	15.8
Property Issues	3.3	8.3	5.3	15.8
Physical Issues	33.3	8.3	0	15.8
Fate/Silly Issues	3.3	5.6	0	0
Character Issues	6.7	11.1	10.5	0
Resolution Strategies				
Psychological	23.3	38.9	63.2	15.8
Communication	10	16.7	21.1	10.5
Other Intervention	30	30.6	15.8	52.6
Physical	10	11.1	31.6	15.8
Collective Action	0	0	0	0
Total Strategies Applied	73.3	97.2	136.8	94.7

Plots

Table 3.1 lists the percentages of different issues and resolutions in adult-conflict narratives by young participants across four positions of the former Yugoslavia. Conflict issues and resolutions account for the full set of narratives, resulting in issues about social relationships, differences of opinion, politics, property/turf, physical altercations, character/emotion, and fate/silly issues. Strategies for resolving those issues include psychological, communication, intervention, physical, and collective action. The conflict issue in the opening narrative by Feniks revolves around a difference of opinion about whether to focus on the past or the future: "Adults find it difficult to forget certain things from the past. . . . My opinion is that we shouldn't forget the past but that we must look forward to the future." The author's resolution strategy is a psychological one of compromise: "This problem can never be solved because it exists subconsciously."

In contrast, this narrative by Narandjica in BiH is about a physical conflict on a bus:

> *One of the conflicts occurred on the bus. I was going back home from school with some friends. The bus was crowded. On the second stop, the door opened and an elderly gentleman was trying to get off, but he couldn't because of the crowd and because in his way was standing another man who himself didn't know where to move! The man who was trying to get off swore at the man standing next to him, who just kept gazing confusedly, not knowing what to do. Then they started exchanging bad words, which was soon followed by hitting each other. The bus driver solved the conflict by pulling over and throwing them both out of the bus.*

The resolution strategy to this escalating physical conflict is the intervention of a secondary character, the bus driver.

The plots of adult conflicts across contexts differ dramatically in ways suggesting youth–environment interactions. As shown in Table 3.1, most conflict-resolution structures in narratives by youth in BiH are physical altercations (33.3 percent) addressed by interventions of secondary characters (30 percent). This pattern differs in the narratives from Croatia, where the majority of conflicts revolve around differences of opinion (22.2 percent) addressed with psychological strategies (38.9 percent). Yet another pattern dominates in Serbia, with a majority of narrative conflicts in social relationships (26.3 percent) resolved overwhelmingly via psychological strategies (63.2 percent). Conflict issues in narratives by youth in the United States are distributed more evenly across strategies including differences of opinion, politics, property, and physical altercations (15.8 percent each), all addressed by the similar strategy of intervention by nonprimary characters (52.6 percent). Also interesting is the overall difference in total resolution strategies applied, with 73.3 percent of the narratives by youth in BiH including strategies to resolve the conflicts, whereas more than 136.8 percent of the narratives by youth in Serbia include resolution strategies, often more than one per narrative.[2]

This analysis indicates that youth in BiH perceive the adult world as unstable and requiring assistance, in Croatia as annoying and requiring reflection, in Serbia as socially divided yet psychosocially intense, and in the United States as requiring assistance. These differences suggest that young people are attuned to environmental circumstances, even in the adult social milieu. Surprising given previous theory and research highlighting adolescents' obsession with personal identity is the finding that they use narrating as a lens to focus more broadly on contentious issues in the local society, which do not always revolve around identity, as is often emphasized in research on adolescence. To examine whether and how young people intermingle more deeply with the effects of political violence and instability, we turn to an analysis of narrative scripts, the implicit organization of icons and plots. Because a script analysis reads beyond the literal text, it offers insights about this generation's ways of knowing and local diversities.

YOUTH–SOCIETY SCRIPTS

"Social script" is a useful concept for examining how young people interpret the significant dynamics in their environments. Identifying social scripts reveals common conceptions among a group of youth in transitional sociopolitical situations, but these methods allow room beyond the frozen scripts circulating among or repressed by those who focus on the past. An analysis of narratives may reveal diverse public psyches around issues of conflict in diverse locations, such as a victim script where most of the killings occurred, a guilt script among major aggressors, or a script organized around another local dynamic.

---

[2] Because some stories included more than one resolution, the overall percentage can be higher than 100.

Despite assumptions about collective memories, no prior research has offered information about such scripts or their complexity from the perspective of young people who have grown up with war.

Analysis of scripts to determine collective and diverse orientations within and across societies is consistent with recent political analysis (Gagnon, 2004). Two major explanations of the extremely violent breakup of the former Yugoslavia are the primordialist account emphasizing the popular eruption of long-standing hatreds among ethnic groups and the constructivist account emphasizing elites' exploitation of intergroup tensions to fuel fighting (Gagnon, 2004). Both explanations acknowledge violence, including ethnic cleansing – the killing, maiming, robbing, raping, expulsion, and other atrocities to remove nonmajority ethnic groups from areas claimed by majorities. Toward our goal of understanding postwar development as a function of the geopolitical circumstances that define children's lives, we draw in particular on the constructivist account that ethnicity is a tool for sociopolitical relations rather than the primary cause for war. Just as this explanation offers insights about why ethnic diversity could be a minor but tolerable issue during some regimes while fueling war during others, ethnicity could be more or less relevant to young people as a developmental issue in different times and places. Although ethnicity became highly salient during the breakup of Yugoslavia, a postwar generation poised for the challenges of the contemporary global market could have very different concerns. Given the dynamic nature of narrating in the physical world, this notion of construction does not mean that *any* account whatsoever is possible but that narrators interact with actual contexts.

A script analysis involves identifying the combined plot–purpose organizing a narrative: conflicts, resolutions, and causal connections among those major plot elements. Of course, we read the young authors' scripts with our own, with questions like, "What scripts do I (researcher) think organize(d) this narrative?" and "What sociocultural forces shape the narrative?" In other words, reading scripts means zooming back from literal statements in the narrative and

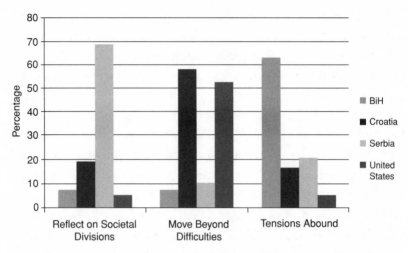

FIGURE 3.2. Percentages of narratives of adult conflicts organized by different scripts.

reading between the lines to gain insights about how a narrator is communicating with the context via the organization of the narrative and other details. Scripts, the taken-for-granted social frameworks organizing local life, embed expectations and logical relations expressed subtly in language (Billig, 1995; Nelson, 2003). Particularly interesting for understanding how groups of young people understand events are the patterns of similarity and difference of conflict scripts.

The graph in Figure 3.2 represents percentages of cross-country adult-conflict narratives organized around similar scripts.

As shown in Figure 3.2, scripts organizing young people's adult-conflict narratives differ dramatically across the study contexts. Reading all 101 narratives revealed three major scripts: tensions abound (in public life), moving beyond difficulties, and reflecting on societal divisions.

"Tensions Abound" Script

Youth in BiH narrated conflicts among adults in terms of tensions as they escalated mostly in public life but also in some private settings (hotel rooms and homes). The range of tensions among adults on public transportation, at events to honor war victims, and conflicts in other public settings like school trips also persists across the narratives. The script organizing conflicts around interpersonal tensions, the escalation of those tensions, and their ongoing nature includes specific types of conflict characteristic in adult-conflict narratives by youth in BiH. This narrative by Ema focuses characteristically on conflicts among adults in public transportation:

> *It is truly difficult to use our public transportation and not to see everyday conflicts between nervous citizens, retired people, drivers and conductors. Usually the problem starts out of nothing, maybe as a result of general unhappiness and stress in people, and then it escalates into something big. In a typical situation everyone is screaming, pushing each other. Conflicts like this one are never resolved, they just serve as a pressure relief.*

Ema echoes tensions in conflicts on public transportation. After identifying "nervous citizens, retired people, drivers and conductors" as participants, the author mentions possible causes, "maybe as a result of general unhappiness and stress in people," and escalations, "then it escalates into something big. In a typical situation, everyone is screaming, pushing each other." The narrator concludes by summarizing the tension-filled nature of such events. As narrator, Ema situates herself as an observer, entering the narrative by attributing psychological states impersonally with the observations "It is truly difficult to use our public transportation" and "Conflicts . . . just serve as a pressure relief."

With a similar "tensions abound script," Diana also narrates a situation as an observer with the impersonal reflection " . . . it is very sad" and via characters' states, such as "parents of those children feel used."

> *There is a debate about building a monument for children killed during the war, and it is very sad to see disagreement whether or not it should be for all children from all of Sarajevo or only for its*

Federation part. They still debate this issue, tensions are really big,
and parents of those children feel used.

That youth in BiH would perceive conflicts among adults in terms
of ongoing tensions, in some cases attributed specifically to tensions of the war, is consistent with the local circumstances of human
destruction, political division, and protracted economic difficulties.
Nevertheless, as in these examples, participants in BiH also reflected
on those tensions for themselves and their readers. Thus, rather than
characterizing youth in BiH as victims of trauma because they echo
tensions in their society, their narrative performances suggest that
they may be using the activity to manage those tensions and to make
sense of them.

"Moving Beyond Difficulties" Script

The script, "moving beyond difficulties," common in narratives in
Croatia, is, in many ways, one that makes sense in a context that
has recovered relatively more from the war, certainly in economic
terms, than the other contexts. Young authors in Croatia are fluent
observers of difficulties resulting from profound problems such as
mental illness among wounded war veterans to petty antagonisms
such as arguments about wayward chickens. Nevertheless, although
participants in Croatia offer great and sometimes humorous detail to
highlight how ridiculous the conflicts among adults can be, they also
craft plots with communication among former antagonists to move
beyond the past.

As shown in the following narrative by Anamaria, young people
understand local conflicts but also distance themselves from them:

My two neighbors always fight over a piece of land. The problem
is that the hens that belong to one of them always go to the piece
of the land that belongs to the other neighbor and she always calls
the police and makes a fuss about it. One day, while I was coming
back from school, I saw them having an argument. I mean, they

are adult women and it is not nice to see them fight and shout and
call themselves names. Everyone who was passing by laughed and
turned their eyes. Ugly! After the long lasting fight, the conflict was
covered up. But every day these fights happen again. Sometimes I
feel embarrassed to be their neighbor.

The narrator moves beyond this recurrent conflict by distancing with
judgments ("it is not nice . . . ;" "Everyone laughed and turned their
eyes;" "Ugly!") and a clear personal statement about her embarrassment to be their neighbor.

A narrative of the "homeland war" by 16-year-old Margareta also
conforms to the "moving beyond difficulties" script. As shown in her
narrative, if given the opportunity to engage with their environments
in several ways, young people integrate the past with present events,
feelings, and goals:

I can't think of anything except the Homeland war. Yugoslavia
fell apart. Then the Serbs, aggressors, destroyed Croatia and my
hometown as well. I don't know how the participants felt. I do know
that in my family there was optimism and hope for a better future.
The Serbs had a plan to become a huge and a powerful nation.
Conflict was solved with Croatia's victory in the war. Today we
have an independent country. These hopes came true. But the life
in Croatia is not even close to the one we expected it would be (bad
privatization, corrupted politicians, low life standards, etc.).

After repeating a frozen narrative of the "Homeland war," which
blames the Serbs for destroying Croatia, Margareta comments on the
unfulfilled expectations of her family, who had hoped the war would
lead to a "better future." Although obviously occurring in Margareta's
subjective repertoire, as well as in those of many others, the script of
the homeland war is permeable to a reality she perceives in her life:
"bad privatization, corrupted politicians, low life standards, etc."
Because it occurred in a workshop, the values of the community
center teaching coexistence, in a critical reflection about the war, the
consequences of the victims and the international researchers are all
embedded in this narrative, perhaps as a somewhat surprising ending.

As in Anamaria's narrative, moving beyond difficulties in Margareta's narrative means distancing from problems rather than surpassing them. Margareta narrates her family's hopes for the war sympathetically ("I do know that in my family there was optimism and hope for a better future") and in contrast to her family's adversaries ("The Serbs had a plan to become a huge and powerful nation") but then offers her narrator perspective in stark contrast to the results of the hopes: "But the life in Croatia is not even close to the one we expected it would be...." The "moving beyond difficulties" script, as illustrated in the narratives by Anamaria and Margareta, are neither counter scripts nor simple resistances. Instead, these youth use literary devices to indicate how they identify with issues, such as in resolutions or comments by characters. Such multiple positioning differs from the "tensions abound script," which leaves interpersonal or intergroup tensions relatively suspended, albeit occasionally commented on, across the majority of BiH narratives.

The majority of adult-conflict narratives by U.S. participants also emerged with a script like the "moving beyond difficulties script" of narratives by Croatian participants. As evident in the following narrative, Fikret narrates multiple sides of an issue.

A major microprocessing company intended to build a multi-billion dollar facility in this area creating hundreds of high-paying jobs. Arguments between local businesses and townships/cities persuaded the company to start its operation in a different part of the state.

Fikret's narrative is set more in the public domain than most others by his U.S. peers, but it is similar in the consideration of multiple points of view and resolution through an agent other than the antagonists, in this case the "state," which is persuaded to "start its operation in a different part of the state." Interestingly, the sense of injustice pervading many of the U.S. narratives is somewhat subtle in Fikret's narrative but present all the same, with losses of "hundreds of high-paying jobs." Advancement is possible, however, for those in the "different part of the state" where the company will start its operation.

"Reflecting on Societal Divisions" Script

The most common script by youth in Serbia, in contrast, describes divisions around opinion or affiliation elaborated further by narrator and character reflections about these reflections. This script builds with landscapes of consciousness (primarily psychological state expressions) rather than with landscapes of action (verbs describing actions). The "reflecting on societal divisions" script tends not to focus on the escalation of observed actions, as in the "tensions abound" script.

> *My neighbors were having an argument about who painted the graffiti in our building. One of them was accusing the son of the other. I think all the neighbors in the building were thinking how bored they were and how annoying it was to have such a thing in the morning. Eventually, they offended each other and left.*

As in this narrative by Vahmata, narratives conforming to the "reflecting on societal divisions" script build with psychological actions ("accusing," "thinking," "annoying," "offending") and reflecting on reflections ("I think all the neighbors in the building were thinking. . . . "). Resolutions tend to combine psychological and physical actions, such as "Eventually, they offended each other and left." The divisions in Vahmata's narrative occur close to home, with neighbors. Such divisions also occur in the workplace, as in Ljubicica's narrative recounting a conflict in employer–employee relationships:

> *Conflict in a company occurred between an employee and her supervisor. There were two factors. The others, who were not directly affected, did not get involved in the conflict which revolved around the expectations of the boss toward the office worker (in the company where I work part-time). I was thinking that I didn't know whose side to take and whether it was expected of me in the first place. Besides, I couldn't even judge, since the matter was related to something which was not part of my job, therefore not something I*

knew well. The others who were present exchanged comments among themselves, and the office worker resigned.

As does Vahmata's, Ljubicica's narrative illustrates the pattern of successive cognitive states ("revolved around," "thinking," "know," "expected of me," "judge"), resulting in a characteristic reflecting on reflections ("I was thinking that I didn't know," "others who were present exchanged comments among themselves"). Again, reflection and action combine in the resolution, although some narratives from Serbia end purely with reflection.

With these summaries, I must reiterate that these interdependent society–youth scripts are not stereotypes. They are, instead, dynamic interactions between young people and elites, who are present although sometimes distant and impersonal. These patterns indicate that young people use narrating to interact profoundly with their environments. Differences in the narrated icons, conflict issues, conflict resolution strategies, and social scripts that implicitly organize narratives indicate, moreover, that these youth are engaged with the *specific* circumstances where they live. The narratives indicate how young people connect personal and environmental experiences. As a generation growing up across dramatically different political systems from wartime to peacetime, how do these young people evaluate the state of their states, in particular in terms of the problems and positive qualities for their transition to adulthood?

YOUTH REFLECTIONS ABOUT THE STATE OF THE STATE

As part of the broader set of activities to create youth social histories, participants had the opportunity to identify problems and positive qualities in their societies, especially the ones affecting youth development (see Chapter 2). When we asked participants, "What are the problems facing youth in your society?" and "What are the positive qualities in your society?" they mentioned a wide range of factors, some surprising, some not. Issues that emerge as salient to young people across the contexts go beyond expectations about damage social reproduction in part because our developmental perspective mentions the future and, in part, because our sampling across the political system allows for context-dependent differences and similarities.

Analyses of participant responses to open-ended questions about problems and positive qualities in society involved compiling all responses into a database, identifying the issue in each response, creating topical labels for each issue, and computing frequencies for each by country context.[3] The problem "Youth's opinion is not understood seriously" is, for example, coded as "social acknowledgment youth." The following positive qualities required combining categories (indicated by /), which were then each coded as follows: "Beauty of nature,/ slower rhythm of life,/ people work less than in foreign countries and spend more time with amusements and pleasures, even despite the lack of money." The positive qualities are "nature," "leisure and entertainment," and "catch-22" (combination qualified positive).

Most participants (124 of 137) responding to the survey items identified problems, resulting in a mean number of different problems in their societies at 2.77 per participant. On the other hand, 129 of 137 participants mentioned positive qualities, with a mean of 2.14. Listed in descending order of frequency, problem categories focus on the social milieu (25.5 percent), substance use and abuse (24.1 percent), infrastructure (such as a lack of centers for youth) (24.1 percent), and developmental opportunities ("lack of resources for youth pleasures like travel") (21.9 percent). The relatively frequent mention of different types of economic issues warranted a separate category for "economic issues" (21.2 percent) and "unemployment" more specifically (20.4 percent). Other problems mentioned in between 10 and

[3] For purposes of comparison, we computed ratios of the number of coded comments per participant to the total number of coded comments for the country group.

20 percent of youth comments include dangers and violence, youth themselves, cultural and moral issues, education, politics, and societal acknowledgement of youth. The one category mentioned in fewer than 10 percent of the comments was family issues.

Participants mentioned fewer positive qualities (12 compared with 14 problematic qualities). Interestingly, the most frequent problematic aspect of society, social milieu (45.7 percent), was also the most frequently mentioned positive quality, with comments like "if something happens, everyone will help" and "a town with a lot of cultural heritage." A second group of positive qualities mentioned by 20 to 30 percent of the participants focuses on urban and rural qualities ("the city offers choices for meeting different people" and "anonymity in the city, everyone knows you in my small hometown"), education, leisure and entertainment ("lots of amusement down by the river"), personal qualities (e.g., "kindness" and "humility"), catch-22 ("most of it is negative" as a positive quality), and institutions and infrastructure ("It is good that there is a center for youth – that offers much amusement").

Participants across positions identified different problems and positive qualities, as shown in Table 3.2 and indicated by statistical analysis.[4] Table 3.2 presents the mean number of participant mentions of problems and positive qualities across the country contexts in the case study.

With these results, we consider the mutual youth–society sensitivities, which are supported and expanded in subsequent chapters. Participants in Croatia mentioned significantly more positive qualities (3.03) than problems (2.61). Participant means in the United

---

[4] Overall, an ANOVA indicated the significance of the different patterns ($p = 0.028$), and post-hoc contrasts indicated differences between $p = 0.03$ responses in Serbia (3.25) and the United States (2.32). Differences in responses to positive qualities were indicated overall at $p = 0.000$, with contrasts between Croatia (3.03) and BiH (1.84) at $p = 0.002$; Croatia and the United States (1.22) at $p = 0.000$; and Serbia (2.23) and the United States at $p = 0.043$.

TABLE 3.2. *Mean Mentions per Participant in Responses to Open-Ended Questions about Problems and Positive Qualities of Local Life*

| Summary categories | Countries across the former Yugoslavia | | | |
	BiH $N = 37$	Croatia $N = 39$	Serbia $N = 31$	United States $N = 25$
Problems in Local Area				
Economic Issues	.16	.26	.38	.14
Unemployment	.21	.29	.12	.27
Education Issues	.08	.26	.27	.18
Societal Acknowledgment of Youth	.11	.11	.23	.05
Politics*	.11	.13	.46	.14
Lack of Opportunity for Youth	.16	.29	.31	.23
Cultural and Moral Issues	.21	.13	.38	.14
Lack of Infrastructure	.13	.39	.31	.23
Dangers and Violence*	.34	.05	.19	.32
Substance Use and Abuse*	.42	.16	.12	.41
Issues of Social Milieu*	.34	.24	.42	.09
Youth Themselves	.29	.24	.19	.09
Family Issues	.11	.05	.15	.05
Positive Qualities	BiH	Croatia	Serbia	United States
Natural Resources*	.03	.24	.08	.15
Urban/Rural Qualities*	.13	.47	.38	.19
Quality of Social Milieu*	.50	.47	.65	.19
Personal Qualities	.24	.32	.27	.15
Values, Cultural Heritage	.03	.05	.12	.04
World of Work*	.13	.18	.04	.04
Leisure and Entertainment*	.13	.26	.54	.26
Education*	.39	.34	.19	.19
Institutions and Infrastructure*	.24	.29	.15	.04
Safety	.04	.11	.00	.04
Catch-22, Qualified Positive	.32	.24	.15	.04

* $p = 0.05$.

States also indicated more mentions of positive qualities, but those differences were not statistically significant. Mentions of problems and positive qualities across the contexts indicate the state of the state from the youth perspective.

As shown in Table 3.2, particularly interesting cross-context differences emerge in the most-frequent categories. The issues most salient to youth in BiH include substance use and abuse, dangers and violence, and problems in social life; on the positive side are frequent mentions of social milieu, catch-22 (qualified positives), and education. Youth in Serbia, in contrast, focus on political as well as social milieu, although their emphasis on mentions of problems in social life indicates a salience of ideological conflicts in the transition away from a "last century" or past "mentality." On the positive side for youth in Serbia are the qualities of social milieu and leisure and entertainment. Youth in the United States compare to those in BiH in their focus on substance use/abuse and dangers/violence, although they mention positively leisure/entertainment, education, and social milieu – albeit with lower overall frequencies than in other contexts. In general, the significant[5] differences of youth mentions of problems across country contexts are in the categories of politics and issues of social milieu, with youth in Serbia most focused on those two categories, while youth in BiH and the United States focused most on dangers/violence and substance use/abuse.

Differences across the positive categories occur for natural resources and urban/rural qualities, especially among youth in Croatia; positive qualities of the social milieu among youth in the United States are significantly below those in the other three countries for frequency of mentions. Youth in Croatia and in BiH mention the world of work most; youth in Serbia and in the United States mention leisure/entertainment most, along with other differences for positive qualities including education and institutions/infrastructure.

Because actual situations across the countries do not necessarily match the youth reports of their concerns, their interactions are with symbolic as well as material circumstances. During 2007, unemployment in the United States was generally lower than in Serbia, for example, and many of the older U.S. participants were employed. Thus, we must consider that the relatively high concern about employment

---

[5] $p = 0.05$ on post-hoc tests after ANOVAs.

among the U.S. participants may be related to the relatively high expectations for opportunities, especially given the sacrifices made by their families to be in the United States that they note elsewhere. Consistent with this explanation that concerns relate to combined symbolic and material circumstances is the relatively low recognition of educational opportunities in the United States, rather than identifying the possibility of attending college well into adulthood and the wide range of part- and full-time community college, public and private universities.

COMPARING YOUTH PERSPECTIVES TO SCHOLARS' ANALYSES

Independent measures of human destruction in the war, political stability, and economic circumstances during the postwar transition offer information for comparing youth perspectives to scholars' analyses of national circumstances. These data account for youth prospects. Drawing on scholarly accounts by political scientists, historians, anthropologists, and internationalists, I present a brief review of the diverse country circumstances. These circumstances are compiled from indicators of political and economic stability and prosperity, but they are also, of course, expressive of the points of view of the various organizations compiling them. Democracy scores, for example, are compiled by a U.S.-based organization with its view of democracy and labor statistics from the International Labor Organization (ILO), which does not consider youth labor as a positive factor. Recognizing such limits, I have drawn on evidence-based sources for comparison to the youth perspectives privileged in this book.

Table 3.3 summarizes measures of political and economic factors relevant to youth development across the countries resulting from the 1990s wars in the former Yugoslavia. These measures are compiled from sources including the World Bank (www.worldbank.org), Freedom House (Goering, 2007), the EU, the ILO (www.ilo.org), the United Nations High Commission on Refugees (www.unhcr.org), and

TABLE 3.3. *Prospects for Youth Development after War*

	BiH	Croatia	Serbia	United States
Positive Measures*	1. International image 2. Increase in democracy score	1. Very near EU membership 2. Middle GNI group 3. International image 4. Political stability	1. Increase in democracy score (constitution advances) 2. Middle GNI group 3. Population stability	1. High GNI group 2. Political stability
Negative Measures	1. Not in EU accession 2. Lowest GNI** group 3. Dealing with high, ongoing mortality 4. Population movements ongoing 5. Political instability 6. Stalled rebuilding	1. Decrease in democracy score (media issues) 2. Population movements ongoing	1. Not in EU accession 2. International image (as major aggressor) 3. Political instability 4. Issues with minorities	1. Highly discriminated group 2. Population movements ongoing 3. Dealing in second language 4. Dealing with high mortality

* 2007 Measures.
** GNI = gross national income.

scholarly reports on the effects of the war in the former Yugoslavia mentioned throughout this book. As shown in Table 3.3, young people in BiH faced the most negative political–economic factors compared to those in other contexts; youth in Croatia faced the most positive. The measures indicate the material prospects for this youth generation to create peaceful, independent lives in the near future, but the measures do not address cultural issues such as the relatively harmonious religious diversity in BiH, the beautiful natural setting of the countryside across the region, or the relatively relaxed lifestyle possible in some places.

Measures of political stability include the score determined by research on the development of democracy in countries shifting from communist and socialist to capitalist systems in the late 20th century (Goering, 2007).[6] Economic indicators determine whether the level of gross national income (GNI) was low, middle, or high, an important measure of employment, resources, and opportunity (www.worldbank.org/website/external/datastatistics).[7] Another measure of political–economic circumstances is the country status for entry into the EU. Beyond being an indication of economic, political, and cultural stability, joining the EU provides inclusion in economic

[6] The circumstances of the postwar Western Balkans, as with the other 22 states resulting from the Soviet Union that broke apart in 1989, are defined in a multi-year analysis of the progress toward democracy (Goehring, 2007). Democracy scores are from 1 to 7, with 1–2 indicating consolidated democracy, which embodies "the best policies and practices of liberal democracy" (p. 19) to 6–7, indicating a consolidated authoritarian regime, which characterizes "closed societies in which dictators prevent political competition and pluralism are responsible for widespread violations of basic political, civil, and human rights" (p. 23). Factors considered include national democratic governance, electoral process, civil society, independent media, local democratic governance, judicial framework and independence, and corruption (Goehring, 2007, p. 10). Country summaries indicate slight improvements in BiH and Serbia and decreases in Croatia from 2006 to 2007. The democracy score for Serbia improved slightly from 3.71 to 3.68 last year, primarily because of improvements to its constitution and electoral process. BiH's score improved from 4.07 to 4.04 for advances in police reform, civil society initiatives, and constitutional reform. By contrast, Croatia's democracy score worsened slightly from 3.71 to 3.75 because of a weakening of the freedom of the press.

[7] The World Bank classifies countries based on the GNI per capita at three levels with two sublevels. According to this classification, low-income countries are defined as those with a GNI up to $905, lower-middle-income countries from $906 to $3,595, upper-middle-income countries from $3,596 to $11,116, and high-income countries from $11,117 and up (www.worldbank.org/website/external/datastatistics). Among the 185 income-ranked countries, Croatia and Serbia are in the upper-middle income classification, Bosnia is in the lower-middle income classification, and the United States is in the higher income classification.

opportunities and a range of international processes that offer a boost of which young people are cognizant. Having passed all but the final step in the "stabilization and association agreement" process, Croatia has the status of candidate member with an expected entry in 2011. Despite not having met some requirements of the postwar period, specifically, turning over war criminals wanted by the ICTY, Serbia has recently received an offer to begin the "stabilization and association agreement" process, although actual membership is unlikely to occur for many years. Because of political and economic issues, Bosnia is not yet in line to begin the process for entry in the EU.

Material and symbolic circumstances include representations of the country and its role in the war as conveyed in the media. For example, television and print media include daily reports of the ICTY procedure status (such as Serbia's progress in turning over war criminals); reports of efforts by the EU (such as updates on Croatia's status as a candidate nation and Serbia's temporary termination of its "stabilization and association agreement" with the EU); the status of ongoing conflicts over shifting borders in the region (such as Kosovo's 2008 declaration of independence); and issues related to ongoing separations by ethnicity in government (such as a government shared by different ethnic groups in BiH) and education (such as in class scheduling by ethnicity in some areas). Media and public discourse in the community, religious organizations, and cultural institutions also address ongoing issues related to the physical environment. Although the physical remains of war, such as bombed-out buildings and bullet-scarred structures, are gradually disappearing, there is also ongoing discourse about how public and private buildings are being rebuilt, about reclaiming ownership of properties (given displacement and returning refugees), about issues of public works and infrastructure (such as reclaiming political processes and about government (such as constitutions, governing bodies).

Several scripts have emerged via the media, political decisions, local responses to those national scripts, and rituals of everyday life.

Such characterizations depict Serbia as the primary aggressor, BiH as the victim, Croatia as somewhat ambivalent (including the Nazi connection in World War II), and refugees in the United States as the fortunate ones.

Sensitive to such environmental circumstances, children and youth focus on leading activities, especially as they present threats and opportunities. After comparing analyses of youth narratives of adult conflicts and youth evaluations of society (problems and positives) with social-science indicators of youth prospects, this chapter concludes by highlighting the threat–opportunity complexes across the diverse contexts.

Youth in BiH Focus on Tensions in Uncertain Conditions

The BiH war script is that of a major victim in the war. Based on the number of deaths and other aggressions suffered in the war; massive ongoing displacements; political instability, in particular with governmental structures in flux; divisions by ethnicity; and the relatively poor economic situation, BiH appears to be especially challenged in terms of future prospects for adolescents. In addition, international and national accounts of Bosnians as the major victims of the war continue, with "the generosity of foreigners" – as stated by one participant – offering positive social support as well as a sense of dependence. Nevertheless, as reported elsewhere, youth in BiH mentioned the strength of their cultural heritage and ethnic diversity, especially in Sarajevo, as a much-valued aspect of society (Daiute & Lucic, 2008).

All groups experienced displacement, including thousands of Bosnian Croats displaced to Croatia by the conflict in BiH (www.Amnesty.org, 5-6-08). Reports indicate that between 1993 and 2003, approximately one hundred forty-three thousand Bosnian refugees and smaller numbers of Croats and Serbs came to the United States, many after having originally been displaced to Germany or other parts of Europe (www.state.gov). War-related killing and other violence has, for the most part, ceased, but the attendant displacements continue to play a role in reconstituting communities and families. Large numbers of displaced people have become returnees, seeking to reclaim property taken from them after their expulsion and to reconnect with more familiar prewar associations. Thousands of Bosnian refugees and internally displaced people returned to their home from Croatia or the West (Amnesty.org, 5-6-08). These statistics provide information about only one aspect of the instability that is likely to be salient to adolescents trying to imagine a future. The "tensions abound" script indicates that young people are interacting with these circumstances, and that they are not necessarily affectively depressed. The relatively lower rate of resolutions to their conflict stories suggests an intense focus on the tensions, perhaps even some suspension of discomfort; however, as illustrated previously, narrators are also mastering the tensions.

These indicators of youth prospects are consistent with analyses of narrative icons, plots, scripts, and commentaries about problems and positive qualities in society. This suggests that salient threats are the precarious quality of the national government and economy, thereby suspending the sense of uncertainty indefinitely. At the same time, the opportunity of ongoing international sympathy and the possibility of creating something dynamic, given strong educational institutions and cultural pluralism, offers developmental support.

Youth in Serbia Focus on Ideological Divisions

Although Serbia's political situation earned it relatively high marks on the democracy scale among the Western Balkan countries in this inquiry, the country continues to be on the hot seat from the international perspective because it has not yet turned over all war criminals sought by the ICTY. This is one factor that led to a temporary suspension of Serbia's stabilization and association agreement with the EU during the study. International, regional, and internal tensions about the declaration of independent statehood by Montenegro in 2006 and the anticipation of a break by Kosovo characterized the political environment, of which youth in Serbia were intensely aware. With an economic situation slightly better than that in BiH and equivalent to Croatia's more on paper than in public perception, youth in the study reported great concern about their employment prospects while also praising the cultural and leisure life that their captivating capital of Belgrade offers. Given these relatively contradictory images of Serbia as aggressor, advocate of political institutions, and economically challenged nation with a vibrant social life, its position at the intersection of international and local spheres of activity reflects of the tension. As summarized by one youth in the study, "We have troubles but we are hedonistic all the same." The mantle of aggressor that is echoed in international courts, the EU processes, and ongoing regional tensions also ushered in the collective will and policies that the martyred Serbian Prime Minister Zoran Djinjic described as the "domestic aim in 'de-emotionalizing' the political discourse" to create a psychological change in national priorities (Bieber & Wieland, 2005, p. 10). Despite ongoing political conflict and instability manifested in Djinjic's murder and divisions related to the secession of Montenegro and Kosovo, efforts toward political change in Serbia have been acknowledged by international reseachers (e.g., Goehring, 2007). No less important is the rational if not hypervigilant analysis of conflicts by a group of youth in Serbia who participated in the study reported here.

Serbians also suffered in the war. Reports indicate that in the early to mid-1990s, three hundred thousand Croatian Serbs were displaced to Serbia by the conflict in Croatia. Indicating the long-term nature of consequences is the report that by 2007, one hundred twenty-five thousand Serbs had returned to Croatia, with some in our data-collection area working to reclaim property and other rights.

The "reflecting on societal divisions" script indicates a uniquely hypervigilant psychological orientation among the groups of participants in our study. The reputation as aggressor and the desires by the youth generation to contend with this image and consider whether and how they figure into it may have heightened their sensitivities to the intersubjective realm of life in their society.

The apparent threat for youth is being suspended between ideologies of the past and present, and between allowing time for creating new options and enjoyments. A stated and implied danger is that the "old guard" could continue to dominate and plunge the country into an adversarial position internationally, thereby by isolating it further and by limiting young people's prospects for the future. Such a clear distinction of past and present ideologies warrants a sense of opportunity to think and act in new ways, as well as to enjoy local geographic and social riches. Commenting about societal problems, one youth, for example, said, " . . . because I need to create something new and express my rebelliousness against anything I consider unfair – globalization, Nazism, etc."

Youth in Croatia Focus on Obstacles to Economic Advancement

Because the process of becoming a member of the EU involves numerous assessments of political, economic, and cultural stability, Croatia's status as a candidate nation, attests to its relatively strong position among the Western Balkan nations in this inquiry. Croatia's connection with the EU has created economic and educational programs that especially affect young people's lives, a factor that we hear about in youth assessments of their society. Although the capital city is geographically and economically close to Western Europe, political and economic indicators from the sources noted previously indicate instabilities, especially in issues of justice related to the media and resettlement of returnees. Reflective of this broader and somewhat ambivalent situation are the diverse views of youth in the more rural areas of Croatia (which experienced intense human and environmental destruction during the war) and those in the capital city who are more directly pointed toward a future in broader Europe.

Echoing throughout the data from Croatia and in the analysis of political–economic prospects is a tension between the opportunity to join the EU, with its attendant national and personal consequences, and the possible intrusions of past mentalities and personal losses related to the shift to a market economy. One young participant phrased it as her generation being "bought out" and thereby risking the beautiful resources her parents had fought to preserve. Offering specifics, this young woman mentioned that a foreign company had recently bought a valuable Croatian dairy company and that youth may have to emigrate to take advantage of Croatia's shift to the West.

Youth Refugees (Immigrants) to the United States Deal with Isolation

The relatively stable political situation and high national GNI of the United States provide refugees from war-torn and transitional nations with relief and hope for the future. Refugees from Bosnia were settled by the U.S. State Department in upstate New York, where housing is relatively affordable; small factories provide employment opportunities; and all levels of public education are good and responsive to the community, for example, by offering courses in the Bosnian language. Although permanent settlement is the exception, many families have remained beyond 2000 and continue to invite others. As with many immigrant groups, however, the positive outlook of the first generation does not always continue with their children, as is apparent with many of those in our inquiry (Suarez-Orozco, Suarez-Orozco, & Todorova, 2004). Although they are aware of and thankful for the opportunities in the United States compared to the situation they left, Bosnian immigrants in the study are in the midst of tensions about U.S. immigration. Discrimination is a major issue for the mostly Muslim group, and lack of social inclusion creates a sense of uncertainty, sadness, and criticism among young immigrants. For youth in the United States, the threat of ongoing isolation elicits nostalgia for Bosnia, with the concurrent realization that they are better off economically in the United States.

Summary

When inquiring about how young people manage the intersecting crises of adolescence and a transitional society, we find insights with the concept of living history. Young people across four positions of a political-violence system integrated issues related to past events with their attention to threats and opportunities in their current environments. The diverse living histories that emerged across these four contexts indicate that adolescent development involves context-sensitive leading activities. Youth experiences in their narratives and evaluations of problems and positive qualities in society are consistent with scholars' analyses of political–economic issues, indicating that youth care about more than identity and peer relationships. The analysis of young people's living histories suggests much greater political sensitivity than we have previously identified. These findings indicate the profoundly interdependent quality of youth–society development, not only because youth focus on what is around them, but also because the organization of these factors suggests the psychosocial nature of knowing. Building on this major insight, we can consider how in rapidly changing societies, young people may express and transform scripts to address societal pressures.

FIGURE 4.1. Symbols of diversity in the aftermath of ethnic cleansing.

4

Critical Narrating

When the nation itself struggles for identity and political stability, those in power exert pressure on citizens to express certain ideas and not others. Pressure to speak in ways that justify a war or prove that the country is moving beyond a violent past, for example, may affect the powerless in society, including young people and minorities, because they have not been privy to decisions governing these discourses. As discussed in Chapter 3, scripts by young people narrating conflicts among adults organize mundane events consistent with societal circumstances. Young people have the right to critique violence in their society, yet it is in just such circumstances that critique is dangerous and narrating becomes a cunning enterprise. With the understanding that youth, like nations, can use story-telling, in part, to manage their relations in society, the DSTY research workshop includes a fiction-writing activity (see Figure 2.6). In this story, Moira, a 19-year-old in Croatia, played with a political script:

> *The Greens and the Blues created this center in order for it to be the main place for social development of our town. The Greens were ready to do everything. They didn't mind the fact that the Blues participated in some other community centers in other towns. The Blues were loyal to the Greens as much as they were to the other partners. They had enough time and will to be active in many places. The news they told the Greens destroyed everything. With time, the Greens showed they weren't open for cooperation with others. They wanted their capital and their success only for themselves. They didn't realize that it was possible to be even more successful through cooperation with others. The Blues weren't able to explain to them how they weren't the traitors and that they didn't operate behind the Greens' backs. In the end, the Blues, cooperating with others, became even more successful, while the Greens failed completely. The projects the Blues and others were writing helped the development of many towns. A few years later, they called the Greens to join them.*

This fable of the Greens and the Blues illustrates the power and play of discourse in a context that promotes diversity. With her story of opposing groups the "Greens" and "Blues," Moira recounts a universal conflict between good and evil, but when we look closely, we see that the plight applies to a particular case. I argue that Moira, like her peers, is using the fictional genre in a way that maintains her privacy to recount a ubiquitous, yet publicly muted story of the 1990s from the Croatian perspective. The fictional genre provides tools for bringing together several tensions Moira and her peers across the region face. To confirm that it is fiction, Moira uses colorful names, intriguing plot development, and emotional tension around the turning point "the news they told the Greens destroyed everything." Perhaps without knowing the name of her literary device, Moira uses the fable for a thinly veiled national script that actual or imagined audiences would perceive as less than ideal or even taboo. Consistent with the argument that the literary genre can serve young people for exploring condemned political narratives in particular, I offer this rereading of Moira's story. The underlined words and phrases are all that I changed to explore what could be the reality in the fiction.

> *The Serbs and the Croatians created this country of Yugoslavia in order for it to be the main place for social development of our region. The Serbs were ready to do everything. They didn't mind the fact that the Croatians participated in some other republics. The Croatians were loyal to Yugoslavia and its capital of Belgrade as much as they were to the other partners. They had enough time and will to be active in many places. The news they told the Serbs destroyed everything. [This news was that they wanted to separate their Republic into a new nation.] With time, the Serbs showed they weren't open for cooperation with others. They wanted their capital [Belgrade] and their success only for themselves. They didn't realize that it was possible to be even more successful through cooperation with others. The Croatians weren't able to explain to them how they weren't the traitors [even though they seceded from the nation and expelled Serbs from the territory they claimed] and that they didn't operate behind the Serbs' backs. In the end, the Croats, cooperating with others [such as the European Union] became even more successful, while the Serbs failed completely [losing Montenegro, other provinces, and having no economic prospects]. The projects the Croats and others were writing helped the development of many towns. A few years later, they called the Serbs to join them.*

This rereading launches a discussion about the use of literary devices to mediate contentious situations. Such a use of cultural tools is no esoteric enterprise; it is, instead, a strategy for thriving in challenging circumstances. Perhaps intentionally, perhaps not, Moira uses literary devices well. She first establishes harmony between the Greens and the Blues. After the news, which the Greens perceive as destructive, their character emerges as stingy, uncooperative, suspicious, and failed, in contrast to the character of the virtuous Blues, with their enterprising nature, loyalty, openness, and attempts to explain their position, and reach out to adversaries. The conflict is a political one that, in conjunction with the resolution, conveys the tone of a moral tale. In addition to this plot, Moira uses time markings (tenses and temporal words) to convey a sense of historical weight to the Blues' patience and persistence, in contrast to the Greens' apparently mean-spirited actions and intentions.

Moira's fable reifies and perhaps also mocks a nationalist account with the expression of strong, even desperate emotions. She then invents a less predictable resolution of a symbolic olive branch to the vanquished: "A few years later, they called on the Greens to join them." Finally, Moira's use of figurative language completes the performance of this story. The double meaning is expressed efficiently with imagery, the true blue versus the less noble green, the ambiguous "capital," which could mean money and/or the national seat, and the similar ambiguity of writing a project, which could refer to a plan for the community center or national constitution. Even if the story is not condemned by current mores, Moira's exaggerated hero story is nationalistic enough that it could arouse the scorn of some of her peers. Setting this tale in fiction does not necessarily mean that Moira endorses it, but she may, instead, recount it as a way of reflecting on its complexities or releasing pent-up tensions. As in Figure 4.1, young people in these contexts of recent conflict can apply myriad, even conflicting, symbols to question old views and to imagine new ones.

Moira is an educated young woman, as were 99 percent of the people in the region before and after the wars of the 1990s (www. worldhealth.org), so it is not that her story-telling skill is rare or that a high national education rate prevents wars. Most participants in the study engaged the story format in similarly creative ways, which supports the idea that young people participate in national production through socially shared subliminal and explicit stories relating to the activities of everyday life. Youth across ex-Yugoslavia garnered the power of literary tools, but, youth in other geopolitical contexts may better apply symbolic media like oral language, movement rituals, or graffiti.

This chapter focuses on how young people use cultural tools to interact with their social milieu. The pull of discourse, in this case diverse narrative genres, involves youth in different social relational activities around a set of relevant societal issues. After discussing the political importance of narrating, I explain the interactive qualities of narrative genres and offer examples to show how young people's uses of literary features lead to critical narrating of hot issues in society.

THAWING FROZEN NARRATIVES

Social scripts generally embody traditional and accepted activities in society, but scripts may also introduce new and diverse ideas. In Western cultures, for example, a common conflict script is one in which adversaries resolve their differences and "live happily ever after." Members of groups may also identify with their own peculiar scripts, like a wealthy person's prerogative to assert, "Everything will work out all right" or a feminist's use of the script that "women are often used as scapegoats in extramarital affairs." Public institutions like government, public schools, and state-sponsored media organizations across the former Yugoslavia (as in other contexts of political violence) have ample means for spreading their scripts, which they sometimes try to do quickly to promote their causes. At the same time that national institutions struggle to spread their stories, numerous NGOs are eliciting young people's participation for a new system in transitional spaces (Popadic et al. 2000; Spajic-Vrkas, 2003a & 2003b). Community-development involves activities like deciding on a rebuilding agenda, participating to rebuild bridges destroyed in the war, clear out lakes near abandoned refugee encampments, and create new institutions like preschools, spread the word about children's rights treaties, create programs to include discriminated minorities, and allow young people to imagine alternatives to what it means to be a citizen. Even in times of peaceful political transitions, however, no one lets go of frozen scripts easily, so there are few opportunities to engage multiple scripts critically.

The goal of a developmental inquiry is to identify not only the nature of new national narratives but also the process whereby narratives can change. We consider, for example, how people respond to actual and imagined audiences creating pressure to conform to nationalist versions of the war and its aftermath. In various cases, those national narratives emphasize moving on, promote victimhood, or explain that the outside world has greatly misinterpreted the story. Although they can reproduce such national scripts, young people apply sensitivities in their activities to transform scripts. The need for contexts that allow such a thawing of frozen narratives is poignantly expressed in the following account by 13-year-old A. from a previous study (Daiute & Turniski, 2005).

> *This conflict started between me and my friend because she lied. I felt awful. She was from a different nation* [ethnicity], *but I have never made any difference because we are all from flesh and blood, and we have the right to say our opinion. While we were going to the "community center" from school, she told me some terrible things about me and my family which have really moved me and I started to cry. I didn't say anything to her in order to cool the situation. But the quarrel continued. Then she threw a snow ball and hit me in*

the eye. My eye got red and I was in pain. I left for home and I told everything to my mother. My mother was very angry and she wanted to call her grandmother, but I told her to wait until her mother gets back to [town]. The day after, I came to school and I was getting ready for the class when my class-teacher asked me to come talk to her. I was surprised because I didn't know why she would want to see me. But, my "friend" had complained about me to the class-teacher. She asked me why did I swear her Serbian mother and why am I saying bad things against Serbs. I started to cry and I tried to explain that that isn't true, that it doesn't matter to me whether someone is Balkan, Romanian, African, Serb, Croat, Bosnian, white, has long hair, has big nose... it only matters to me that he is a good person. It doesn't matter how he looks like, it is important to have a good heart.

This narrative hints at prohibitions against talk about ethnicity. The author's friend, for example, is portrayed as having used a report of ethnic talk as retaliation, most likely knowing how the teacher would respond. As noted by A.: "... I was surprised because I didn't know why she [the teacher] would want to see me. But, my 'friend' had complained about me to the class-teacher. She asked me why did I swear her Serbian mother and why am I saying bad things against Serbs." When the teacher reprimands A., this teenaged girl reacts, openly declaring her different "nationality" and her belief, exaggerated in ways that flaunt the sanction, that she can use nationality to decry its sinister application: "I started to cry and I tried to explain that that isn't true, that it doesn't matter to me whether someone is Balkan, Romanian, African, Serb, Croat, Bosnian, white, has long hair, has big nose... it only matters to me that he is a good person. It doesn't matter how he looks like, it is important to have a good heart."

This teenager's teacher was apparently concerned about more than the mere mention of ethnicity in a Croatian public school. As a candidate nation to the EU, Croatia is weathering pressure to prove social inclusion of minorities, among them Serbs, and this is often translated into pressure against not only mentioning ethnicity but also avoiding "saying bad things against Serbs." Such control of discourse also plays out among peers directly, as illustrated in narratives by teenagers in Serbia and BiH. The following narrative by 16-year-old Nancy expresses the contentious nature of nationalistic talk coded in folk music:

> *I had a conflict with a friend about the most stupid thing in the world – folk music. She'd been trying to convince me that I was faking it and lying when I would say that I don't know these "songs." That irritated her a lot. I simply didn't pay attention to such comments because I didn't want to waste my time on such nonsense.*

The peer monitoring implied in Nancy's story is echoed by Diana, age 22, in BiH in the following narrative:

> *The discussion was about Yugo-nostalgia. The girl that I was talking with thought that it was stupid to love something you never saw or experience, thinking about my nostalgia for Yugoslavia. I was thinking the same for her religion. We did not talk to much about it, everyone has its own view on life and I respect that as long it does not harm others.*

In addition to illustrating processes of silencing undesirable discourses, these excerpts suggest the possibility of creating new scripts. Much is at stake in thawing frozen narratives via story-telling in dramatically changing contexts. As suggested in the following statements by a legal scholar and developmental theorist, the need to juggle implicit scripts always applies because tensions among diverse scripts may be particularly salient in situations of injustice: "our very success in making things narratively believable often seduces us into unintended conventional stances toward the world" (Amsterdam & Bruner, 2000, p. 113); and during times of war, " ... psychological warfare consists in the determined continuation of general conditions which permit them [leaders] to indoctrinate mankind within their orbit with the simple and yet for them undoubtedly effective identities of class warfare and nationalism" (Erikson, 1980, p. 99). When young people have opportunities to narrate from diverse perspectives, they can use cultural scripts creatively; that is, they can use discourse to mediate their relations in society. How do young people use narratives to scrutinize "What's going on here?" and "How do I fit?"

CREATIVE USES OF CULTURAL GENRES

To explore whether and how young people involved in community workshops would use, thaw, and transform scripts, the DSTY activities introduced fiction, among other genres, as a tool for development. In the context of community participation, the research design and analysis focus on the breadth, depth, and diversity of narratives to mediate relationships. As presented in Chapter 2 (see Figure 2.6), we asked participants to write three narratives in response to systematically varied prompts. The fictional prompt begins by inviting participants to complete a story starting with a vignette that describes the scene at a groundbreaking for a new community center:

> _____ and _____ (from two groups) met at a ground-breaking of the new town center building. Everyone at the event had the opportunity to break the earth for the foundation and to place a brick for the building. It was an exciting community event and everyone was pleased that the new building would mark a new future. As they were working to begin the foundation, _____ and _____ had a conversation about how they would like to make a difference in their town so their children could live happily together. All of a sudden, someone came with news that changed everything! What was the news? How did everyone involved think and feel? How did it all turn out?

This opening vignette is realistic, implies characters, and introduces a climatic turning point that may or may not develop into conflict, requiring some sort of resolution or an ending, but it also leaves considerable room for imagination. Most participants read the prompt accurately and recounted to events that could have and may have happened. The focus is on participants' uses of this activity, like Moira's, as they engage with the qualities of fiction, plot, and emotion to integrate the material circumstances of news that is often bad.

Aesthetic Hooks for Political Expression

Something about sleeping–waking cycles and the passage of time between them translates well into the beginning, middle, and end structure of narrated experience. What is particularly powerful about narrating is, however, the fertility of this apparently mundane cultural tool for creating "landscapes of consciousness" (Bruner, 1986) that make sense of the "landscapes of action." The specific interweavings of narrative action and meaning differ across cultures, but all children grow up learning about their worlds, at least in part, in oral storied forms and then in artistically transformed products via literature, religious rites, and other media.

The various features of narratives create not only a recognizable structure indicating that "this is a story" but also interactive devices that individuals can use to achieve their goals. Beyond any literal meanings negotiated by conversants are the implicit meanings, the words between the words that members of a culture understand as expectations or possibilities. In this case, the narrative, "there was a war here and everyone feels bad about it," conveys some literal and also implicit meanings in Bosnia, where a young person wrote it. The passive construction, "there was a war here," for example, implies that the war was imposed on the Bosnians when they were attacked by Serbia, and "everyone feels bad about it" applies to the local people, the commonly accepted major victims of the Balkans in the 1990s. In contrast is the superficially similar narrative written by a youth in Serbia: " . . . the news is that we are again under an embargo. They all got scared and mad and started . . . fights about whose responsibility it was. . . . " Although these narratives are both about war and express painful emotions, one allows passivity of the declared victim, whereas the other makes explicit the issue of responsibility. These nuances are embodied in the texts but also inextricably linked to contexts. Foregrounding responsibility in the one case ("fights about whose responsibility it was . . . ") and foregrounding lack of control in the other ("there was a war here") evolve relative to the local living history. The political aesthetic of narrating, especially in challenging situations, unfolds in the interactive quality of story-telling.

LITERARY CONVERSATIONS

Stories are communications with a variety of features that narrators use not only to share specific messages but also to hint at why they are telling *this* story in *this* way at *this* time. Table 4.1 presents dimensions of this interactive quality, also referred to as "addressivity" (Bakhtin, 1986). The idea is that writers and thinkers, like speakers, direct language to audiences who are sometimes implicit, such as others who may judge us, as well as to actual audiences in the immediate context. Because we select what to say, what not to say, and how to say it in relation to our views about expectations of these audiences, they become part of each text. As shown in Table 4.1, the basic relations involved in addressivity are the narrator stance, the narrator–audience relationship, and character interactions.

In fiction, narrators are often omniscient, presenting the story from outside the action, while in autobiography, narrators are also characters in the story. To compare implications of narrating in contexts of political violence, workshop activities allowed for an omniscient stance, like that of Moira who presented "Greens and Blues" without interjecting herself explicitly. Two autobiographical activities, narrating adult and peer conflicts (see Chapter 2), offer two other possible narrator stances: observer and participant. Narrator stances,

TABLE 4.1. *Literary Conversations with Addressivity*

Addressivity feature	Fictional community conflict	Autobiographical peer conflict	Autobiographical adult conflict
Narrator stance	Omniscient	First person	Third person
Narrator–audience relations	Open, potentially equal power	Direct, narrator exposed	Indirect, narrator can observe
Character interactions	Narrator free to play	Defined, constrained	Available for selective play

in turn, have consequences for narrator–audience relationships because the fictional story allows the narrator to remain anonymous, whereas the autobiographical account exposes the narrator directly to audiences. Whether the narrator of personal experience assumes the stance of participant or observer, the expectation of listeners and readers is, with some cultural variation, that the story is more rather than less true. The actions of characters are thus relatively free or constrained with each genre. Although cultures differ in the specifics of their narrative genres, scholars have explained that addressivity is a universal process (Bakhtin, 1986; Labov & Waletzky, 1997).

These variations in narrator stance, narrator–audience relationships, and character interactions provide tools for young people to use when considering desirable and undesirable information. The fictional story is particularly interesting because the omniscient narrator stance is a potential tool for creating and/or expressing unique or silenced scripts. Focusing on the fictional stories in comparison to the peer- and adult-conflict narratives offers information about the interaction of politics and aesthetics as a developmental strategy.

Plot

Young people across contexts used the fictional-community context in similar ways but differed in how they narrated adult conflicts and, to a lesser extent, peer conflicts. As discussed in Chapter 2, several questions motivated the inquiry, with multiple opportunities to narrate conflict. Worth pondering is whether young people use the narrative tasks to engage different types of conflicts. In particular, would these youth growing up in the context of violent wars fought, at least in part, in relation to narratives of hatred among ethnic groups select those issues or would they focus on other issues; and would they narrate with rigid resolutions or sensibilities unaccounted for in previous research? The fictional prompt sets up potential for a range of conflicts and strategies to resolve them, either peacefully or not. Interestingly, although participants named groups that oppose each other in some aspect of local life, such as sports teams and political parties, they used the fictional story starter to identify bureaucratic obstacles, abuses of power, and democratic means to counter such abuses. Some, like Moira, focus on identity-group conflicts; many others do not.

Table 4.2 indicates the most common conflict issues and reso-lutions across fictional and autobiographical narratives. Participants used these narrating activities for different purposes, conveying com-plex knowledge and engagement with conflict.

As shown in Table 4.2, most participants across the country contexts organize their fictional stories around problems of insuffi-cient infrastructure to support community development. Across these 77 stories, "the news that changed everything" is bad, most entailing political obstacles to the building of a community center. For the most part, the narrative plots turn on a range of political issues and strategies to resolve them. Many of the political issues involve abuses of power, such as "the Mayor . . . said he had bought the land from a man and had been planning to build a house," "air strikes started!!!!," "the man took the money [for the center construction] and ran away from the country," "cancelled because they didn't like everyone in the community," "both sides got involved in a bad argument which

TABLE 4.2. *Most Common Plot Conflicts across Narrative Contexts*

Plot feature	Fictional community conflict	Autobiographical peer conflict	Autobiographical adult conflict
Conflict Issue			
Social relations		X	
Differences of opinion		X	X
Physical altercations		X	
Politics–infrastructure	X		X
Property/turf			
Character/emotion		X	
No reason, fate, no conflict		X	X
Resolution Strategy			
Psychological	X	X	X
Communicative			
Other intervention			X
Physical			
Collective action	X		

ended in cessation of any type of collaboration," "was being built on land that does not have the ownership status resolved," "the center would be owned by a foreign company and that no Croats could go there anymore," "a loud factory that would pollute the environment instead," "the government didn't allow immigrants into the U.S. anymore," and Moira's "with time the Greens . . . wanted their capital and their success only for themselves."

Many obstacles revolve around bureaucratic issues, such as "the building did not meet the standards of the local community," " . . . does not have a building permit," and "property illegally purchased." Many others recount competing needs for resources or a general lack of resources: "the money was supposed to be spent . . . for reparation of a dam destroyed in recent bombings," "the state has to finance more profitable endeavors," and "12 million KM (Bosnian currency) was received to build a new embassy." Some of the political–economic issues interact with issues of conscience, such as "the Fiat factory participated in the project only because of a tax reduction, not out of genuine concern for the community" and "participants lost their motivation." Some obstacles evolve as twists of fate: "Fire . . . nothing could help – the fire was gigantic," "found dinosaurs under the foundation of the building," "the construction site was a landfall," and "foreign nationals found a massive graveyard."

Along with conflict, the narrative genre presses for resolution tying together the major elements of the plot. Narrators face the pressure to resolve as the time or space for conclusion approaches. The resolution can also become an emplotment with which the narrator indicates the significance of the story by integrating the diverse temporal strands of activity (Ricoeur, 1984). Participants' uses of these literary devices enact their conversations with complex environments.

Because cultures convey values in narrative genres, children begin early to engage those values and figure out how to resolve conflicts by interactive story-telling with parents (Nelson, 2003). Scripts are well-known conflict-and-resolution combinations and account for children's earliest narrating, but they proceed to create original stories by school age. In cultures where parents first narrate children's lives for them, then with them, as in most Western cultures, autobiographical narratives correspondingly begin as scriptlike even when using fictional material as a basis (Miller et al., 1993). As children mature, however, they seize fiction as a safe space for departing from expected scripts by introducing novel conflicts and resolutions (Daiute, 2004). The portrayal of highly dramatic scenes with great emotion suggests that young people may also use this veil of fiction to master issues that are personally difficult, like remembering "air strikes!" and other frightening events.

As shown in Table 4.2, the most common resolution in the fictional narratives across contexts is collective action. Examples of strategies for overcoming obstacles include collective political strategies, such as "they signed a petition and demonstrated peacefully... since the elections were close," "two years of signing petitions, demonstrations, appearances of their representatives in the media, filing complaints, seeking for public support on the Internet and other media, the City finally decided...," "citizens decided to strike," "they tricked him [the mayor] into signing a document about donating the land for the youth center because he was drunk," "demonstrations were organized," "in the end, by strike, they won," "they agreed that everybody was going to give 10 percent of their salary," "they went up against the mayor and they won and the mayor went to prison for discrimination," and "environmentalists required a more sincere approach." Some strategies are pragmatic, like "they were trying to redirect the fire digging trenches," "they began collecting money," and "some generous people from the Balkans decided to help." Other responses are passive, such as "fortunately a representative of the construction company managed to negotiate terms with the owner" and "the lady from the local government office said she will try to find another location for the project." Of course, there is some giving up, as in Nothing happened – everything remained the same, and "minorities were offended."

This story by 18-year-old Lolita in Serbia illustrates the plot structure of a political conflict with a collective-action resolution strategy:

Marija and Marko
They had run out of funds and the construction of the foundations had to be delayed or perhaps cancelled if they did not succeed in finding additional support. Marija and Marko, their neighbors, were disappointed. Another failed hope. Nothing again.... They decided to talk to the neighbors and to take initiative. They agreed that everybody was going to give 10 percent of their salary (surprisingly enough, everybody was willing to do it). If somebody couldn't afford it, they might have contributed the amount

they could. They raised considerable funds and the municipality
agreed to make a contribution to the full amount. The building
had been finished. It is now an orphanage. Apart from several
people who are employed there, the children are being helped by
the neighbors who contribute things they no longer need.

Lolita identifies the political–economic issue, "the construction
of the foundations had to be delayed or perhaps cancelled if they
did not succeed in finding additional support," with a corresponding
political-resolution strategy, "They decided to talk to the neighbors
and to take initiative. They agreed that everybody was going to give
10 percent of their salary." Their effort prevails with political acumen:
"They raised considerable funds and the municipality agreed to make
a contribution to the full amount." Lolita's approach is similar to
that of most of her peers, although some differences emerge across
country contexts.

The following story by 21-year-old Juro in Croatia also includes the
common plot structure with financial obstacles and correspondingly
introduces issues of rights and responsibilities in a democracy:

The news was that the main investor wasn't able to provide the
money he had promised and that the building process would be
postponed for an undetermined period of time. The citizens felt
betrayed. They had the right to protest; they chose this government
and now the government didn't want to give them the money that
was essential for the town. The citizens decided to strike and the
government was forced to give them the money.

Juro presents relatively new knowledge in his society with his
statement in the hypothetical context "The citizens . . . had the right
to protest; they chose this government and now the government
didn't want to give them the money that was essential for the town.
The citizens decided to strike and the government was forced to give
them the money."

A somewhat different strategy for overcoming obstacles to the hypothetical yet realistic building of a community center to benefit future children is 19-year-old Adin's psychological approach in his narrative from BiH:

> *The only bad news that could come at this point is the prohibition of the construction of the Center. The participants would feel awful and that would eventually lead to protests.*

Adin includes protests as an eventual strategy but expresses it as a potential consequence of feeling "awful" rather than as actual action. A difference across contexts worth mentioning is the relatively large percentage of young narrators in the United States and BiH who wrote stories without conflicts or, more typically, who claimed that no conflict would occur in such a situation. Some participants used this story activity to deny conflict (23.1 percent in BiH and 26.7 percent in the United States compared with only 6.1 and 5.9 percent in Croatia and Serbia, respectively). The frequency of strategies to resolve conflicts also differed, with 80.8 percent of the fictional narratives by youth in BiH including resolutions compared with 109.1 percent[1] in Croatia, 88.2 percent in Serbia, and 53.3 percent in the United States. The considerably lower percentage of resolution strategies in the U.S. stories could be due to the fact that many of the Bosnian immigrants were still learning English. Although several participants wrote in Bosnian, daily struggles with a foreign language may make it difficult to resolve plotlines in a written story. Results like those discussed elsewhere herein suggest that the young people felt alienated in the United States, so the lack of resolution may itself be a strategy.

The following stories illustrate the most common resolution strategies by youth in the United States: the physical strategy in "Huso

---

[1] Because some stories included more than one resolution, like the story about the Greens and the Blues, the overall percentage can be higher than 100, as in the stories in Croatia.

and Haso" (26.7 percent) and the psychological strategy in "Amy and Mary" (26.7 percent) (the collective-action strategy is most common in stories by the other three groups of participants):

Huso and Haso
The news were that there was going to be some charities who would help them have the construction done.

Amy and Mary
The news were bad (Death) everyone felt so bad, they couldn't think or even feel but at the end everything turned out to be good because we all were strong and got out of it (moved on).

Participants include a much broader range of conflict issues in their peer-conflict narratives than in the fictional-community narratives. As shown in Table 4.2, common plot conflicts in the peer-conflict narrative were about relationships, differences of opinion, physical altercations, issues of character, or silly reasons. Differing also from the fictional narrative, issues in the peer-conflict narratives are most commonly resolved with psychological strategies, often with characters reflecting on the reflections of their peers, as was most typical in narratives by youth in Serbia.

Unique conflict issues and resolution strategies appearing most commonly in the adult-conflict narratives compared in particular to the peer-conflict narratives are issues of politics and infrastructure and the intervention of a third party to resolve conflicts. As discussed in Chapter 3, adult-conflict narratives differ dramatically across contexts, and from the perspective of this analysis focusing on differences across narrative genres, we gain independent insights that participants used the scenario of conflicts among adults to address political conflict and the incompetence of the war generation. These young authors are not without sympathy for their elders but recognize the problematic nature of the history they inherit and reflect on the consequences and need for assistance to help adults who argue about fences between their properties, a presidency that must rotate several times a year to give each ethnic group power, meddling neighbours, or governments perceived by the United Nations to require intervention for ensuring human rights.

In the past, creative discourse was seen as less than appropriate for serious situations, but insights about political aesthetics could advance the design of research and practice in situations of political violence. The different plot-structure patterns across narrative genres show how young people use narrative genres interactively to share different perspectives on conflict. Although relationships figure prominently in peer-conflict narratives, other issues do as well. When given the opportunity to narrate beyond their own personal perspectives, adolescents and young adults seize those opportunities to consider opinion, physical issues, public and private space, and a range of resolution strategies. With the focus on political issues at the center of conflicts in the fictional-community event and country-sensitive issues in the adult-conflict narratives (see Chapter 3), these results cast doubt on the over-determination of identity and peer relationships as the primary focus of youth.

Emotion

Another quality that young people readily employ in literary scenarios is emotional expression. The context-sensitive nature and function of emotionality has received little attention in developmental research. Because it is relevant to questions about the effects of political violence on youth well-being, I have gathered tools to study emotional expression. To examine youth authors' uptake of affective expressions across the narrative genres, I computed the three major types of psychological states per narrative. Given the different addressivities, in particular, the relatively open space for marginal expression when the narrator can remain omniscient, I expected to see relatively frequent affective expression in the fictional narratives.

The expression of characters' and narrators' psychological states, such as "thinking," "being upset," "knowing," and "wanting to do something," is a poignant narrative feature (Labov & Waletzky, 1997). Numerous researchers have found that these expressions, often along with other linguistic devices, indicate the significance of a story. Psychological states are expressed, for example, by favored characters, because these features bring characters to life as they speak for themselves. Young people across cultures are exposed to emotional expression in their local literatures, but they also hear autobiographical tales of woe, especially where there has been violence. Affective expression looms large in the fictional narratives of conflict but is secondary to cognitive and sociocognitive expressions in the autobiographical genres.

Emotion, also referred to as affect, is, of course, possible in autobiographical writing, but third-person renderings in education, community activist, and research settings may make young people feel that emotionality in those contexts is not totally appropriate. Young people may, of course, be reading the signs correctly. Alternately, rather than any specific taboo on expressing a full range of emotions in first-person writing, expectations in those public settings with specific political agendas may emphasize rationality, which we see emerging especially in the autobiographical genres. The literary context lends itself to heightened drama and emotional expression and may offer a narrator a safe distance from potentially negative judgments for violating any explicit or implicit expectations in the context and thus may be an ideal space for examining one's own intense emotions.

Table 4.3 summarizes the results of an analysis that indicates the relatively intense use of emotion in the literary narratives.

As shown in Table 4.3, expressions of cognitive/sociocognitive states ("think," "know," "decide," etc.) were generally more prevalent than affective states ("hope," "was upset," "etc.") and intention states ("wanted to," etc.). When writing fictional stories, however, participants in this inquiry balance affective states with cognitive states more

TABLE 4.3. *Psychological State Expressions across Narrative Contexts*

Psychological state	Fictional community conflict	Autobiographical peer conflict	Autobiographical adult conflict
Affective	195	239	175
Cognitive/sociocognitive	275	497	410
Intention/anticipation	134	136	98

than in either of the autobiographical-narrative contexts. The greater balance between emotion and cognition means that emotion functions more prominently in fictional genres. The difference between cognitive and affective state expressions in the fictional genre is 80 but in the autobiographical genres 158 and 240, respectively. In addition, although negative affect is more prominent than positive affect across all the narrative genres, the difference between positive and negative affect is considerably less in the community-context narrative (Daiute, 2008).

The story starter for the community narrative did not explicitly mention conflict, but most participants spun stories around conflicts. Because a corresponding proportion of those narratives lament "news that changed everything" revolving around some type of conflict, the relatively high ratio of affective states and high positive affect relates to the way young people used the affordance of the genre to engage self–society relations. U.S. youth write with the fewest psychological states compared to the other groups. Their psychosocial-state patterns are roughly the same, except for a reverse in the relationship between cognitive and affective states in the community narrative.[2]

In addition to examining the frequency of affective-state expressions relative to cognitive/sociocognitive and intention/anticipation,

---

[2] The nature of empathy via psychological states across the peer- and adult-conflict narratives differs across the country contexts. Youth in Croatia and Serbia express greater differences in valence skewed toward negative affect in the peer-conflict narratives than in the adult-conflict narratives, whereas the ratios are more similar in narratives by youth in BiH and the United States.

I identified a range of broader emotional orientations. Psychosocial-state expressions are coded by word or phrase; emotional orientations represent, in contrast, the entire narrative. When a majority of the affective-state expressions converge, the narrative is oriented affectively in one of the following ways emerging from the analysis of the data set for this inquiry: sadness, fearfulness, anger, happiness/excitement, unfulfilled expectations, and desire/hope. The following narrative by 21-year-old Thor from Serbia demonstrates emotional intensity.

> *Rockers and posers*
> *An anxious guy came running. He was breathing so heavily that he could hardly speak. "Fire," he whispered. Both rockers and posers started to run, trying to rescue the people who were in vicinity. The fire was approaching us. They took to a safe place all the onlookers. They redirected their attention to a construction site. They were trying to redirect the fire digging trenches. Alas, nothing could help – the fire was gigantic. When the fire ceased, they came to where the construction site used to be. The sight was devastating. For the rockers, it was like a battlefield where their destiny was completed. For the posers, it was like a destroyed path. They went their own separate ways. They no longer hated each other, but they didn't love each other either. There's still hope.*

In his highly literary narrative, Thor builds to an overall expression of unfulfilled expectations with the emotion words "anxious," "whispered," "devastating," "destiny completed," "destroyed," "no longer hated each other," "didn't love each other either," and "still hope." Each of these expressions implies an expectation. Anxiety, for example, includes anticipation as a foundation for the unsettled emotion; "no longer hated each other" includes the expectation that hating would have continued indefinitely;" and "still hope" implies that people had stopped or might stop hoping.

Thor's narrative of a conflict among peers shifts quickly from a good mood to a negative orientation.

> *A couple of days ago, there was a small gathering at my friend's place. As usual, there were several, carefully chosen people. The atmosphere was totally relaxed and cheerful. However, like everything else in life, even a good mood has an end, which happened when one of the friends started bullying one of the female friends who was very dear to me. We exchanged some really bad words and I almost left the gathering. I couldn't stand sitting at the same table with this friend. However, the host helped us calm down. The gathering went on, however, not as cheerfully as before the incident and I will never forgive this friend for doing what he did.*

A scene with "carefully chosen people" in an atmosphere that was "totally relaxed and cheerful" transforms into a disappointing scene where one friend started "bullying," leading to the exchange of "some really bad words" and lasting resentment, "I will never forgive this friend." The intervention of a secondary character, the host who "helped us calm down," preserved the gathering, albeit "not a cheerfully as before." The polite calming down "not as cheerfully" differs from the passionate resolution of the fictional "Rockers and posers," characterized by "hate," "love," and "hope."

Stories embodying unfulfilled expectations are also often expressed as betrayal and bitterness, as in the following story by 22-year-old Ema, also in Serbia:

> *A man came and told them: "Why are you laying the bricks? You are building a better future for your opponents. Their children will have a better future thanks to you." All of a sudden, everybody forgot the reason why they were there in the first place. So, the conflict started. The building remained unfinished and everybody was happy for "at least the others won't have it either."*

The sense of bitterness builds from a series of affective-state words and phrases. The story begins by questioning the collective-community activity: "Why are you laying the bricks?" elaborated by "everybody forgot the reason why they were there" and mutual pleasure about the abandonment of the project, albeit for very different reasons. For example, "everybody was happy" is a cynical emotion because it is qualified by "for 'at least the others won't have it either.'" This fascinating use of quotes around "at least the others won't have it either" suggests that this is a common phrase in the context as well.

Ema's story builds not only on the story prompt but also responds to it critically by qualifying a very positive characterization of collective action with the bitter "at least others won't have it either." Beyond clusters of emotional expressions, we must read how young people use the entire narrative to do something – that is, to mediate the near and far social relations. In this case, the response turns on the story starter in a sophisticated way to respond to an international audience as well as to the local audience, which appears to be expressing regret about unexpected effects of the war in Serbia. It may not be that there was an expectation of gratitude to the Serbian Republic for providing the capital of Yugoslavia, but perhaps that they would at least be offered the same international compassion given to the seceding nations like Croatia. Instead, the bombing of Belgrade in 1999 was a seminal event witnessed firsthand by these youth, thereby forging not only a sense of bitterness but also an apparent need to understand and address societal divisions. Ongoing inquiry into the effects of violence can further examine young people's uses of reflective media (narratives and others) to mediate issues, opening them for discussion rather than allowing them to remains closed as group or personal conclusions.

The sadness orientation is most characteristic among fictional narratives by youth in BiH. Fifteen-year-old Lajla, for example, explains characters' responses to the bad news that "the new youth center could not be built" with a combination of sadness and unfulfilled expectations.

> *The news was that a new youth center could not be built due to the fact that funds were planned for different purposes. The participants were very disappointed and felt uncomfortable. Nothing happened eventually – everything remained the same.*

In this relatively short narrative, Lajla states that the characters were "disappointed" and "felt uncomfortable" and concludes with the depressed sentiment "everything remained the same."

Zejna, who is 21 years old, describes the characters in her story as "crushed" and "upset" among other emotions, including "angry".

> *The news that the building could not be built came because the property was illegally purchased, and government does not approve building on that place. People were crushed, angry, and upset. At the end, by strike, they won and building will be built.*

Zejna's narrative also shows that the sadness pattern did not necessarily mean that there was always a completely negative outlook. Although she acknowledges sadness, as do her peers in BiH, Zejna expresses other feelings, like hopefulness, which is most prevalent in the fictional stories. This finding is especially relevant to counter the ongoing emphasis on trauma.

That young people vary emotion with other psychological-state expressions across narrative genres suggests that they share their experience with more control and goal directedness than implied in the damage and social-reproduction models dominating conflict studies.

Speaking with Time

The literary feature of "emplotment" identifies meaning in the time expressions a narrator uses to weave a story. This analysis extends previous literary observations of emplotment as a symbolic device to create a "concordance of discordances" or to "grasp" together the myriad elements in terms of their personal significance (Ricoeur, 1984). In time-sensitive languages (like those in this study), time has proved to be a powerful dimension that narrators use, among other linguistic devices, to indicate how they are making sense of scenarios, at least when narrating. The following story by Aida is a representative peer-conflict narrative:

A student brought a gun to school and threatened another student asking from him a small amount of cannabis. Some students were appalled by the possession of weapons, others by cannabis, and some by both. As for myself, I was a bit disgusted by the gun but, at the same time, it could be expected from such persons.

"A student brought a gun to school and threatened" is the material and symbolic center of the conflict. Not all participants who may have witnessed this fact of life chose to share a story about it, and any narrator who deemed it worthy of sharing could have developed it in myriad ways. Aida, however, offered a range of judgments about the event, the object, and the gun-wielding person. The psychosocial dynamic to reflect morally on an event becomes most evident in the sequence, "I was a bit disgusted by the gun but, at the same time, it could be expected from such persons." Aida makes her point by connecting events in the past to a hypothetical "at the same time" from her perspective as narrator in the present time. Narrative psychologists suggest other devices for such evaluation (Bamberg, 2004; Labov & Waletzky, 1997), including uses of time, which is central to our inquiry with youth for whom there is much at stake in history.

The emplotment analysis is designed to explore how young people use narrating as a symbolic mediator of self and context. This analysis involved identifying psychosocial dynamics for insights about what was salient to youth across the contexts and how they used narrating to make sense of the challenging circumstances in which they lived. The idea is that individuals focus on circumstances in their environment that challenge, confuse, upset, satisfy them, or that serve some other function worthy of narrating. This analysis thereby builds on theory that narrating is a mediation process guiding perception, interpretation, and development rather than merely reporting on events or personal experience. This dynamic is psychosocial motivation for telling the story in the way it is told. Using the pressure that a story must end at some point, ideally resolving issues in a culturally satisfying way (which could be shocking as well as expected), young authors create turning points (or climaxes) to tell themselves and their readers what they understand in the storying event. In other words, they not only resolve the story plot but also address the issue of why they are telling this particular story in this way.

After identifying the emplotment in each narrative in the database, we identified the psychosocial dynamics: the goal-directed way in which the narrators resolved the various elements of the story they chose to tell (Daiute & Lucic, 2008). Psychosocial dynamics accounting for all narrative emplotments in our database include:

- clarify affiliation/relationship
- express uncertainty/ongoing challenge
- identify contradiction/irony
- clarify identity
- suggest injustice/unfairness
- express hope/desire
- consider process
- consider moral/cultural issues
- minimize
- justify

Analyses of narrators' psychosocial activity in the emplotment sequences identified ten different narrative goals. Table 4.4 provides examples of the eight most frequent categories of psychosocial dynamic expressions.

Table 4.5 lists the percentages of narrative emplotments expressing different psychosocial dynamics by youth across narrative genres. As shown in the table, these youth used narrating to express very different psychosocial orientations across story-telling contexts. Similarities in young people's uses of narrating across these contexts include clarifying relationships, especially in the peer-focus narratives, and the exclusive use of the community narratives across all settings to express hope and desire.

TABLE 4.4. *Diverse Psychosocial Dynamic Categories and Examples*

Psychosocial dynamics	Examples in narratives by youth across the former Yugoslavia
Clarify relationships/ affiliations	*"I had a feeling that they felt the same way I did but didn't want to admit it."* *"The gathering went on, not as cheerfully as before the incident and I will never forgive this friend for what he did."*
Identify contradictions	*"Whenever he [the retired man] enters the trolley he rudely tells someone to get up so he can sit . . . he [feels] he always gets the 'shorter end of the stick'."*
Express uncertainty ongoing challenges	*"However, the major issue was the mentality which we have not been able to change so far."*
Clarify identity	*"I always feel as if I were preaching all the time . . . I'm thinking about stopping worrying about irrelevant things."*
Express hope/desire	*"Later they made an agreement with the Municipality and the construction continued."*
Suggest injustice	*"They had the right to protest; they chose this government and now the government didn't want to give them the money that was essential for the town."*
Consider process	*"I didn't feel bad because we spoke with calm; we didn't argue."*
Consider broader issues	*"I was a bit disgusted by the gun but at the same time it could be expected from such persons."*

What is most notable in this analysis is, however, within context differences across the narrative genres, suggesting the use of complex tools to mediate a range of psychosocial dynamics in especially complicated contexts. A common goal is to identify consistent psychological orientations in narrative turning points for maturity in the narrated self (McLean & Pratt, 2006; Thorne, McLean, & Lawrence, 2004). This approach informs us about developmental uses of narrating within-group and within-person variations, in particular by young people negotiating contentious environments. Across the following narratives below, Juro, for example, narrates for purposes of clarifying relationships and identity, identifying injustice,

TABLE 4.5. *Percentages of Emplotments Expressing Psychosocial Interactions*

Psychosocial dynamic	Fictional community conflict $N = 85^*$	Autobiographical peer conflict $N = 87$	Autobiographical adult conflict $N = 85$
Clarify relationships	1.2	36	11.8
Identify contradiction	17.6	0	22.4
Express uncertainty	7.1	5.7	18.8
Clarify identity	0	31	7.1
Express hope and desire	36.5	0	0
Suggest injustice	9.4	6.9	21.2
Consider process	8.2	9.2	11.8
Consider broader issues	7.1	10.3	9.4
Minimize/distance/justify	1.2	9.2	8.2

* $N =$ number of narratives with emplotments.

and expressing means for desired outcomes. The emplotment in the peer-conflict narrative (in the underlined sequence), which "grasps together" several past and present times, integrates differences with friends into a collective, "we." As Juro shifts from "I" and "they" to "we," he marks the purpose of identity clarification for the group of students at the center of his narrative:

> *My friends and I were discussing the issue of how hard it was to be in college. I thought it was as easy as being in high school but they thought differently. I had a feeling that <u>they felt the same way I did but didn't want to admit it. Now, being students in college, we have to say that it's hard and that we have to study a lot.</u>*

This relatively common pattern of psychosocial orientation of clarifying identity in peer conflict narrative by youth in Croatia also differs from the use of the adult-conflict narrative to observe and comment on injustices, as in the following narrative by Juro:

> *We were at the cinema. We were watching some new movie about Mayas. I found the movie extremely boring, too long, typically*

American. Some older people praised the movie. I said that the way they described some things about the life of Mayas was OK but that the stupid American <u>story about a super hero who runs days and nights through the entire jungle to save his family was completely unnecessary. I felt that no one understood me. They were quite sure that the movie was good.</u>

Although using the peer-conflict narrative for identity clarification, Juro uses the adult-conflict narrative for distancing from others and, in particular, for pointing out an injustice, "I felt that no one understood me. They were quite sure that the movie was good." Quite different an orientation is Juro's proactive connection with a solution to the problem posed in the fictional-community narrative:

The news was that the main investor wasn't able to provide the money he had promised and that the building process would be postponed for an undetermined period of time. The citizens felt betrayed. They had the right to protest; they chose this government and now the government didn't want to give them the money that was essential for the town. The citizens decided to strike and the government was forced to give them the money.

Replete with agency ("They had the right to protest," "they chose this government," "citizens decided," "the government was forced"), this story provides a context for a very different Juro to explore and express himself. Diversity in psychosocial dynamics among youth in BiH may be particularly important because, as the major victims in the war, one might expect a relatively restricted range. Even brief narratives by youth in BiH engage a range of psychosocial orientations, not always the same as the range by youth in other contexts but internally diverse nonetheless, as we observe across these narratives by 3xl.

I can't remember quite well for it happened long time ago . . . it was the person who used to be my best friend . . . to cut a long story short, it was about a girl. . . .

In contrast to the friendly and romantic focus in the previous narrative, 3xl expresses the common orientation of uncertainty in the following adult-conflict narrative:

> *Last year in Vogosca – I don't know exactly what the reason was – a couple of "brutes" attacked a boy much younger than themselves and hurt him badly. I'm writing about this because it happened in front of the police station, and it took 10 minutes for the police to respond.*

Especially given the tensions abound script (see Chapter 3) and the psychosocial orientation of uncertainty, the fact that 3xl, like others, uses narrating to shift to a more positive orientation is not only promising for their development but also indicative of the importance of leaving open the psychosocial figures of childhood and youth for potential development.

> *The news was that two more identical buildings were going to be built near the existing one. Everybody was excited because it meant that more youth would be engaged in similar projects.*

CRITICAL NARRATING

This analysis offers insights about tensions between the public and private formation of life in language. Young people's uses of narratives of conflict mediate the particularly challenging circumstances of their generation growing up in the context of political violence and transition. The mutual creation of story, event, storyteller, and audience means that we should begin to take the narrating process more seriously as a developmental tool. Learning critical uses of political discourse could always be an educational goal, and encouragement to use cultural tools flexibly (such as in fiction writing) could aid in that process. The cultural–historical theory of discourse as a mediator offers a way to transform the psychodynamic process of repression into active development. Shifting priorities from autobiography to multiple diverse genres is an important step in that process.

The mediational uses of discourse illustrated herein are central to processes of social relations, social change, and human development, where the stakes for communication to rebuild society are high. Mediation is the creative use of cultural genres. Differences in how young people use narrative genres and aesthetic devices in the fictional narrative in particular highlight the use of discourse to mediate relations in society, not only personal relations but also political relations of power, such as conforming to or transforming national scripts. This view differs dramatically from the use of narrative for representation (of self), release (of emotional stress), or postmodern intentionality. It is a contrast to the more typical approach of conceptualizing discourse and even social activities as media for reporting singular views, in some cases as "dominant discourses" and in others as "authentic individual" perspectives. Both the former notion of dominant discourse and the latter of individual discourse belie views of social discourse as transparent of knowledge that resides elsewhere, on the one hand in powerful institutions and on the other in individual subjectivity.

How do we explain common patterns of narrative structures in these fictional narratives? The compelling explanation is that young people use literary features to express what they assume to be less acceptable in autobiographical contexts. In addition to what the fictional story starter implies, the use of fiction to portray political issues like corruption, misuse of power, or other problems is one that may require an image-protecting veil of omniscient narrator. These stories are tied to real circumstances, relying on facts like the need to get permits, "men in dark suits who are buying up local land for multinational corporations," and so forth, but the context also offers affordances of a story with literary devices like drama for extending into imaginary or forbidden terrain. By using those literary features, probably not so consciously, these young people appear to be creating possible worlds. The fictional genre lends itself not only to exploring taboo issues, as we saw in Moira's narrative, but also to exploring unlikely ones, like dreams. Also important to note in relation to this strategic use of fiction is that the specific issues addressed differ across the country contexts where, understandably, the issues differ. It is not surprising, then, that these fictional stories also allow for more positive affective orientations than some of the autobiographical narratives. To address the process of mediation via uses of cultural tools like narrating in context, we consider corresponding analyses of plot structure in narratives of adult and peer conflicts.

SUMMARY

Observing young people's flexibility as communicators, as we have with their differential uses of narrative genres to mediate conflict, raises questions about several common assumptions about discourse. The first common assumption is that narrating is valuable because it offers authentic voices, especially those of the powerless in society. Narrating *is* an empowering communicative process, but the power is relational. The strategic use of narrating is, for example, to critique social abuses, to repeat an unpopular story in fiction, to critique remnants of the past, and to offer reasonable solutions to conflicts among peers. The second assumption that these analyses serve to question is that narratives are either societal scripts *or* the reflection of unique personalities. Reducing discourse to society *or* the individual ignores constant interaction of individual in society. Our examination of young people's responses to several narrating activities systematically varied for addressivity illustrates the complex interaction of storyteller, story, and context. The three narrative genres offer pieces of a puzzle yielding a picture of contemporary youth–society issues.

Scholars with other theoretical perspectives have observed the importance of emotionality as a particular enterprise of adolescence:

The dynamic quality of the tempestuous adolescences lived through in patriarchal and agrarian countries (countries which face the most radical changes in political structure and in economy) explains the fact that their young people find convincing and satisfactory identities in the simple totalitarian doctrines of race, class, or nation. Even though we are forced to win wars against their leaders, we still are faced with the job of winning the peace with these grim youths by convincingly demonstrating to them (by living in it) a democratic identity which can be strong and yet tolerant, judicious and still determined. (Erikson, 1980, p. 98)

In addition to acknowledging the pressures of conformity to national scripts, especially during times of change (which the United States also faced during the time and perspective from which Erikson was writing), tensions among multiple competing scripts are always in play.

Adolescents may be particularly tempestuous not only because of biochemical changes during puberty but also because of choices they must make about education, employment, mates, and much more during transitions to adulthood. Psychological intensity may be related to the interaction of changes in the body and social roles, but we have learned that, rather than because they are emotionally out of control, adolescents may be particularly tempestuous because they are so in control, as we have seen in their mediational uses of cultural tools that serve in the sense-making process. What we once noted as adolescent rebelliousness or impetuousness, we can identify as a context-sensitive use of cultural tools to address particularly contentious issues in society.

FIGURE 5.1. "Future prospects:" Are they on the horizon?

5

Participation Matters

YOUTH OF THE WORLD, WE ARE ASKING YOU TO FILL OUT OUR SURVEY AND ALLOW US TO FIND OUT WHAT YOU WOULD LIKE TO CHANGE IN YOUR COMMUNITY. WHAT ARE THE POSSIBILITIES FOR CHANGE, AND DOES YOUR COMMUNITY HELP YOU IN ACHIEVING THOSE GOALS?

This announcement, created by a group of four 15- to 17-year-olds working together in Croatia, offers insights about the role of participation in human development. As discussed in Chapter 2, designing a survey for other youth across the former Yugoslavia was an activity to promote connection and reflection from increasing positions of youth power. Employing skills of critical reflection, adolescents' ongoing development involves participating for the benefit of others as well as themselves. Increasingly complex collaborative activities can support that development.

Figure 5.1 and the accompanying invitation to complete a youth survey illustrate how participants in the DSTY workshop communicated, in this case magnanimously, with "youth of the world" to "fill out our survey" and "allow us to find out what you would like to change in your community." Like other participants creating their own surveys across the political-violence system, these teenagers appeal directly – "we" are asking "you" – no abstraction or passive expression here! Choosing uppercase letters, they emphasize their enthusiasm. These friends converse among themselves about what they would like to know from the children of their parents' former adversaries and how they should ask such questions. As they do so, these young people make quite clear that they are knowledgeable rather than naïve and forward looking rather than stalled in the past, posing questions such as "What are your goals?" and "Does your community help you in achieving those goals?" These young participants acknowledge that not all is possible and that people who could be helpful sometimes are not.

Having explained how participants echo national scripts in Chapter 3 and thaw frozen narratives in Chapter 4, we focus in this chapter on how workshop participants use discourse genres to interact directly with public officials and one another. All discourse is interactive, but these activities are designed to have an impact beyond the personal sphere of friends and family. Asking questions of former adversaries extends beyond answering questions about the state of the state. Interpreting results of a survey extends beyond completing a survey, and writing letters to officials extends beyond narrating. Discussing a public story with peers allows for debate with other youth. In addition to interpersonal communication, young people's interactions with powerful people, especially during the adolescent and young adult years, provides experience interacting with the social structures that influence their lives, learning about the course of public engagement, and responding to obstacles.

We begin this discussion about power stances by considering conversation by a group of young people who created an advertisement in a small town in Croatia. Several male and female participants wrote the "future prospects" announcement after working together to pose questions for a survey titled "By and for Youth," as did 16 other groups of participants in DSTY research workshops in four countries. This group of young people worked in a computer lab of the community center transformed with redevelopment funds in the postwar period. Participants include one boy who identifies as Serbian, a girl who identifies as a Croat from Bosnia, another as a domicile Croat, and one who says simply that he is Bosnian. In addition to these ethnicities, others make references to their various religions as orthodox Christian, Muslim, and Roman Catholic. This diversity characteristic of Yugoslavia, uncommon and dangerous during the war, is gradually re-emerging in the region and in the community center where "future prospects" was created.

When discussing what to ask peers in countries on the other side of the war, some mentioned their own experience, like a youth who said "I was in Serbia during the war, so I know how they think," while another added that she could imagine questions from Bosnia, where she had lived. All were annoyed, yet amused, when someone mentioned that respondents might call them, "villagers, like some guy I know in the city." Although not sounding particularly powerful, the shift to active stances as questioners, advisors to public officials, and commenters about youth activism (as in their discussions of the public stories), these young people, like others across the workshops, summon different knowledge and issues in these explicitly activist genres.

The group who made the "future prospects" ad, like half of the other participants, was involved in community-development activities, including attending workshops on human rights, building play structures for younger children, and raising funds for the center by tutoring. Whether intensely involved in a community center or not, all participants work together to pose compelling questions to their international peers.

Despite ideological and playful disagreements while proposing survey questions, the youth never question the goal-directed nature of their inquiry. Interestingly, in this context, numerous contentious issues emerge related to the war, the effects of the war, worries about becoming adults, and numerous personal issues from health to drugs to sex. Questions like "Do teachers abuse you if you are from the 'wrong' group?" are particularly poignant. Also by consensus, albeit achieved in debate, this group orients toward societal critique via their focus on change, with questions like "What would you like to change in your community?" and looming challenges like "Would you live with your parents if you get married and there still are no jobs?"

As a few members of the group edited a draft of their announcement, one member used computer-drawing tools to create the accompanying image, Figure 5.1, with a sunrise representing future possibility and a sunset far off on the horizon expressing threats to possibilities for change. Although not all groups across the four countries had access to computer tools, they created equally compelling illustrated invitations to their segments of the youth-designed survey. With a few markers and paper, participants working in a Bosnian bakery in a small city in the United States created the image in Figure 5.2 to accompany their questions about displacement after the war.

FIGURE 5.2. U.S. survey.

The teenager who drew this picture was one among several young people whose families had fled Bosnia during acute phases of violence or in the aftermath of political–economic instability. The groups in the United States focus on consequences of displacement: the apparent opportunities and obvious losses. Despite the benefits of living in the United States, this image of "US" burning from inside expresses the lingering pain of those youth as they reflect in the safety of the Bosnian bakery. The ironic nature of these and other advertisements supports the argument initiated in Chapter 4 that multiple positioning with diverse genres can support the development of critical thinking.

With these vivid logos to announce their original survey questions, I introduce a discussion about the orientations young people shared about community participation. After a summary of youth reports about their participation in community activities, I review how young people use inquiry genres (interpreting youth survey responses and creating a survey for peers across the former Yugoslavia), an advisory genre (writing a letter to a public official), and collaborative story-telling (rewriting a public story). Results indicate the potential of power genres to scaffold development through participation in community change.

PARTICIPATION AND DEVELOPMENT

Participation in activities with goals beyond personal and interpersonal interests is developmentally appropriate for adolescents and young adults. More than "learning by doing" (Dewey, 1929) or scaffolding in the zone of proximal development (Vygotsky, 1978), participating in world affairs (Erikson, 1980) is exciting for young people, although the powerful elite rarely draw on youth as resources. During adolescence, it is important to gain control over the environment to the greatest extent possible, and it is precisely those interactions with the "concrete conditions of the child's life . . . [when]

some types of activity will be more prominent, and more significant for the further development of the personality; and others less
so" (www.marxists.org/archive/elkonin/works/1971/stages.htm, p. 5).
Waiting too long to foster youth participation in meaningful societal processes, however, can mean waiting until their insights are less
astute because of habit, conformity, or some other phenomenon that
undermines childhood and adolescent plasticity.

Exploring similar proposals, research on adolescents' civic participation and political understanding has increased in the last 20 years
in part because of the new post-communist democracies and the
transformations of older democracies (Flanagan, Gallay, Sukhdeep,
Gallay, & Nti, 2005; Helwig, Arnold, Tan, & Boyd, 2007; Sherrod, 2003;
Tourney-Purta, Schwille, & Amadeo, 1999; Youniss, Bales, Christmas-
Best, Diversi, et al., 2003). As stated by one scholar, "When the structure of government and the form of the economy are in flux, citizenship can no longer be taken for granted as a plain matter of the older
generation passing tradition on to the younger generation" (Youniss
et al., 2003). Catalysts for this increased interest in children's sociopo-
litical development include numerous wars like those in the former
Yugoslavia, the ratification of the UNCRC (Ruck, Abramovitch, &
Keating, 1998; United Nations, 1989), and broader contemporary globalization processes, including increased communication via the media
(Nilan & Feixa, 2006), migration (Suarez-Orozco, Suarez-Orozco, &
Todorova, 2004), and conflict (Daiute, et al., 2006).

Previous research on young people's understanding of political concepts and practices, including citizenship and democracy,
has occurred primarily within cognitive–developmental frameworks
equating development with chronological age or ethnic culture.
Researchers found, for example, that 14-year-olds across 28 different
countries express basic knowledge of democratic values and practices
like voting (Torney-Purta et al., 1999). This research also identified
diverse societal activities supporting youth civic engagement, such
as supporting programs of children's rights, fostering enthusiasm for

voting, requiring national service, and modeling democratic process in schools (*ibid.*). Research focused on the interaction between
context and development found, moreover, that children growing
up in the very different political systems of Canada and China preferred democratic to nondemocratic forms of government and used
principles like majority voice and representative rule to explain their
preferences (Helwig et al., 2007). One reason for these preferences is
the participatory nature of democracy.

One United States–based study identified gaps in youth knowledge
about democracy. Researchers who asked adolescents to respond to
the question "What does democracy mean to you?" found that only
half of the youth in their sample gave what the authors defined as "correct" definitions (53 percent) (Flanagan et al., 2005). Of that 53 percent, their definitions of democracy mentioned principles of representative rule (40 percent), individual rights (30 percent), and civic
equality (30 percent). Given such results, scholars have argued that
civic engagement is a catalyst for ongoing development of political
understanding. Another analysis of young people's political attitudes
and socialization experiences in the United States showed that some
were concerned about issues like poverty and injustice; others were
concerned about politics as it impinges on self-protection (Sherrod,
2003). Shifting from methods that elicit young people's abstract political knowledge, another study asked high school and college students
to indicate their preferences for different types of activities, revealing their motivation to participate in local, personally meaningful
causes, like protecting the environment and helping those in need,
rather than voting and other formal processes (*ibid.*).

Several recent studies focused on political discourse as the embodiment of social relations. A discourse analysis of texts for citizenship
education in the United States found differences between political
ideology and practice, identifying specifically that the majority of
citizenship textbooks in use from 1990 to 2003 defined citizenship
in ways relevant to prior centuries but were silent on the more

contemporary issues of citizenship practices (Knight-Abowitz & Harnish, 2006). Another study examined democratic education relative to different societal conceptions of "the democratic person" in several Western societies, which has recently shifted from emphasizing the production of democratic individuals to preparation for democratic action and participation (Biesta, 2007). Also relevant is how individual young people interact with such changing discourses, not only in textbooks but also in everyday practices. Although there are increasing opportunities for youth participation worldwide (Hart, 1999), a need exists to examine the nature and effects of different forms of participation. Toward this end, a cultural–historical explanation is useful for considering sociopolitical development. Consistent with this view, development occurs through participation in society, discursive interpretation, and activities appealing to youth.

A dramatic result of previous research, as a matter of fact, is that most civic-education projects focus on voting and official political practices, but teenagers report being most informed by and passionate about volunteering in community organizations, where they can connect with other people, make a difference, analyze when activities go awry, and fix them. Considering this dynamic with youth who are at least minimally active in a community organization is a step in the inquiry into development in transit.

YOUTH PARTICIPATION ACROSS POLITICAL-VIOLENCE SYSTEMS

Youth participation sometimes involves violent activities, like those of child soldiers or the supporting roles of messenger and cook. Reviews of research on child soldiers reports on recruitment processes and their dire consequences. Serving roles in violence is a tragic abuse of children's rights and seriously tests expectations of human morality, two factors that explain the intense focus on child soldiers. This research on participation in violence is extensive (and not the focus of this study), in part because the number of child soldiers is small compared to the millions of children interacting with the effects of war (displacement, poverty, orphaning, exploitation, and so forth). Parallel to analyses of rehabilitation activities of child soldiers, we consider the involvements of youth who have been exposed to violence in other ways. Children become involved during acute phases of violence by helping to acquire resources, like one youth who reported running behind the barricades in Sarajevo to get water from one of the few functioning wells at the edge of town, supporting family members, bringing messages, obeying parents' attempts to protect her, and staying out of the way. Young people also report enjoyable, mischievous times in tunnels during air raids when their parents' watch strayed amidst the chaos of violence. Those who grew up during and after war also have access to organizations beyond public education, religious services, and family where they can develop their interests and skills.

In the myriad violent and nonviolent political transitions at the beginning of the 21st century, NGOs are playing a central role, especially for the generation growing up during major changes. Challenges to young people in transitional nations occur in part because their parents, teachers, and political leaders were educated in a different political system, experienced a violent war, and now have few resources to address the prolonged consequences of the war, such as the destruction of factories, railroads, and other infrastructure. Teenagers in rural and marginal urban areas do not see many adults working in town during the day, so they are acutely aware of their own financial vulnerability and the possibility that in order to become independent, they will have to leave home for higher education or employment.

At the same time, multinational organizations like the UN, World Bank, WHO, UNICEF, UN Commission on Human Rights (UNCHR), United National Development Program (UNDP) and many local NGOs focusing on the plight of children in war provide funding for spaces, technology, workshops, and social activities where young people can play a role in developing their communities and their own skills. Participation in community activities, especially in Europe, is important as a means of socializing youth with models of human rights, intergroup tolerance, and democratic participation, since this post-war generation is in an historically unique position. Their parents had, for example, grown up during the socialist era and survived or perished in the wars of the 1990s.

The role of organizations like those involved in our study is, however, not without contention, as are other international institutions like the UN, which is a reference point for many contemporary civil-society groups. Transnational institutions model values and practices of democracy and activism. Given the pressure to demonstrate success and thereby gain ongoing funding, these organizations also promote children's dependence on them rather than empower their independent action, as critics have recently emphasized (McMahon, 2009). For example, families and children learn that claiming trauma can garner resources. More prominent, however, is the issue of promoting youth participation in their communities despite the power relations that accompany formal organizations. The NGOs in our study provided a liminal developmental space for those interested in developing their societies and serving more personal goals. With this fact of individual in context in mind, we ask, How do young people engage powerful stances to make sense of society and their role in it? What role can such resources play in the face of recalcitrant ideologies and economic stagnation? Research on the nature and consequences of such conflicts should be defined as an interactive developmental process.

PARTICIPATION MATTERS

Consistent with the idea that active participation in organizations would heighten young people's engagement in and determination of relationships beyond their interpersonal spheres of activity, the research workshop explored relationships between active participation and evaluations of society. The question "Do you participate in a community organization?" was followed, for those responding "yes," by questions about reasons for participating and the importance of the relevant programs, whereas for those responding "no," the follow-up question asked their reasons for nonparticipation. The number of young people stating they were active in a community organization (72) was roughly equivalent to the number who were not (63) on a forced-choice item.

Results of comparisons of young people reporting involvement and noninvolvement in community organizations indicated that active youth are more attuned to problems in their societies (3.10 mentions per person) than youth who are not (2.43 mentions per person); $p = 0.015$.[1] More and less active youth did not, however, differ in their mentions of positive qualities. This seemingly simple finding supports the idea that participation in organizations engages critical thinking. If all higher-order thinking and acting are developmental sociocultural interactions, then those within collectives focused on community as well as personal goals would involve participants with the tools of those organizations. Although involvement in formal organizations is not necessarily always positive, perhaps because of pressures to secure funding or activities that may use such funding in inadvertently coercive ways, participants would be exposed to the types of analyses, obstacles, and strategies in an organization's discursive activities.

Young people who are not active in community organizations are aware of unemployment, and those who are active offer a series of issues: "There are no jobs, no one is taking us seriously, we are giving the opportunities to the citizens of our neighboring countries, but

---

[1] Details of these and subsequent statistical analyses to be presented in Daiute & Lucic, in preparation.

do they invite us over there? Politicians are corrupted and they are not doing anything for our well-being. With two entities, how can we have a normal country which will have laws from whom youth can benefit?" In addition, when examining such critiques, we find that active youth not only mention more problems but also analyze, for example, causes of the problems: "With two entities, how can we have a normal country which will have laws from whom youth can benefit?" and ".... In fact, it all stems from the poor government (politicians, government, and parliament) who are not qualified for such a responsible job, and about economy they have no clue. The solution we will only find if in the higher state powers come highly qualified professionals and especially from fields such as economy, because that is the only way to get out of a situation like this."

These two excerpts both mention a political problem with an explanation of its implications and, in the latter example, the cause. Such issues are, of course, available to adolescents and young adults in educational contexts, the media, and conversations in the family and among peers, but the greater incidence among those active in community organizations suggests that participation in organizations may relate to critical thinking. The lack of difference in mentions of positive qualities of society also lends support to the developmental nature of active engagement in community organizations.

How Do Youth Participate in Community Organizations?

Open-ended questions about participation were followed by a series of Likert-scale items asking about the importance ("very important" [1] to "not important" [4/5]) of reasons to participate, including to learn skills, improve society, meet new people, pass time, have fun, and fulfill school requirements.

Analyses showed that young people across the four case study settings responded that participation in community organizations is important. Differences emerged, however, in responses to the importance of several reasons for participating: "to learn new skills," "just to spend time," and "to fulfill school requirements." Youth in Croatia indicated the highest rationale "to learn new skills" (1.94) compared to those in Serbia (1.26), with a difference score of $p = 0.008$; this was indistinguishable from the youth responses in BiH (1.62) and the United States (1.50). Youth in Serbia distinguished themselves with the explanation "just to spend time," rated 3.70 compared to youth in both Croatia and the United States (2.86), with no difference from youth in BiH (3.36). Youth in Serbia also rated the reason "to fulfill school requirements" as relatively important (3.74) compared to youth in Croatia (2.86), BiH (2.79), and the United States (2.08), which also differed from responses in Croatia.

Open-ended questions to youth about their participation in society yielded responses about organizations, activities, and reasons for participating in organizations in their communities and societies. Those who stated that they do not participate in community organizations offered reasons with a majority having other commitments to family, school, and work. Analyses of responses to these questions resulted in categories listed in Table 5.1, including community and service organizations, learning, cultural/religious, leisure, and sports activities, and reasons for participation such as social, educational, and personal or other opportunities.

Participants provided several names of community centers run by NGOs, cultural groups, sports teams, and religious organizations. Activities within those organizations included service ("helping others and myself and to spend quality time"), educational enrichment ("volunteering in this organization I think that I gain skills necessary for diplomacy, that I maybe intend to pursue considering that I study law"), cultural and religious ("we also learn to preserve our own cultural heritage which is very important today in the times of unstoppable globalization"), leisure ("spending time/hanging out"), and sports ("playing in the sports field to get some exercise"). Participants

TABLE 5.1. *Mean Mentions per Participant in Responses to Open-Ended Questions about Participation in Community and Other Activities*

	Countries across the former Yugoslavia			
	BiH	Croatia	Serbia	United States
Participation Categories				
In Community Organizations	.41	.20	.04	.05
Other Organizations	.22	.11	.13	.03
In Service Activities*	.26	.40	.13	.13
Learning Activities*	.04	.26	.54	.24
Cultural/Religious Activities*	.11	.06	.33	.34
Leisure Activities*	.04	.17	.75	.34
Sports Activities*	.00	.03	.54	.45
Reasons for Participating				
Social Reasons	.33	.54	.46	.29
Educational Reasons	.37	.31	.29	.26
Not Participating and Other Obligations	.22	.17	.08	.21
Intention to Participate	.15	.03	.00	.00

* $p = 0.05$.

offered reasons including the desire to educate ("to help others in their academic improvement, such as tutoring"), to learn, and to develop one's own skills. Between one-fifth (United States), one-third (Croatia and BiH), and slightly more than one-third (Serbia) of respondents indicated that they did not participate in community organizations because they had no time, had other obligations, or did not have the opportunity. Especially poignant examples include "I try my best to be involved, lack of involvement would possibly be because I work full-time and go to school full-time," and "my grandparents don't speak the language so I have to help them all the time."

As shown in Table 5.1, analyses indicated different percentages of respondents across contexts in the nature of and reasons for participating. Youth in Serbia report participating in relatively more leisure and sports activities than youth in the United States and

BiH, and youth in Croatia also participate to a large extent. Analyses revealed differences across contexts in the nature of participation activities, with youth in Croatia indicating more service activities than youth in BiH, and youth in the United States indicating more educational activities than youth in Serbia, BiH, and Croatia. When reporting participation, respondents in the United States also noted more cultural and religious activities than youth across the other three countries. Differences in sports activities also emerged in responses between youth in Serbia and BiH, who also differed from youth in Croatia.

The significance of these results is that young people across geopolitical contexts are involved in different personal and collective activities, although their motivations may be similar. Those reasons are, most frequently, social and, secondly, educational. These patterns of difference and similarity suggest some broad common orientations to self-development and social contact dependent on opportunities in the local area. To this information about participation, we learned how these young people used the active position of writing letters to public officials as another means to participate.

YOUTH ADVICE TO PERSONS IN POWER

Writing letters to public officials positions young people as experts. Elites in society must take the lead in changing political, economic, and social structures to ensure ongoing development, but their work depends on the agency of the youth generation. The project of preparing young people for a better future is, therefore, a collective enterprise traditionally skewed toward the powerful. In letters to public officials in government, education, and other fields, young people growing up in the context of dramatic political–economic change shared their firsthand knowledge about their own goals and needs, as well as difficulties in achieving those goals. For those already in power, gaining youth advice is a practical matter; for young people, sharing their expertise is a developmental matter. The development of the society hinges on increasing the power of the upcoming generation.

By connecting youth and public officials, whose job is improving the collective good, the letter-writing activity potentially engages understandings and goals that we reasonably assume to be developmental. Generations growing up during times of political–economic transition express a desire for something different from what they know to be a troubled past. As with all discursive activities, this activity engages youth at the intersection of multiple, sometimes conflicting scripts, reaching out to the leaders still in control from the past to bring awareness of contemporary realities that they may not perceive. The youth role of expert in this activity reorients them to future goals. Questions about this process include, How will young people project that future in letters to officials? How, if at all, does youth advice to officials echo societal scripts, including those of adult conflicts, the newly formed states, and the EU?

As part of the DSTY research workshop, 103 participants wrote letters to a variety of public officials, including prime ministers, presidents, mayors, university deans, and school principals, among others. These youth organized their letters around a range of discursive functions, including complaints, explanations of causes, thwarted goals, suggestions of how to address those complaints, explanations of why and how those solutions would work, and various personal appeals. In addition to these rhetorical activities, the letters mention several domains (including education, politics, environment, community/family, media, social/personal, work), the scope of issues (national, international, technical, systemic), strategies to remedy the problems, and values (such as human rights, peace, social order/ politics, morality/religion, praxis/relevance, quality of life/fun). This list itself indicates the scope of young letter writers' concerns and agency. I also applied the concept of script to identify common patterns of complaints and solutions.

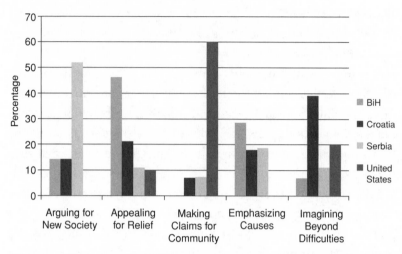

FIGURE 5.3. Percentages of different scripts organizing youth letters to leaders.

Figure 5.3 shows that participants in different locations organized their arguments according to different psychosocial scripts. Because the analysis identified authors' orientations to issues rather than only the issues, the resulting scripts reveal young people's ways of knowing, perceiving, and interpreting problems and solutions in their societies.

"Imagining beyond difficulties" is a script emphasizing complaints and solutions related to improving the quality of life. A high school student wrote the following example, organized in terms of the "imagining beyond difficulties" letter script:

> *Dear minister, I ask you to please do something with the development of our society. Great help would be a donation for computers or similar. In teaching the curriculum it should be more applied, prepare youth for life. In some topic areas add as many experiments, organizing excursions, preparing school with basic equipment.... I hope that the letter will not end up in the trash and that we will become "wealthier."*

The letter-script analysis identifies the pragmatic purpose in this letter to the minister of education: to transform the current impoverished state, which is lacking in technology, applied curriculum, and excursions. The letter writer builds to that general goal by making specific requests for "a donation for computers" and a curriculum that is "more applied" and includes "many experiments" and "excursions" for reasons including to "prepare youth for life" and to "become 'wealthier.'" That set of entailments comprises an "imagining beyond difficulties" letter script, most common in letters by youth in Croatia and, to a lesser extent, in letters by participants in the United States.

As shown in Figure 5.3, the most common script organizing letters by youth in Serbia was by far, at 51.9 percent, "arguing for new society," followed by "emphasizing causes," with three other scripts each accounting for only a few letters. The "arguing for a new society" script implies causes while focusing explicitly on changing from old to new ways of thinking, acting, and believing in life, as in the following letter by a high school student in Serbia:

> *Dear Head of Interior Affairs:*
> *I would like to ask you to be very careful when you recruit new employees. Do make sure that your employees do not have a criminal record. If there is no criminal among the guardians of order, we will all be much better off. Capturing juvenile petite criminals is not a big deal. Dig that?*
> *Yours sincerely,*

The most common script organizing letters by youth in the United States is "making a claim for community" (60 percent), followed by "imagining beyond difficulties" (20 percent) and a few "appealing for relief" scripts. The "making a claim for community" script focuses on local, national, or international community building as a means and/or an end. Letters conforming to this script do not typically make specific complaints, and the narrator implied values of peace, social order, morality, social connection, and well-being in the future. For example:

> *President Bush,*
>
> *Can you please attempt to make our country & other countries a better place? Instead of speaking about how this world could become peaceful, do something about it. Go to several locations (countries, etc.), see what the civilization is like there. See what their issues are and do your best to correct them. Thank you.*

As illustrated in this letter, communication, especially across diverse perspectives, is often a means to community, as stated by 16-year-old Narea in the United States when she counsels President Bush to "go to several locations (countries, etc.), see what the civilization is like there." Seventeen-year-old Haso and Mujo offer a slightly different emphasis within the same community-oriented script: "Build a community center for people from the same countries, that way they can interact with each other in their mother language" and "find out what many people need and want to make a better community."

The script that accounts for most of the letters (46.4 percent) by youth in BiH is "appealing for relief, protection," followed relatively closely (28.6 percent) by "emphasizing causes" and more remotely by the other three scripts. This letter by 20-year-old Admir makes such an appeal:

> *Dear Mr. President, how much more time do you need to see all corruption and criminal that is happening and surrounding us in every sense. Unemployment is high, many young people are leaving the country purely because of that. There is no sense to continue like this any more. Very soon our country will crumble, and who will stay after us to hold it together and on its feet. The country will remain to us, but because of your negligence and cynicism you do not think how everything will be for us. Thank you.*

Finally, the two most common scripts in letters by youth in Croatia are "imagining beyond difficulties" (39.3 percent) and "appealing for relief" (21.4 percent), followed closely by "emphasizing causes" (17.9 percent), with several letters for the remaining scripts. For example:

Dear Primier Ivo Sanader,

The programs of preschool and school and higher education has to expand the program of cultural and art contexts, learning about interpersonal relations, and cultural and social differences of the population of the whole world, so that young generations are guided towards real human values and preventing ignorance, disinterest, and all kinds of discrimination.

Honored minister of education, with this opportunity I ask you to weigh the suggestions for a better school curriculum. Youth in Croatia need a chance to participate much more in the practical work of the subject that they observe (learn) in high schools. I think that the subjects are aimed for future work because there is not time for understanding and exercises. Students need financial help to perfect their area of study because there is much capacity and one can go far. Please consider the suggestion that I am sending in the attachment. This will be the first step in connecting students from those same departments on an international level and I think everyone will benefit. Please reply by the end of June to the email address in the attachment.

The diverse scripts across letters by youth in different positions around the Yugoslavian war shed additional light on young people's engagement with political issues and directions of transformations for their societies. Each script involved awareness of activities and responsibilities of public institutions, including government and education.

ACTIVE INQUIRY: YOUTH INTERPRETATIONS OF SURVEYS

Participants also interacted with one another using excerpts from survey responses (See Figure 2.4). The focus of this collaborative activity is to reflect on responses by youth in the other countries, in particular to summarize the responses and comment on surprises in those responses. This innovative activity involving young people in reviewing results by transnational peers does not include all of the data that the research team used because that would be overwhelming in terms of training and time. Rather than being comprehensive, the guided review of research results serves the important purposes of fostering explicit connections among youth locally and transnationally, as they consider the same sets of important issues, share their insights, and debate.

In their conversations, participants across sites indicated how this activity elicited second thoughts about their own reasoning and extensions to other issues, as in this excerpt from several participants discussing survey responses by youth in other locales.

> FEMALE 1: *We have something to say about question #10. It shows us how differently people think.*
>
> MALE 1: *No, I thought how much the same as me they think.*
>
> FEMALE 2: *It surprises us that it's not crime and legal issues that they found important.*
>
> MALE 2: *We have something different about that . . . it surprised us that for young people crime is important at all, which is important for the future. . . .*
>
> FEMALE 1: *It's interesting that young people think about crime, unemployment, and that they are concerned about the future . . . things which are to come. That's not typical for a young person to think about. It would be more the way adults think, which is not to say that one should think about the future.*
>
> MALE 3: *Yeah, well I thought the question was just arrogant! Of course, in a small town, we have things to do, no way to make money. In the city, it's crime.*
>
> FEMALE 3: *And it's surprising that for young people it's more important to find a job than the issue of security. Maybe, that's the difference, where you are even in the same country, who has opportunities, who doesn't.*

In that context, the issue that emerged in conversation was whether young people like them would be thinking of the future, which all of them did! In a sense, their own concerns surprised them. In another workshop, the issue of gender relations emerged, which was not mentioned spontaneously in other contexts. Another notable comment underscores the purpose of this activity: to engage youth in thinking about youth in other places, as well as to assess their present thoughts. One female participant in a city said, "I feel powerful thinking about others' responses to a survey I completed a little while ago." One related issue important to her and others in her group was that the discussion divided ideas by those who had come to the city from smaller towns and those who grew up in the city. Someone commented that this is, after all, stereotyping, which launched yet another debate.

These excerpts of conversations about youth responses to surveys about problematic and positive qualities in their societies illustrate the complexity of any single strand of data and, thus, the need to engage diverse social–relational contexts for expression. Responses to survey questions were, in different ways, consistent within and across countries, but, as is evident in the conversations about young people's surprises each new, social–relational context becomes part of youth knowledge.

ACTIVE INQUIRY: CREATING AN ORIGINAL YOUTH SURVEY

This chapter began with an advertisement and a conversation by young people involved in contributing to the "By and for Youth" survey. This section continues with a discussion of the nature and significance of the youth survey design as a powerful genre. Creating questions challenges young people to identify their own curiosities, not indiscriminately but those curiosities that uniquely and provocatively could be addressed by peers living in different political positions. These inquiries bring contradictory and compatible ideas together, such as that adolescents across sites of political conflict experience ongoing discrimination. Answering questions engages young people in ideas and stances that they may not have come to spontaneously except when asking questions of other youth, shifting them into intense, interactive reflection.

As discussed in Chapter 2, this activity has several purposes, including to generate youth-designed surveys on the general question "What do we want to know from young people in the other areas about important issues in their lives as they move from being children to being adults?" Other purposes are to foster communication among youth from different areas, to provide an additional context where participants can reflect on the issues facing them, to generate information for youth leaders and educators about issues of importance to young people, and to provide an opportunity for learning and using features of the online research tool.

The process involves a group generating topics for the survey questions they would contribute and deciding on the subsequent process for their group, such as whether they would all work together on one general survey topic with different sections or whether each small group would generate questions about areas of interest. Instructions suggested that participants write a draft of their survey on paper, following the guidelines to "Create a Title for the Survey," "Write questions," and "Decide on a format for each question" (reminding them of formats in the survey they completed at the beginning of the workshop). After writing the survey on paper, participants enter it into the online survey-maker application program if computers and the Internet were available, and if not, they handwrite or dictate to a volunteer scribe. (See Figure 2.5.)

Participants were especially engaged when working in small groups to create questions for the "By and for Youth" survey to be distributed across the workshop sites. Approximately sixteen groups of three or four participants each created several hundred survey items. Groups were, for the most part, self-selected and, to some extent, fluid, meaning that occasionally someone left one group and joined another. Analyses of the original youth survey focused on the issues and pragmatic relationships expressed by participants when actively posing questions to international peers. The significance is that youth questions foster reflection and indicate what is on young people's minds relative to their own goals and needs and what they are curious about in the lives of peers across the region and beyond to the United States. This activity shifts the speaker–audience relationship in two ways: first, by including diverse specific interlocutors, and second, by provoking a discursive stance that requires imagining those new interlocutors in ways that may be similar and unique. As question askers, young people can, thus, expand their perspectives. Participants were enthusiastic and productive in their creation of questions for a survey of youth across the country positions involved in the study.

Analysis of the survey items focused on topics, issues, and pragmatics stated and implied in the questions. As discussed previously, the contentious nature of certain issues across this system means that certain speaker–audience–context interactions generate different types of knowledge and concerns. Participants may not have expressed concerns about societal divisions in autobiographical contexts where they are exposed as actors and/or where they think the audience such as international researchers or NGO directors might not be interested and/or responsive to interaction about certain issues. Just as the public-official audience generates information about policy-related issues and solutions, peer interlocutors from across countries implicated in the broader political context elicit novel knowledge. Young people across the region know, for example, of certain events that led to the wars, albeit from the perspectives of their own country contexts, as well as any understandings they may have about how people in other countries perceive them. Information in the media and from travelers across the region, for example, provides such insights, but direct and diverse interactions can engage youth perspective more critically, as we see in the complexity of DSTY activities. Given the opportunity to inquire about the lives of youth in other areas of the region about whom they have some knowledge, some assumptions, and ideally some interest could spark curiosity and, perhaps, empathy. The specific nature of curiosity expressed in youth-designed surveys provides insights about concerns emerging uniquely in this genre reaching out to those in former adversarial contexts.

As listed in Table 5.2, participants across the settings generated questions encompassing a wide array of topics. The most frequent topics include politics, education, violence, marriage, and health. Also popular were questions suggesting curiosity about youth culture, including media, music, money, entertainment, and friendship. Some of the topics are predictable given that participants are poised toward adulthood, including marriage (mentioning issues of timing, economic ability to set up a home and have a family, issues of who can marry ("okay for gays?"), issues of intergroup marriage (cross-religion, ethnicity, different country, different values and goals), health, health care, politics, money, occupation, employment, success, shopping habits, male–female relationships, and education. More self-revealing issues either not mentioned or not mentioned as prominently in other contexts were current issues of violence, abuse by professors, homosexuality, and prostitution. The range of issues for topics is broad. For example, hot issues are probed in questions about abuse by teachers, professors, and politicians; causes and effects of violence; and reasons for or results of immigration.

When identifying problems in society or narrating conflicts, participants mentioned issues with teachers or professors, most critically about their unfairness in grading or listening to youth perspectives. The youth-survey questions, however, probe deeper into war-related issues, such as whether teachers discriminate against youth based on their ethnic or religious identity. Topics including homosexuality, prostitution, and philosophies of life also emerged uniquely in the original youth-survey questions. It is unclear whether the small-group collaboration at the end of a long day was the primary impetus for new ideas in the surveys and invitations to potential responders. It could also have been the shift to the authoritative

TABLE 5.2. *Results of Analysis of Original Youth Survey Questions: Issues and Pragmatics*

Topics	Pragmatics
Alcohol, cigarettes, drugs	Act
Approaching marriage	Advise
Community	Analyze
Dance	Choose
Differences	Experience
Education	Explain
Environment	Feel
Extracurricular activities	Hypothesize
Fairness	Imagine
Friendship, peer social	Play
Gay	Notice
Having fun/entertainment	Prefer
Health	Project to future
Health care services	Remember
Immigration	Think
Male/female relationships	
Media	
Money	
Music	
Occupation/employment	
Parents/family	
Philosophy	
Politics	
Prostitution	
Purchasing	
Relationships with professors	
Society (broader)	
Success	
Tensions	
Violence	
War	
Yourself	

youth stance that provoked the change or some other aspect of the activity.

The pragmatic analysis focused on the speech act implied in the question (Searle, 1970), that is, the functional intention of the question. Beyond the topic of the question, the pragmatics imply activities like analyzing, imagining, remembering, and choosing, as indicated in Table 5.2 and in the following questions:

> *15. What type of music do you listen to?*
>
> *16. Do you listen to that type of music only because your friends listen to it, because you think you can that way enter a "better" circle of friends?*
>
> *17. What do you think about music as an art through which you express your emotions?*
>
> *18. A lot of people only listen to one type of music and do not accept other types; what do you think about that?*
>
> *19. The last concert that you attended is . . .*
>
> *20. Name three bands from your country:*
>
> *21. Would you go to the Exit festival in Novi Sad?*
>
> *22. What music reminds you of your childhood?*

These questions are not only about music but also about the role of youth culture in the broader scope of social relations. These questions ask about preferences as mediators of social relations: "A lot of people only listen to one type of music and do not accept other types; what do you think about that?" In this question, as in others, participants insert a projection, "a lot of people listen to only one type of music," thereby sharing a perspective as well as asking a question. Others imply a view, such as that music reminds them of childhood or that art expresses emotions. Many questions also simply ask about preferences: "the last concert you attended . . . " and "list three bands in your country." In this way, participants used the inquiry genre to mediate understandings about their country in relation to those of the peers with whom they were interacting at a distance with this survey.

In addition to the range of topics and pragmatics in the original youth survey questions are issues of division and choice that permeate the survey. Many of the questions unearth the issue of intergroup divisions and youth choices for their future. Societal divisions are prominent in questions related to "violence:" "Are you verbally abused at school because of your nationality (ethnicity)?" "Who is a more frequent perpetrator of violence? Men/Women." Divisions also organize questions about marriage ("Would you marry outside your religion. . . . Your ethnic group?"), immigration ("When you moved to a new country, how did people react to you?"), education ("Do you mind that you attend school with mates of other nationalities?"), and health ("Would you rather go to a male or female doctor?"), among other topics. Most explicit are questions like "Does the society you live in differentiate among people of different religions and nations? How are those differences expressed? Are there differences between rich and poor?" A notable communicative relation begs for interaction: "Would you like to know facts about the life of youth in other countries that were once part of the former Yugoslavia? If yes, which ones in particular?"

This stance of youth power engages different information about youth perspectives. Future research and practice could follow such lines of inquiry to examine the nature of interaction that emerges across groups and changes in young people's thinking and action as a result of participating in this specific power genre.

DEBATING PUBLIC STORIES

Public stories were adapted from news reports of youth activism on issues of political violence or societal change (see explanation in Chapter 2 and summaries of public stories in the Appendix). Participants had the opportunity to engage with these stories in several ways: first, by working with peers to debate the views of characters in the stories, and, second, through collaborative reflection about an event where other youth acted politically on their behalf. Guidelines to launch the conversations asked participants to read the stories, to write notes about what each major character in the story might have been thinking, and to say how they personally would respond to the characters. The culminating activity is a group discussion to rewrite the story, elaborating it from the point of view of the group. Encouraged to disagree as well as agree, participants would position themselves authoritatively in relation to the story, the issues it raises, and their own potential role in public events.

Although a major public story across these contexts could be a history of the wars of the 1990s, a relevant developmental approach was to provide a context in which young people could reflect on local youth activism. A local event of youth activism provides a context for participants' reflection on a major national issue relevant enough to young people to create a spontaneous demonstration or another active engagement. Beyond that, such events also most likely involve a range of youth perspectives, thereby articulating young people's increasingly mature reflection on political issues. In addition, discussing the events from different perspectives in small and large groups during workshop activities provides a unique stance considering participation in public life not only in terms of personal philosophy (which may model family members or other adults with personal influence) but also relative to one's own generation. Thus, the public-story activity involves practice discussing youth activism related to current events as well as insights for research, education, community-development activities, and young people's debates about these issues. For adolescents and young adults, such civic engagement is a relatively unexamined developmental process deserving support and warranting inquiry.

Ideally, discussing public events with peers can engage debate and reflection beyond political issues in the family, school, or religious institution. If the public stories elicit a range of perspectives about an important political event, young people can provoke one another to think beyond their most easily accessible thoughts (or frozen narratives) to consider a broader range of options that may complicate their own. For example, after groups of three or four read and discussed a public story about a recent youth demonstration related to increasing government control over the media, including exclusion of women and minorities, all the groups gathered to share the major points of their conversations (see Figure 2.7 for instructions and the Appendix for synopses). Participants voiced different views about motivations for youth activism, obstacles to youth participation, and the possible achievements. Summarizing various perspectives in the story, one female teenager offered the following:

> We have the organizer of the demonstrations – the one who had been organizing it for many years... engaged because he believes that youth have the right to express their ideas... an organizer who said you cannot prevent youth from voicing their opinion. The director of the TV station got upset... the policeman, who was present at the meeting, saw the scene in which the man was beating the woman with his fist and said he was going to bring it up later at the commission meeting... for him that fight was senseless....

A male peer in the group interjected the following when someone asked about the character named "Marijana:"

> Marijana thinks that older people should not have control over media just because they think they are smarter than youth...

The evaluative statement "older people... think they are smarter than youth" provoked the following debate:

YOUTH 3: *The friend thinks that there are much bigger issues than media issues and the problem that a guy runs a TV station... things like famine, water scarcity, violence, and other world issues....*

YOUTH 4: *We have a question if the youth were successful in the demon-strations and if so, how the older people reacted to their success. And how the commission responded when the policeman said what he did!*

Another group in the same country raised questions about the motivations of young people who make such public declarations. In a more urban context, a group of older youth focused on the motives of characters in the public story.

YOUTH 1: *People are generally selfish and all they do is for gaining some benefits including the leader of the public reunion in the story.*
YOUTH 2: *He was fighting for qualified leaders for the selfish reason of wanting to be a leader himself.*
SEVERAL OTHERS: *Not all motives come from selfishness.*

Even when participants debated the quality of a particular story, they thought it was a good catalyst for addressing issues that are not normally expressed in their daily social milieu.

Conversations of the U.S. public story generated especially passionate and diverse interactions. Following is an excerpt of responses to the U.S. public story about the "Catch an Immigrant Game." The most contentious debate arose in response to the comments of a woman identified in the story as a "Muslin-American graduate student in the media studies department" who explained: ... social exclusion has become such an issue in the U.S. after 9/11 that students should really do something lasting, like creating a radio program devoted to youth inclusion and collective action about democratic citizenship. The activities of such a radio station could touch a nerve. This media devotee commented, "They can include debates, for sure, but also diverse music, spiritual activities, comedy, and other stuff." His friend, Sara, said that as a Muslim-American, she thinks a radio station would be good but we can go further than that. "Why," she asked, "does it make sense for each little group from south Asia, Latin America, the former Yugoslavia, and every little state in the union to have its own club? What sense is that? We have to figure out how to unite around political issues, not identity politics."

Although most of the participants in the discussion cited herein identified as Bosnian immigrants and practicing Muslims, the story elicited a diversity of opinions. Comments by numerous participants across different groups meeting in the Bosnian bakery indicate that this statement touched a nerve among these young people. Debated across the comments are issues of migration, intergroup relations, and the role of the media.

> YOUTH 1: *David Laska of the Young Republicans brought up an important issue in the wrong way. I disagree with all of the people in this article. They all look at the problem at hand, illegal immigration, without looking at the core reasons it happens. They need to study the actions of international governments and corporations to see why it really happens.*
>
> YOUTH 2: *I do not agree with the young Muslim-American because she doesn't know why the groups are divided in the first place. Serbs and Bosnians cannot "bond." Things have to heal, time must pass. I think she was being ignorant and stating an overused lame idea, "we should all get along." I lived through the war which is probably why I am so biased. I completely disagree with David Laska. I believe he has deep-rooted hate but he is trying to seem politically correct. He makes me sick. It's ignorant people like him that I had to put up with my whole life here in the U.S. I would not let him get away with that fabricated answer. I agree with the NYU President, I think educated youth should be better than that. No one wants to leave everything they know behind and move to a foreign land. Once we do, people such as the College Republicans do not make our life any easier.*
>
> YOUTH 3: *I agree with David Hancock because immigrants make a big part of every community in USA. So separation of immigrants would result in separation of the community. . . . I disagree with the young Muslim-American. Not all groups can get together and provide the best outcomes. Working together results in most efficient outcome, however, for instance, I cannot work with any Serbian people because of our past experience.*

YOUTH 4: ... *I agree with Maja* (who said we should have a youth radio station where we can debate important issues) *because people should talk more about the war and other topics, that maybe all of them realized "you are not alone."*

YOUTH 5: *I agree with Maja, because talking to someone over the Internet for example will broaden our mentality/knowledge of other cultures and their way of life, doesn't necessarily mean they will form a club and interact but just get some personal background info. In the end, it's easier to talk to someone you can relate to.*

Faced with a difficult situation in the United States, these participants, like Krusko (youth 2), a 19-year-old in the United States who identifies strongly as a Bosnian immigrant, are dealing with discrimination as immigrants (which during 2007 was extremely strong, as indicated in the public-story event) and most as practicing Muslims in the aftermath of the attacks on the New York City World Trade Center 9/11. In several narratives of her own experience, Krusko decries intolerance against Muslims in American in one discussion yet is completely against arguments that Bosnians should try to get along with Serbs in another discussion. Although Bosnians' suffering somehow looms across these expressions, their diversity is enriched when we consider their scripts in the context of their performances. Krusko's intolerant script against Serbs was expressed in a context she identified as phoney political correctness, while her comment against the intolerant script of Americans toward Muslims was expressed in a context about a family's sadness, and the script of opportunity was expressed in the context of commenting on positive as well as negative aspects of her society. If searching for coherence, one could reduce these comments to the collective memory of Bosnian suffering, but this developmental approach foregrounds the performance of multiple, seemingly contradictory, transformative living history. Somewhere between the pressure to repeat frozen narratives of war and youthful desire to have a future is a developmental dimension of living history, where young people are especially attentive to social relations in real time and space. These types of conversations create the sense of audience inherent in more apparently solo discursive activities and, ideally, occur in increasingly frequent and supportive contexts to promote development. In these excerpts of conversations about important issues, we heard young people becoming acquainted with cultural tools such as "freedom of speech," "youth activism," and "illegal immigration," using those terms not only casually but also critically. The excerpts of debate about youth engagement in public stories offer insights about human development contributed by the practice-based research presented in this book. Consensus and disagreement ignite complex debates that relate to the issues in the public story, as well as the issue of how young people represent one another. These brief examples illustrate youth capacity and interest that merit continued support. Implications for ongoing activism related to this activity are intriguing (albeit beyond the scope of this inquiry), but the conversations would be foundational activities to awaken critique and agency that render the public personal.

SUMMARY: POWER GENRES

The power that young people could have involves imagination, intention, and action. The various activities discussed in this book were designed to promote those orientations in a workshop connected to varying degrees with community organizations. The focus on explicitly participatory genres in this chapter adds several generalizations to those of previous chapters.

Participation reified in purposeful discourse activity engages young people's knowledge and critical thinking in the context of action. Researchers increasingly seek youth perspectives, but interviews separated from the field of practice may reveal quite limited versions of those understandings. On the other hand, practice that does not challenge young people to use their critical abilities may also miss developmental opportunities. Certainly the present inquiry also has limits, but the project of eliciting young people's intellectual power with the various dynamic story-telling activities demonstrates that we can go beyond drawing and play-acting when working with young people in challenging contexts. The following summary of results across the DSTY activities indicates the potential power, moreover, of making complexity rather than coherence a goal of inquiry. Table 5.3 lists the preferences of youth across countries in several major workshop activities.

As shown in Table 5.3, youth in BiH used adult-conflict narratives to embody societal tensions, carried over to the fictional narrative as expressions of uncertainty, while adding a sense of hope and desire. In their letters to public officials, the participants in BiH appealed for specific types of relief to tensions and uncertainties. The Serbian letters add to laments of "last-century mentality," contradictions in the present time, and specific ideas of what this new society might be like, thereby transforming complaint to concern to, finally, their own praxis.

In this way, the participatory intentions of the letter genre, as with youth survey question design and other activities, promote power orientations. Youth in Croatia used their letters to public officials to suggest enhancements that would enable them to experience the promise proffered in the contemporary national narrative of recovery in the EU. In a more nostalgic tone but with no less conviction, letters by participants in the United States moved beyond their important identifications of the various dangers and injustices they perceive in this place that does not yet feel like home. The poignant contrast is that the U.S. letters ask not for equipment or opportunities but for the president, the mayor, and other officials to create a community of honesty and inclusion.

These discursive genres interact, of course, with physical activities, which is why we see more critical and powerful engagements

TABLE 5.3. *Compilation of Emphases across Youth Positions*

	Evaluations of society	Narratives of adult conflicts	Narratives of fictional community	Letters to public officials
BiH	• Dangers/violence • Social milieu • Substance abuse	• Tension abound	• Express hope/desire • Express uncertainty	• Appeal for relief • Focus on causes
Croatia	• Economic issues • Education issues • Social milieu	• Moving beyond difficulties	• Identify contradiction • Express hope/desire	• Imagine beyond difficulties to prospects for skill building, travel, etc.
Serbia	• Political issues • Economic issues • Social milieu	• Reflecting on societal divisions	• Consider process • Identify contradiction	• Argue for new society, with a new mentality and praxis, without old abuses
United States	• Dangers/violence • Substance abuse	• Moving beyond difficulties	• Express hope/desire • Express uncertainty	• Make claims for community • Imagine beyond difficulties

among those youth who reported being highly involved in community activities. To current literature on civic participation and rights, this historical analysis of diverse youth engagements indicates the need for research and practice accounting for complex context-sensitive definitions of problems and solutions from youth perspectives.

FIGURE 6.1. Personal variations.

6

Sociobiographies

War influences generations, in large part, through how people talk about it. Having considered the cultural–historical process of script making across a political system, we now explore how individual young people transform national scripts into personal stories. Stories are variations on shared scripts, still social but specific in experience and choice, as expressed in the youth drawing in Figure 6.1. Although not asked to talk or write about war, some participants chose to do so, albeit in very different ways that provide a segue for discussing how young people define themselves in the inescapable shadow of political violence.

> There is a debate about building a monument for children killed during the **war**, and it is very sad to see disagreement whether or not it should be for all children from all of Sarajevo or only for its Federation part. They still debate this issue, tensions are really big, and parents of those children feel used.

Consistent with the "tensions abound" script, 22-year-old Diana narrates a conflict in her hometown of Sarajevo in BiH. In this brief story, Diana foregrounds the war and its consequences as influencing "all Sarajevo." As narrator, Diana embodies the tension, "it is very sad to see . . . " and implies her view that the monument should be "for all children from all Sarajevo." Although not explicitly *about* herself, Diana's story presents a self-image. She expresses the local emotional context with comments about sadness, tensions, and feelings of being used. Diana's younger peer, 18-year-old Curica, invokes war in a very different way with her account of a conflict with an American youth about a war far from Sarajevo.

> *A couple of weeks ago I had a conflict with a young American guy, who was my age. We talked about the American economy and their president, and he said that all nations in the world want to be like America. He added that their economy is the strongest one and that he supports the war in Iraq because of the terrorist threat. What he said made me angry because I am very weak on the topic of **war**. I said that everyone knows that the real reason for ongoing **war** is oil, and that Bush's propaganda is a smart one, but his nation (people) is either stupid or they do not want to understand. He asked me how I know all this, and that the reason for the **war** is oil? I responded that everyone knows what is really going on but they do not want to admit it because it is easier to believe how the **war** has a good intent. Innocent people are killed there because of nothing, just like we were here. He did not have anything else to say. I did not want to fight with him since he my good friend, but I still felt superior to him because I knew I was right ☺. I spent my whole life in the **war** and I am always sympathetic towards people who are going through the same thing as we have.*

It is not clear what a young American was doing in Sarajevo, but Curica draws on his presence and friendship to display her knowledge and compassion, both for people in Iraq who are killed "because of nothing" and to the antagonist in her story, with whom she "did not want to fight." Curica distances herself from people who are "either stupid or they do not want to understand" how they have been fooled about their country's war. She then shifts to her personal experience in a city that was the site of a prolonged siege when she was a child. Diana's authorial voice embodies war-related tensions, while Curica crafts a global perspective connecting her experience to the plight of children suffering elsewhere and objecting to those causing the suffering. Diana and Curica weave different personal stances into the "tensions abound" script, one using herself as an instrument of sad feelings and the other presenting herself as an informed interpreter. One situates herself locally, the other transnationally.

Mentions of war by participants in the United States appear in a letter to a president and in a fictional narrative, among other places, as in the following examples:

> *Dear Mr. President,*
> *Please get our troops out of **war**. There is no point for our troops to be fighting for a hidden reason. If we got out of **war**, there would be no more dead troops.*

In his letter, 15-year-old Mujo i Suljo informs the president of the United States that he knows "our troops to be fighting for a hidden reason" and explains that the solution to "dead troops" is to get "out of war." The self-perspective here is Mujo i Suljo's definitive statement of a cause (fighting for a hidden reason), a problem (deaths due to a hidden reason), and a solution (get out of war). Although critical of the war, this teenager identifies with the president by invoking "our troops" and using the word "we." Sitting near him at the workshop, 16-year-old Narea writes a letter organized with the same "moving beyond difficulties" script but using the language of emotion.

> *Jim and Bob*
> *The news was that a **war** was coming & everything that they wished & dreamed for, is going to be ruined. Everyone involved thought about it as a tragedy never again will they're lives be*

the same. In the end Jim & Bob had to leave and start their foundation elsewhere.

Narea's letter is emotional in contrast to Mujo i Suljo's practical approach. Emotional approaches to the community narrative are common across country contexts (see Chapter 4), but individuals also made more personal choices about the genres they found appropriate for certain types of expressions. For example, Narea assumes an emotional approach with her drama of the "war ... coming," "tragedy," "dreams," and "ruin;" repetition in "everything that they wished & dreamed for ... " and "never again will they're lives be the same;" and resolution in "they had to leave and start their foundation elsewhere." Although she stands outside this consistently third-person story, Narea the narrator presents herself all the same. She engages the all-too-familiar war in a dramatic story. At the same time Mujo i Suljo chose a letter, Diana chose a narrative about adults, and Carmen a narrative about a conflict with an acquaintance.

The following two responses differ in how they reflect on divisions in Serbia. In her response, Ljubicica expresses intolerance for passivity in the face of political challenges.

> *Problems include: the lack of motivation and awareness that one can direct his or her own destiny, i.e. that some things do depend on us; **war**, consequences of the **war**, poverty; the influence of the church interfering with the state affairs, which must not be so.*

Interjecting herself as co-responsible, "some things do depend on us," Ljubicica connects with the fact of war and its numerous consequences, from poverty to intrusions of the church in politics. That sense of agency differs strikingly from the response by her peer, Medeja, to the same question about problems in society:

> *Problem: Bad education (lack of motivation of professors – insufficient funds), biased media, **war** in Kosovo, the fact that nothing can be done, the fact that one cannot study what he or she wants*

*(either because of corruption at a particular college or because there
are not opportunities after graduation from a particular college),
corruption, favoritism, lawlessness.*

Medeja also embeds war in a litany of problems, but, unlike Ljubicica, she displaces blame to others. According to Medeja, others –
the professors – lack motivation, with not a hint of self-inclusion as
an agent. The "fact that nothing can be done" extends to academic
choice, "corruption, favoritism, lawlessness." The mention of "war
in Kosovo" is also nested between blame on the "biased media"
and a global statement of troublesome facts. In addition to select-
ing the inquiry genre focusing on problems in society, these two
young women in Serbia differ in how they connect to the issues they
raised, one implicating herself in the solution and the other distancing
herself from solutions.

Works by two youth in Croatia also vary along self-presentation
dimensions. In his narrative about a dinner in Belgium, Egroeg is
a character with personal feelings about his "boring and annoying"
host and shares his intentions as a representative of Croatia whom
others question about "participation in the Second World War and in
the Homeland War."

*During one dinner in Belgium there was a discussion about nation-
ality issues. A man was constantly questioning me about Croatia's
participation in the Second World **War** and in the Homeland **War**.
He was boring and annoying. I tried not to say anything about the
political constitution of Belgium. At the end I mentioned something
about Belgium and the man got offended. The dinner ended in
silence.*

To what he clearly perceived as an attack, this 21-year-old from
a candidate nation to the EU visiting its capital in Belgium presents
himself as the image of self-restraint: "I tried not to say anything
about the political constitution of Belgium," but he finally "mentioned something," in response to which the "man got offended."

Egroeg's "moving beyond difficulties" strategy was thus a passive one, accepting that the dinner ended in silence. Choosing a different genre for a spontaneous mention of war, Carmen also assumes a defensive position, in this case to a national institution.

> *Honored Minister of Education, Culture, and Sports: Continuously in all medias [it] is mentioned how education is one of the main components for development of our little nations. However, in education less and less money is invested, you blame the government, the government blames the previous government for debts, and the previous government blames the Homeland **War**. Everyone has some excuses. The problem is not approached seriously enough and we are offered short term solutions that only hide the problems and do not solve it. . . .*

Twenty-one-year-old Carmen presents herself in this letter as an insider, in part by references like "our little nations" and "we are offered short term solutions." As someone committed to a longer-term solution, Carmen also identifies herself in the goals she suggests for the "little nations." Her approach to the "moving beyond difficulties" script differs from Egoreg's. While he presents as self-restrained, Carmen is involved in part, as embodied in the direct sender–receiver connection of the letter genre, the first-person perspective of "we," and "our," and the detailed litany of problems, implying personal knowledge.

These examples illustrate young people's uses of "war" as a cultural tool, that is, a symbol serving individuals seizing an opportunity to insert their personal positions within broader landscapes. Across the excerpts, war seems taken for granted, with various meanings embedded in young people's interactions in families, public institutions, peer groups, and their own private thoughts. Nevertheless, these young narrators use "war" as a symbol in unique ways, bringing into view the details that matter to them by telling stories, writing letters, or responding to a survey about problems in society. As a cultural tool, war has meaning in society, sometimes in frozen narratives but also, as in these examples, in nuanced ways amidst the din of specific places and times where individuals apply scripts in terms of their personal goals and challenges.

War is real and its material effects long lasting. Also real, yet rarely considered, is the symbolic role of war as a focal point for social relations and change. Neither completely fixed nor open, the meaning of war evolves as children and nations grow together, a process we examine in this chapter from the perspective of individuals.

It is clear that war-talk tends to be ideological or forbidden, but what is less clear is how it might serve individual goals for self-development. The comparative transformations of national scripts illustrated in these various uses of "war" indicate individual motivations, such as claiming versus shunting responsibility to resolve conflicts, restraining oneself versus getting involved in conflicts, identifying with versus distancing from the issues provoking conflicts, and practical versus emotional connections to issues. Such diverse personal positions in shared national scripts are evocative for a theory of sociobiography, that is, development through inquiry into how one fits within the broader scene of what is going on. As a way to fill in the gaps in understanding collective–individual development, I build on these examples of war as a cultural tool to consider how young people used activities in the research workshop to perform an ideal or possible self in the context of political change. Connecting with previous inquiry into individual differences, personality, and personhood, I argue that sociobiography is the crafting of personal positions in material and social relations.

Drawing primarily on peer-conflict narratives, I discuss the relevance of sociobiography for young people's self-development in a context where social relations are relatively equal and poignant, thereby especially appropriate for self-presentations. This explanation sets the scene for case studies to identify dimensions of diversity *within* national groups. In addition to contributing to theory about the social nature of self and identity, I present this analysis to consider the variability of individual responses to war to offer more detail about responses beyond damage and risk, as well as variations of national orientations.

Sociobiography is a concept positing that individuals have unique perspectives *in relation* to the social and physical world (Daiute, 2004). Contemporary case-study methods emphasize social dynamics of institutional cases as units of analysis, such as in classroom literacy practices (Dyson & Genishi, 2005), workplace activities (Engestrom et al, 1999), or interactive technology systems (Engestrom, 2009). In this inquiry, the political-violence system is the broader case consisting of interacting nations and community centers where individuals presented themselves across the wide range of activities in the research workshop. Sociobiographies bring those relationships to life.

As discussed in Chapter 3, young people organize their understandings of conflict relative to the circumstances where they are growing up. A script analysis showed that the young people whose families escaped the war and its aftermath, eventually settling in the United States, organized conflicts in terms of "moving beyond difficulties." The U.S. orientation is similar in some ways to that of youth in Croatia. In contrast, youth in Serbia organized narratives responding to the same prompts as "reflecting on societal divisions," and youth in BiH responded with a "tensions abound" script. Those scripts define culture via their consensus, but cultures are also complicated by individuals' ways of experiencing life from their perspectives in unique locations, families, communities, and journeys. While scripts are cultural consensus, stories are individual and idiosyncratic variations. This notion of "story" compared to "script" is not limited to narrative discourse and applies to personal inflections of consensus across genres. As discussed in Chapter 5, for example, participants' letters to public officials conformed to national scripts *and,* as we observed above, could also be used to express personal stances about societal issues.

Sociopolitical factors like war are not backgrounds, influences, or ways of knowing that individuals internalize. Rather, individuals integrate their environments within and across time and space, as we saw in the diverse uses of war at the beginning of this chapter. Because a sense of self infused in cultural products is, thus, not isolated, fixed, or completely malleable, we consider the range of options for an individual in sociobiographical activities. Narrative has become a metaphor for the self, presumably with personality forming in the life story (McLean & Pratt, 2006; Polkinghorne, 1991), and the sociobiographical approach extends this view to define narrating as a tool for engaging person–context dynamics. In situations of major conflict and change, these relations are attuned to threats and opportunities.

BEYOND IDENTITY

Defining self-understanding in adolescents and young adults is a high-stakes process because this is a turning point in life, whether in situations of threat or comfort. Previous theory would suggest that autobiographical narratives of conflicts with peers would involve explicit self-statements. Pressure to consolidate identity and to name an authentic consistent self exists (Erikson, 1980), but theory about the relational complexity of human behavior indicates that self-concept is a transitional object (Winnicott, 1971). The variety of expressions in the DSTY workshop indicates how young people use self-presentations to mediate relations in their environments. Serving to connect, distinguish, or distance, self-concept is thus a cultural tool, like other dynamic concepts, including war. To the extent that society demands the coherent self, most young people will eventually comply, but in revolutionary contexts where the ideal is still to be determined, youth may have more freedom to perform a range of positions drawing on their experience and goals to exert authority over the troubles and potentials in their environments.

As shown in Table 4.5, only 31 percent of participants across contexts used autobiographical narrating of peer conflicts to clarify identity, 7.1 percent when narrating adult conflicts, and none at all when narrating hypothetical conflicts in the community. Although the young narrators are present as characters and evaluators in events, the psychosocial purpose of their telling varies across genres (as discussed in Chapter 4). The following example illustrates self-identity in a peer-conflict narrative:

> *It happened one afternoon when my band gathered to practice the repertoire for the show. One of the members of the band was trying to persuade me to include in it "Tamara," a song by Bajaga. He was quite determined to include it. The two of us starting quarrelling. Soon the other two members of the band got involved in the argument as well. I was thinking of convincing him that it was not a good idea. At the same time, I was trying not to impose my opinion on him. I'm not sure how the other two felt about it, but I think that they were listening to us, trying to figure out what is right and what is wrong.*

Vahmata chose a social activity that was important to him at age 19 in Serbia. In that setting, he begins by recounting events: "It happened one afternoon," "my band gathered," "the two of us started quarrelling," and "other two members of the band got involved." At that point, Vahmata shifts into a psychological realm by reflecting on reflections (quite common of his peers in Serbia): "I was thinking of convincing him" and "At the same time, I was trying not to impose my opinion on him. I'm not sure how the other two felt about it." The narrative ends with the narrator's reflection, pulling together events across time from the distant past to the present: "I think that they were listening to us, trying to figure out what is right and what is wrong." Vahmata clarifies his own position in his role as leader as it relates to others.

In the next example, 20-year-old Milicia in Serbia arrives at a self-statement through the perspective of another in an argument:

A new acquaintance, with whom I'd been spending a lot of time (in the dorm where we were staying), would have some chocolate every time our roommate bought it and offered it to us, which he did on a daily basis. Once she bought some herself and ate it in front of us without offering it to us. The following day, after we were shopping for food, she secretly had her candy when I couldn't see it. I felt irritated and I asked her if she wanted my candy because it happened more than once. I was infuriated and asked her how she could be so selfish. I was making a reference to the situation from the night before. "Women . . . " was her answer. I was enraged for I couldn't believe that a person with whom I was spending so much time during the day could behave like that – day in day out, with different people. Since this selfishness was noticed by other people as well, we exchanged our impressions in conversation with one another. "Hm, Serbisch . . . " – I'm sure she thought, so my response might have been: "Hm, Italienisch . . . " Stereotypes without prejudices.

After working through details of her conversation with a peer and feelings about this conflict, Milicia offers self-reflection ("Hm, Serbisch") based on perspective shifting throughout the narrative. Milicia, like Vahmata, uses character reflection in the context of division, not only to assert herself but also to loosen any fixed self-presentation, as she does with the ironic self-critique "Hm, Serbisch" and the contradiction "stereotypes without prejudices."

In the next narrative, written in a workshop in BiH, Catwomen inserts herself prominently across the story:

A year or so ago, a very unpleasant event occurred in a PE class. I had a conflict with some girls from another class with whom we had PE classes. The situation was extremely tense – it could be felt that something had to happen. For some reason, the girls didn't like me, and they started a conflict. While I was looking, they hit a ball at me. Luckily, I turned around and caught the ball. I felt it was unjust and I thought about it. It seemed to me that the solution to the situation was that I hit with a ball the girl who had done it to me. So I did. That was NOT a solution, but it was a necessary thing to do because the situation required it. Sometimes, one should not just keep quiet and not respond. After I responded the way I did, they stopped torturing me because they realized they could not do to me anything they wanted, and that I was able to defend myself. After that conflict everything was in a way easier. Simply said, they respected me. I myself changed too since that day. I realized that I should not be submissive to other people, and that I should lead my life the way I wish (here, I mean people close to me).

Catwomen explains her actions and their consequences, showing her use of narrating for self-realization and presentation: "I myself changed too since that day." Similarly, Admir in BiH uses the following narrative to explore beyond relating events and characters to telling the story using adversarial perspectives:

I remember the event from my middle school that happened during my chemistry class. One of my classmates stole the book and did not want to admit that he did it. As a result, a couple of my other friends and I had a verbal conflict with him. Other students did not want to get involved, they did not even listen or pay any attention to our conflict.

In this way, 21-year-old Admir employs the privilege of the narrator perspective to perform an ideal self, in this case one who stands up for justice using various strategies. Admir presents his actions as the object of possible critique: "they . . . did not pay any attention to our conflict." This is similar to Vahmata's "I think that they were listening to us, trying to figure out what is right and what is wrong;" Milica's "'Hm, Serbisch . . . ' I'm sure she thought, so my response might have been: 'Hm, Italienisch;'" and Catwomen's "I myself changed too since that day. . . . I realized that I should not be submissive to other people." In these ways, young people across very different national and cultural contexts use narrating to craft self-statements. Although the previous narratives are some of the most explicitly self-focused examples in a large database, the self-object present in them is contingent on narrative social relations. Although such a self-focus is precisely what previous adolescent-development theory would predict, the majority (69 percent) of peer-conflict narratives in the database expresses very different motivations, perhaps because of the challenging nature of the narrators' situations.

A second major psychosocial function (36 percent) of the peer-conflict narratives is to clarify relationships, as in the following peer conflict by Twilight in Croatia:

> The conflict was between me and a colleague from my class. The discussion was about killing, and use of animals because of their fur, for the testing of the cosmetics and other products. I represented my point of view which is: against unnecessary killing of animals, and for with a reason and for human benefit. I didn't feel bad because we spoke with calm, we didn't argue. Other participants either felt like me or otherwise.

More than 10 percent of the participants used peer-conflict narratives to consider broader issues and processes present in the environment or to justify actions. Considering broader issues (10.3 percent) is an especially interesting category for peer-focused narratives because it indicates youth connection and concern in the troubling circumstances. Visnja, for example, focuses her peer-conflict story on issues of discrimination prevalent in her country of Serbia:

> The relationship with certain Roma people, in my city, is very bad. Children suffer from all different sorts of oppression, and abuse. It is hard for them to fit in and live "normal" when they are marginalized from the start. In schools, cinema, theatre, and even in cafés they suffer from evil looks and spiteful comments. A large percent of them falls under the pressure to leave school and to become independent. There are too many of those examples to mention.

Similarly, Ela in the United States embeds a peer conflict within the broader treatment of immigrants in the United States.

> *In high school, American kids would always pick on Bosnians telling that we get everything for free from the government, we don't pay taxes. They thought that they are right and that they know everything. I tried to explain the way it is but they wouldn't listen.*

Ela portrays the rigid views of Americans against Bosnians in terms of kids picking on them and falsely saying they are freeloaders who do not pay taxes. What begins as a peer conflict, "kids would always pick on Bosnians," is an issue beyond interpersonal relations.

Given the numerous difficulties these young people observed and experienced directly growing up in political violence, issues beyond self and identity may loom large or may, as in Ela's narrative, be a minor factor within a larger issue, like discrimination against Bosnians in the United States. It is interesting that among those concerned with broader social issues are the extremely reflective narratives by youth in Serbia. The analysis shows that living in a country that had a major role as aggressor or victim can foster intense perspective taking among the young, rather than render only flattened affect or aggressiveness. When in control of such stories, young authors present themselves in relation to the environment, like Vhamata, who is almost hyper-reflective when involved in a conflict with his band, and Ela, who focuses on effects for her group rather than herself. These and other examples illustrate self-presentation rather than the myopic self-focus implied as an adolescent characteristic in much research. Next, a discussion of within-person complexity contributes to understanding the range of responses to conflict in development.

PERSONAL STORIES IN SOCIETAL SCRIPTS

Case studies of individuals highlight personal motives within a political-violence system. Sixteen case studies illustrate diverse engagements with national scripts in various discursive activities. The focus on individuals' goals, needs, and confusions foregrounds the personal stories in political scripts. The story phase of discourse addresses the question "How do I fit?" not necessarily explicitly in terms of a first-person character but also via third-person characters or other discourse strategies. When examining personal perspectives, guiding questions include: What is the subjective perspective that turns this script into a story? and What are the nuanced variations of the script that express the significance of this telling for the teller?

A script-story analysis is consistent with the dynamic notion of self as defined by theorists using the concept of "leading activity" and its function during adolescence: "The leading activity in adolescence can be described in terms of the relationship between intention and realization" (Polivanova, 2006, p. 83). In this view, the adolescent not only experiences the world and interacts with people, events, and things in it but also learns to control those interactions in tool-like ways:

> ... text ... something within which the author of this text is first born as a personality and as a living person.... Prior to the text, deed, or gesture, it is not only the meaning of the latter that does not yet exist, but also the speaker, the person who addresses us and himself with this deed or gesture... in this sense... the adolescent finds himself at the point of his subjecthood (Polivanova, 2006, p. 82).

This view is consistent with theories explaining that all discourse is social because it embodies meaning in activity (Bakhtin, 1986; Bamberg, 2006; Bruner, 1986; Harre & Van Langenhove, 1999).

> Returning to the idea of the nonidentity of the content and plot of play, we can say that the adolescent too re-creates some whole that is manifest to him in reality, but then discovers something different from what he has re-created.... This modeling is akin to artistic modeling, which re-creates reality by means of art (Veresov, 2006, p. 81).

Consistent with this idea that development of a self-perspective is akin to artistic creation is the concept of *transitional object*. If children are to develop, " . . . a world of shared reality is created which the subject [the child] can use and which can feed back other-than-me substance into the subject" (Winnicott, Shepherd & Davis, 1989, p. 227). According to one view, developing a personality occurs first by relating to an object such as the presence of the mother during infancy, toys during childhood, and the world during adolescence and, second, by being "found in the world," such as through expression and finding oneself in a text. Next, the child "destroys" the object, that is, by comparing self-expression with that of others and identifying limits; surviving the destruction, such as with collective goals; and finally, by being able to use the object. This capacity "to use an object is more sophisticated than a capacity to relate to objects" because relating can be subjective or mere projection and thus not shared, whereas "usage implies the object is part of external reality" and is thus out of the child's "omnipotent control" (Winnicott et. al., 1989, p. 227).

The idea is that during adolescence, we extend our view beyond the immediate context to inquire and to gain some mastery there, as in "play with world politics," where one can connect to broader issues, "feel intensely, and shame the adults by really minding" (*ibid.*, p. 63). This process goes beyond defining the child's increasing interaction in the world to defining personally important issues (Stetesenko & Arievitch, 2004). Because this dynamic process is *polyphonic* conversation directed to and by numerous audiences, figuring out what one wants to express involves confusion, complexity, clarification, and commitment wrought from making sense of experience.

SOCIOBIOGRAPHICAL CASE STUDIES

Case studies of how individual young people make national scripts their own inform us of the interactive nature of human development and social change. I identified individual cases from contributions

TABLE 6.1. *Case-Study Design*

Country/individual	Age group	Gender
United States		
Narea	Younger	Female
Himzo	Younger	Male
Adela	Older	Female
Dzemo	Older	Male
Bosnia and Herzegovina		
Amer-Ci	Younger	Male
Ilda	Younger	Female
Diana	Older	Female
Admir	Older	Male
Croatia		
Anamaria	Younger–rural	Female
Rejo	Younger–rural	Male
Georgia	Older	Female
Jeronim	Older	Male
Serbia		
Pseudonumia	Younger	Male
Nancy	Younger	Female
Francesco	Older	Male
Ema	Older	Female

by participants across their activity in the DSTY research workshop augmented by observational information from my interactions and conversations with young people and the adults who work with them. The following criteria guided my selection of the cases: Participants completed all activities in the workshop; one or more of the narratives conformed to the local script pattern; and the resulting four participants from each country include a male and a female in the younger cohort (ages 12 to 18) and a male and a female in the older cohort (ages 19 to 27). Table 6.1 lists the pseudonyms of participants per country position included according to these criteria.

After compiling the data for these individuals, I compared the approach of each individual to the relevant national scripts. Analyses reveal several dimensions of variation for transforming scripts into personal stories: the location of the narrator (direct or indirect), narrator connection to the conflict (emotional or rational), historical orientation (past, present, or future), tone (earnest or ironic), and any other notably unique discursive elements. Questions guiding the case analysis included: How is the national script enacted differently by this individual? and What variations, consistencies, and contradictions appear across the data for this participant?

I discuss four individuals in most detail, with support from results of the three other case-study individuals in their country cohorts: Amer-Ci in BiH and Pseudonumia in Serbia and two female participants, Narea in the United States, and Anamaria in Croatia. These 16- or 17-year-olds experienced acute events of the war as young children, as well as one or more of the following major consequences: displacement, poverty, social exclusion, and/or a politically and economically unstable environment.

VARIATIONS ON THE "MOVING BEYOND DIFFICULTIES" SCRIPT IN THE UNITED STATES

Narea (female, age 16), Himzo (male, age 17), Adela (female, age 20), and Dzemo (male, age 21) are youth in the U.S. postwar position who expressed the "moving beyond difficulties" script in different ways. Analyses of these young peoples' narrative, inquiry, and advisory genres revealed very different renditions of the "moving beyond difficulties" script.

Narea, Coping with Moving Beyond

Narea's family fled Bosnia during the siege of Sarajevo, remaining in Germany until she was six years old when they came to the United States. Among the variations on the moving beyond difficulties script, Narea expresses resignation about living in the United States, which she portrays as mostly "negative" other than "but umm some positive things may be, education." As shown in Figure 6.2, Narea expresses

Participation: Describe how you participate in the community, reasons for participating, or reasons why not.

I enjoy drawing, singing, writing poetry. I enjoy school & sports.

I participate because it makes me a little more familiar and comfortable within the region I live in. My view is that I live in [this place], might as well make the best of it.

Evaluation of Society:

What is the biggest difficulty for young people in your city/town/country?

The biggest difficulty is that young people don't handle criticism very well & don't want to learn from their mistakes. They don't want to listen to elders when told it's for the better.

What are the positive or best qualities of life in your city/town/country?

Positive? Most qualities of this city are negative. But umm some positive things may be, education. There is a good education system installed.

Narratives:

Peer-Conflict Narrative:

Conflicts occur every single day within my family. They usually occur because people cant handle the truth and if someone speaks their mind, and they might not necessarily agree with what your saying, they get mad. (EX) me and my cousin got in an argument because I disagreed with her about a personal situation. In the end nothing was resolved.

Adult-Conflict Narrative:

Conflict was between my mother & my aunt. They fought about some personal issues. They yelled & screamed. I was involved at a point. I spoke my mind about the situation & they just canceled me out. But in the end they hugged & said sorry. The same situation occurred a week later.

Fictional Community Narrative:

Jim and Bob
The news was that a war was coming & everything that they wished & dreamed for, is going to be ruined. Everyone involved thought about it as a tragedy never gain will they're lives be the same. In the end Jim & Bob had to leave and start their foundation elsewhere.

Letter to Public Official:

President Bush,
Can you please attempt to make our country & other countries a better place? Instead of speaking about how this world could become peaceful, do something about it. Go to several locations (countries, etc.) see what the civilization is like there. See their issues are and do your best to correct them. Thank you.

Group Participant in Conversations: Guided Review of Survey Results, Public Story Re-write-Debate, Small Group Creation of Original Youth Survey

FIGURE 6.2. Data for Narea, 16, female, United States.

in the fictional narrative what could represent the seminal event in her life: "Jim and Bob:" " . . . a war was coming & everything that they wished & dreamed for, is going to be ruined. Everyone involved thought about it as a tragedy, never again will they're lives be the same. In the end Jim and Bob had to leave and start their foundation elsewhere." Although she may not remember much about living in Sarajevo, Narea's characters dramatically declare, "never again will they're lives be the same." Jim and Bob, like Narea, had to leave and start their foundation elsewhere." This narrative is evocative of the sense of resignation, coping, persistence, and sarcasm across Narea's contributions.

In a fatalistic way, Narea expresses resignation about living in the United States: "I participate [in school, sports, and cultural activities] because . . . I live in [this place], might as well make the best of it." Several references to ongoing problems end two of her narratives, with "in the end nothing was resolved" and "the same situation occurred a week later." Having moved also provides a global perspective on political events, which Narea shares in a letter to President Bush, suggesting that "instead of speaking about how this world could become peaceful . . . go to several locations (countries, etc.), see what the civilization is like there. See [what] their issues are. . . . " Although her stance is defensive, Narea also expresses strong and persistent stands against obstacles, as in interpersonal conflicts where she represents herself as someone who "speaks their mind" and states, "I disagreed." Jim and Bob and President Bush prevail as characters, with Jim and Bob leaving to "start their foundation elsewhere" and with her assumption that the president might "see their issues and do your best to correct them."

Narea's implied self-orientations also speak through others: "people can't handle the truth;" "people don't handle criticism very well & don't want to learn from their mistakes;" " . . . they get mad;" and "me and my cousin got in an argument because I disagreed with her." Persistence is a quality that permeates Narea's imagery as her forthrightness is met with interlocutors who "canceled me out" and "the same situation occurred a week later," even after "they hugged & said sorry." Narea's self-presentation is, moreover, specifically one relying on reason: "I disagreed," while others "yelled & screamed." She expands beyond her own myopic perspective: "I live in X, I might as well make the best of it," compared even to a president whom she must direct to "See their issues and do your best to correct them."

Other Approaches to the "Moving Beyond" Script

In contrast to Narea's resignation and persistence, Himzo expresses an otherworldly sense of right and wrong as his guide to understanding problems and moving beyond them. Writing in Bosnian, the 17-year-old lists as community activities going to the mosque "to pray, and imam talks about good behavior, and how youth should respect older adults." The importance of this participation is "To give younger people one more reason to be better, live healthier lives and have better future, religion is very important." Unlike Narea, who mentions other older adults in a different, negative way, "They don't want to listen to elders when it's for the better," Himzo highlights heroism. Defining obstacles in terms of conflicts between "extremists," Himzo focuses on divisions in terms that mingle political and cultural factors, as in "extremists from West Bosnia. After all they have done in their country, they are brave enough to organize Bosnian Association in order to raise the money for a new trial." Himzo comments in several contexts about divisions, "I remember one fight among Bosnians from two groups," extends to the worldly problems of extremist groups raising "money for the new trial," and states, "They showed again which side they were and that everything that happened was consciously organized." Himzo's self-presentation is consistent: "I am only Bosnian on the 'right' side." With these details, we see that Himzo breathes nuance as well as declaration of cultural/moral values into a narrative: "After all they have done in their country they are brave enough to organize Bosnian Association in order to raise the money for the new trial for... of course I am talking about Bosnian leader, who was the member of the political party called DNZ [Democratic People's Community], Fikret Avdic. They showed once again on which side they were and that everything that happened was consciously organized."

Twenty-year-old Adela recounts her own and others' struggles to move beyond difficulties socially in consort with "friends" rather than as on the "right side" of moral and cultural issues like Himzo or with persistent coping like Narea. Expressing an intrinsic value in "participating" because "I think to [do] something every day it's important...," Adela, who speaks Bosnian with her parents and English with her brother, situates herself as someone who does not "have time because of work, school, and help in the house." After establishing this credential in response to a survey inquiry at the beginning of the social-history workshop, Adela focuses on others, in some cases on her peers: "my boyfriend's sister she has strong personalities and I do so we fight all the time for everything, but at the same time we hang out the most;" on situations like "fighting over money two people...;" on the fictitious "Amy and Mary who felt so bad, they couldn't even think or even feel;" on those who have "lots of fights and drugs going on the street;" and on "a lot of Bosnian people [who] changed here in the U.S.A. [and] they are more want to be American now they are forgetting where they came from and who they really are." With the occasional insertion of a first-person pronoun ("we are all strong and got out of it [moved on]"), intensifying adverbs and repetitions ("they are *more* want to be American *now*... and who they *really* are"), Adela conveys her connection to the social milieu for resilience. This is stated most explicitly in her advisory letter to the president: "There should be more places to hang out, more employment. Something to make people to go to school, law to be more fair." Adela's gathering of others both like her and different from her is social strategy: "Bosnian concerns, friends, etc.," "to have fun, hanging out with other people, friends." Her claim is not of individual strength (like Narea) but of collective strength: "we all were strong and got out of it (moved on)" inserted in an emotionally poignant fictional story about news that was "bad (Death) everyone felt so bad, they couldn't think or even feel." Ultimately, consistent with the "moving beyond difficulties" script echoed by many of her peers, Adela culminates each conflict with a collective coming together, as in "but we hang out the most;" "it was stressful but they got over it and moved on;" and the comparison of "better life than in Bosnia (more money) here, better place to hang out there."

Twenty-one-year-old Dzemo, who has lived in the United States since he fled the war in Bosnia, expresses a more explicitly individualistic approach to moving beyond difficulties than his Bosnian American peers. Focusing on his "job, further learning, and educating myself," Dzemo reports spending "time in a useful manner," specifically as a police officer who works "full time" and does not see many activities in the city that "attract me." Guided by a "right path," Dzemo identifies the dangers "on the streets" in his "small city with a very limited amount of activities for people my age which results in young adults doing other things, which may not be good/legal." In contrast to Himzo, who defines right and wrong in terms of adversarial groups, Dzemo focuses on good and bad activities. Albeit not named specifically other than with his declaration of favorite pastimes, to "play soccer with friends target shooting, skiing," Dzemo mentions the need for young adults to have "relationships with family and other friends that try to stay on the right path." Expressing these values more subtly in three narratives, Dzemo recounts an event in his activity as a police officer: " . . . when I was jumped by three people as a result of a conflict. I was able to defend myself until backup arrived. They were all apprehended and arrested." Focusing on the broader community, he then recounts a conflict among neighbors over music: "They started an argument. They resolved the conflict by talking to each other and remained friends." These narratives focus

on processes among people in local proximity, including the procedures for "backup" among police and "talking to each other" to
resolve conflicts. The psychosocial dynamic here is (as among many
of his peers) considers processes, as he does in his advice to the mayor,
asking him to "add more social clubs targeting younger people and
attracting younger people. More fun things that will result in bringing
activities."

VARIATIONS ON THE "TENSIONS ABOUND" SCRIPT

Amer-Ci (male, age 16), Ilda (female, age 15), Diana (female, age 22),
and Admir (male, age 20) are youth in the BiH postwar position who
expressed the "tensions abound" script in different ways.

Amer-Ci, A Cheerful Voice amidst the Tension

Amer-Ci identifies himself as active in cultural events in Sarajevo: "I
take part in social events (concerts, screenings, exhibitions, hanging
out, etc.)," which are embedded within a local cultural context, "I
attended folk dance classes for two years, and now I am engaged in
the activities within this organization . . . to gain new experience and
make friends." As shown in Figure 6.3, Amer-Ci also encourages the
school principal to expand the curriculum: "Curriculum should be
entertaining – it should be more than just official, mechanical dictating. . . . I am almost (?) satisfied that we have this dance night at
school – it's cool. . . . School is not a torture chamber. . . . " Although
clearly engaged and positive, Amer-Ci uses the inquiry genre to identify tensions when he mentions that "school is not a torture chamber"
with a lighter tone than most of his peers. In response to questions
focused on problems in society, Amer-Ci says, "I think it's drugs –
there are dealers everywhere. Besides, school is much more difficult
than in other European countries." Amer-Ci's engaged and agreeable
self-presentation is highlighted in his three brief narratives, where he
positions himself in considerably diverse ways. For example, although

Participation: Describe your projects and activities of major interest, reasons for participating, or reasons why not.
I take part in social events (concerts, screenings, exhibitions, hanging out, etc.)
I attended folk dance classes for two years, and now I am engaged in the activities within this organization.
To gain new experience and make new friends.
My engagement depends on how much time I have.

Evaluation of Society:
What is the biggest difficulty for young people in your city/town/country?
Well, I think that it's drugs – there are dealers everywhere. Besides, school is much more difficult than in other European countries. Not enough high schools . . . perhaps we need more discotheques with security.

What are the positive or best qualities of life in your city/town/country?
Good thing is that we have cultural heritage, but there are those who ruin the culture of Bosnia and Herzegovina.

Narratives:
Peer-Conflict Narrative:
I am OK with everybody; it's not that I have never had a conflict with peers, but there has never been any violence – just misunderstandings which could be solved through a conversation.

Adult-Conflict Narrative:
Simple arguments about stupid things.

Fictional community narrative/conflict:
Well, everybody was pleasantly surprised because the news resonated with the opinions and arguments of both groups, so that everybody was satisfied.

Letter to Public Official:
To the Principal . . . Curriculum should be entertaining – it should be more than just official, mechanical dictating. There should also be more extracurricular entertaining activities. I am almost satisfied that we have this dance night at school – it's cool. Well, these are my suggestions for our school. School is not a torture chamber; when I ask friends from my primary school how it is at high school, they usually say, "OOOOOHHHHH, DON'T ASK." I think it's telling . . .

Group Participant in Conversations: Guided Review of Survey Results, Public Story Re-write-Debate, Small Group Creation of Original Youth Survey

FIGURE 6.3. Data for Amer-Ci, 16, male, Bosnia and Herzegovina (BiH).

having identified tensions in society around drugs and education, he writes, "I am OK with everybody; it's not that I have never had a conflict with a peers, but there has never been any violence – just misunderstandings which could be solved through a conversation."

Positioned more judgmentally toward adults, he adds that their conflicts are "simple arguments about stupid things." He expresses again positive orientation toward conflict resolution in a fictional story: "Well, everybody was pleasantly surprised because the news resonated with the opinions and arguments of both groups, so that everybody was satisfied." Framing the specific nature of problems he notes and his cooperative orientation to conflicts is his response about positive qualities in society: "Good thing is that we have cultural heritage, but there are those who ruin the culture of Bosnia and Herzegovina."

Other Approaches to the "Tensions Abound" Script

Ilda's discourses are especially consistent with the national script to focus on tensions by expressions of mostly negative ongoing tensions. From various discursive positions, Ilda expresses tensions in her own relationships ("I felt I wasn't important to her") and observes tensions among adults in her city (" . . . adults were having arguments on the public transportation. They didn't resolve the conflict, but left the bus feeling angry at each other") and among characters in her fictional story ("Everybody felt disappointed and betrayed"). We cannot characterize this response as traumatic, however, because when asked to talk about participation, she offered, "I use the facilities and services the Center offers . . . to meet with friends, participate in numerous programs, to learn." When asked about positive qualities in her society, Ilda wrote, "Good thing is that it's a beautiful town with lots of cultural heritage," although she qualified her response to reveal, as do her peers, the ongoing tensions: "Bad side is that we had a war here and people feel bad about it." Ilda expresses a contradiction between her experiences of negative emotional tensions permeating her society with a more positive counterclaim.

With characteristic sadness and compassion, the older Diana integrates emotional tensions with cognitions and intentions across the genres, expressing the complexity of a struggling society and the individuals within it. A quote characterizing Diana's approach is, "They still debate this issue, tensions are really big, and parents of those children feel used." This approach is consistent with the "tensions abound" script from the more personal position of someone attempting to understand and deal with these tensions in ways that the other (younger) case-study participants did not. In particular, Diana expresses tensions around a range of diversities: "people put you into groups," "old wounds freshened again," "what is left from the old spirit," "foreign nationals," "should be for all children from all of Sarajevo or only the Federation part," that remain unresolved. These tensions reach across time as well as exist within the contemporary period. While pointing out such divisions, Diana also attempts ways to bridge them, such as by writing that "everyone has his/her own view on life and I respect that as long as it does not harm others." "Tensions are really big," but according to Diana, people "still debate;" people "work on the tomb" (for children killed in the war); "even if you want to remain neutral;" there is a "willingness to fight together for the right goals;" and "it is important to renovate . . . follow modern trends."

Admir focuses on sensible processes that can be used to address tensions, some of which he writes "will never be resolved" and, about others, that "we always find ways to achieve these things." Throughout Admir's expressions, it seems that resolvable issues are those that people attend to reasonably, whereas issues that cannot be resolved are left unattended or wallowing in corruption, as stated in his letter to the president of BiH: "There is no sense to continue like this anymore. Very soon our country will crumble, and who will stay after us to hold it together, and on its feet. The country will remain to us, but because of your neglect and cynicism you do not think how everything will be for us."

In another characteristic approach, Admir distributes tensions and stands outside them: "I do not like to be involved in other people's conflicts;" "One of my classmates stole the book and did not want to admit it" (in spite of the author's view that the classmate did steal it, as suggested in assumptions that he had to admit it); and "Other students did not want to get involved, they did not even listen or pay any attention to our conflict." Admir uses another position to control a potentially negative judgment about participation: "Honestly, I do not know why, I think I am really lazy, hahahah." He implies his own reasonableness "to see" and "to listen" via the success of those who do or could try to do so across genres. This is mostly evident in the peer narratives via a negative case and in the letter via "should."

VARIATIONS ON THE "MOVING BEYOND DIFFICULTIES" SCRIPT IN CROATIA

The responses of the case-study participants in Croatia including Anamaria (female, age 16), Rejo (male, age 16), Jeronim, and Georgia varied in the characteristic "moving beyond difficulties" script in several ways. Anamaria and Rejo live in a small village, whereas the older Jeronim and Georgia live in the city. Those differences are important and stated in their evaluations of society, but these youth in Croatia all organize around a common general script in personally unique ways.

Anamaria, a View from the North

Anamaria moves beyond difficulties with a focus on opportunities. As illustrated in Figure 6.4, Anamaria was a frequent participant in the local community center. Having experienced displacements and other hardships, this gregarious youth has been involved with international efforts to "help[s] the development of youth" across the region like the Red Cross, which, along with her local organization, sponsored a youth exchange with an organization in Sweden. Moving beyond difficulties through the means of such international opportunities differs from those who focus on personal improvement and

Participation: Describe your projects and activities of major interest, reasons for participating, or reasons why not.

At the center each year a volunteer camp is held that I participate in. Volunteers from all over the world come. They were from USA, Japan, Sweden, UK, Spain, and many others. Locals together with the volunteers fix up the town. We conduct various surveys, and then I was in Sweden through the organization and NGO that helps development of youth through the Red Cross. Those were the 5 best days of my life because I learned so much and met new friends. There we had cpr class where the volunteers there and leaders taught us first aid in case of danger. So I learned something and had a crazy fun time. There were many other activities but I think these were the most important [also the wish to learn to know other cultures and people and countries.]

Evaluation of Society:

What is the biggest difficulty for young people in your city/town/country?

This is a very small place and youth do not have enough opportunity to do anything. Something should be done with regards to the social life because it is on a level zero and the brain is even lower. It all leads to the same. In each place the problems are the same but in smaller places like mine the biggest problem is the lack of opportunities to do activities.

What are the positive or best qualities of life in your city/town/country?

It is positive that it is a smaller town and there is no crime (there is but not as much as in bigger cities). Security and perspectives, and for every young person the most important is the opportunity to get employed.

Narratives:

Peer-Conflict Narrative:

It happened recently. Actually it happened in the first grade in high school. I still didn't know anyone that well. One girl annoyed everyone (it was due to her indecent behavior). She was spreading false information and by doing it she made everyone angry. Finally one day I shouted at her and told her what I thought of her. We started to have an argument. Others started to participate in it, too. I felt sorry for her, but I simply couldn't stand the fact that someone was making a fool out of me. To tell you the truth, I won't allow it. This conflict was soon forgotten. She is still today the black sheep of the class.

Adult-Conflict Narrative:

My two neighbors always fight over a piece of land. The problem is that the hens that belong to one of them always go to the piece of the land that belongs to the other neighbor and she always calls the police and makes a fuss about it. One day, while I was coming back from school, I saw them having an argument. I mean, they are adult women and it is not nice to see them fight and shout and call themselves names. Everyone who was passing by laughed and turned their eyes. Ugly! After the long lasting fight, the conflict was covered up. But every day these fights happen again. Sometimes I feel embarrassed to be their neighbor.

Fictional Community Narrative/Conflict:

Iva and Goran met each other at laying foundation of the new Community center building. All participants in the event had a chance take a part in the work. It was an exciting moment for the entire community and town. Everyone was happy because the new building meant new future. While they were working, Iva and Goran were talking about the ways in which they would like to influence on their town so that their children could live happily and have a better future. Suddenly, someone arrived with news that changed everything. The news was that the construction work had to be stopped because the land was bought by a foreign company of store chains. Everyone was disappointed because they knew their only project for the town's well being would be ended.

FIGURE 6.4. Data for Anamaria, 16, female, Croatia.

employment; Anamaria's approach, for example, involves awareness of and contribution to a greater good. Anamaria complains about problems in society, like most of her peers across the region who are involved in community rebuilding (compared to those who are less involved): "youth do not have enough opportunity to do anything" and "the most important opportunity is to get employed." She also, however, mentions numerous contributions, her own and others', including fictional characters': "locals together with the volunteers fix up the town;" "All participants had a chance to take part in the work;" "disappointed because they knew their only project for the town's well-being would be ended."

As shown in Figure 6.4 Anamaria uses the fictional story to make the starkest contrast between the market and social-justice mentalities thriving in her country today: "Their dreams about a better community fell apart. The day after, demonstrations were held. Is it possible that someone thinks that a store is more important than a center in which young people will have all the support they need and have all the possibilities to achieve something in their lives? I.... In today's world, all that people care about is money."

Generally, Anamaria's analysis of the good and bad occurs within the broader perspective of a better world in which she wants to participate. As a national minority and refugee in her current home (Bosnian Croat), this young woman is not unaware of her image, the positive and benevolent one she is developing and the other possible images serving as foils across her contributions. Portrayals of the characters in her peer-conflict narrative are critically humorous yet connected ("I simply couldn't stand the fact that someone was making a fool out of me...she is still today the black sheep of the class"). This is also the case in her adult-conflict narrative ("The problem is that the hens that belong to one of them [the neighbors] always go into the piece of land that belongs to the other.... it is not nice to see them fight and shout and call themselves names.... sometimes I feel embarrassed to be their neighbor").

Other Approaches to the "Moving Beyond Difficulties" Script

Anamaria connects with context through text as more of a moral judge or evaluator, while Rejo inserts himself explicitly as participant and catalyst to events, objects, and issues across the genres. He moves beyond difficulties with confidence, projection, and strategy using plot developments. This approach lives in plot development elements such as the narrator/character's statement that he would speak with the adversary in the peer-conflict narrative ("I will talk to him") and in the narrator/character's report of what he did in the face of a perceived injustice by a teacher ("I asked the teacher to explain . . . "), confronting a person in power and later on engaging an even more powerful other on his behalf ("I went to the principal. He had an argument with the teacher and she almost got fired.") An agentic approach for transforming difficulties that Rejo used in the fictional task was for community youth to trick the mayor into approving the community center when he was drunk:

> *Luka and Ivana came up with a plan. They came to the birthday party and saw that the mayor was drunk. They decided to use this opportunity. They tricked him into signing a document about donating the land for the youth center because he was drunk. He signed it unaware of the plot and by doing it he made the building of the center possible.*

This strategy not only showed inside knowledge about community residents, including those in power, but also the use of such information on behalf of the community. In some ways, this approach is more self-centered than others in terms of the active and explicit narrative character and voice, but it is not only literally self-oriented. Theory explaining that narrating a coherent story helps create a healthy personality implies consistent psychosocial functions. These case studies reveal some consistent psychosocial orientations but more context sensitivity than other theories would suggest. Rejo typically projects an agentic main character in narratives, reflections in the inquiry genre, and explicit reasoned solutions in the advisory genre. With this agentic orientation, Rejo connects with difficulties that are often injustices he perceives in the environment and applies desires and talents to exert control over those circumstances. This highly engaged approach could appear to be myopic if content analysis or literal discourse features are the primary lenses. In contrast, with the lens of discourse as mediation, we observe a dynamic that is relatively unique and highly agentic for social as well as personal benefit.

The older Jeronim prefers a different way of moving beyond difficulties. This characteristic use of the study genres to mediate self–subject–context is to project to third characters as transformational foils for reflection and commentary. In narrative plots and in a letter to the prime minister of Croatia, individuals or other forces (e.g., politics and the EU) intervene in a conflict, issue, or process (such as higher-education reform) to complicate interactions, deter protagonists, and interrupt progress toward moving beyond the difficulties. Examples of these intervening characters and forces who deter progress for a while, thereby indicating the author's negative evaluation, include the following in the peer-conflict narrative: "The principal penalized him [the aggressive older boy who punched the author] but the embarrassment I experienced was much worse to me than the punishment to him;" eventually, however, "now the entire event looks ridiculous to me." Similarly, in Jeronim's adult-conflict narrative, "My grandmother was extremely angry because Danica hadn't been there when they needed her the most [when the author's grandmother was ill]. So she [grandmother] told Danica to go away." The final resolution is, "As time passed, they [grandfather and father] became distant from each other" – an unpleasant moving beyond – "All ... because of their wives." In the hypothetical-community narrative, this pivotal deterrence to moving beyond difficulties is the use of money for "the reparation of a dam destroyed in recent bombings." According to the story, this meant that for those who had worked for the center, "their sweat and effort would be useful to others rather than to them" in the interim, until "Ten years later, the Center was finally finished."

Interestingly, in the very different advisory genre, where youth were asked, that is, given permission to offer advice to powerful adults about how to support youth transitions to adulthood, Jeronim used the affordances of that genre for a similar type of mediation. After clearly stating his position that, although elementary- and secondary-school reform had gone well, the problem at the university level is the "consistent implementation of the Bologna reform!" Jeronim holds the minister responsible for "insufficient preparation before it was implemented." In his characteristic twist, Jeronim blames "the EU model" and its device of grades that "disturb the primary goal of education, and that is knowledge" "and not the capitalistic competition" being promoted by the European community and, implicitly, Croatia's bypassing local needs to satisfy requirements to pass the final steps toward EU ascension. Finally, however, and characteristically, there is a solution on the horizon despite this deterrence: "through this connection, solidarity between students would increase."

VARIATIONS ON THE "REFLECTING ON SOCIETAL DIVISIONS" SCRIPT

The case-study participants in Serbia varied on the characteristic "reflecting on societal divisions" script. Pseudonumia (male, age 17), Nancy (female, age 17), Francesco (male, age 23), and Ema (female, age 22) express themselves in intense, socially engaged ways, albeit with different unique emphases.

Pseudonumia, Young Politician Fighting the Past

Pseudonumia assumes an activist stance on societal divisions in Serbia. Across the inquiry, narrative, and advisory genres, he focuses on ideological rifts in society, often criticizing the "last century's mentality" and "degraded mentality;" "collapse of institutions, collapsed values, morals . . . corruption, disrespect of youth, intolerance, bad manners, and bad education;" "ex-cops;" and detractors who challenge "with no argumentative support." As shown in Figure 6.5 Pseudonumia works to separate himself from this past when "a couple of friends and I were a minority regarding political orientation. Apparently, our problem was that we were 'too open minded' and 'insufficiently conservative.'" The sarcastic tone may defend against the weight the young man feels because "the major issue was the mentality which we have not been able to change so far;" "there has been a lot of argument, but the status quo has prevailed;" and even the "wonderful" building "does not meet the standards of the local community."

Not ready to give up, at least in his rhetorical world, Pseudonumia organizes music performances, humanitarian activities, and the youth initiative "Vote!" In his brief but forward-oriented letter to an education official, he firmly suggests the "modernization of educational resources and the educational system," as well as "more influence of students." The direct narrator involvement and interactive stance throughout Pseudonumia's contributions are characteristic of the narratives by participants in Serbia, although there are variations in how his peers play out societal divisions.

Other Approaches to the "Reflecting on Societal Divisions" Script

Francesco engages more affect to mediate narrator–character in context relationships: affect in psychological states balanced across first-person singular, first-person plural, other, positive, and negative, as well as in evaluative devices, adjectives, intensifiers, negations, and repetitions. There tend to be affective plot pivots and resolutions. Differences over opinion, with cognitive explanations played out quite a bit, and cognitive codas, except for the fictional narrative. Nancy,

Participation: Describe how you participate in the community, reasons for participating, or reasons why not.

I am president of the Student's Parliament at the Grammar School in Zemun; I organize music performances, humanitarian activities, etc. Youth initiative: "Vote" To contribute to the development of the society and the restoration of values.

Evaluation of Soceity:
  What is the biggest difficulty for young people in your city/town/country?

Civil rights, collapse of institutions, collapsed values, morals, degraded mentality.

  What other problems are there? Please explain.

Corruption, disrespect of youth, intolerance, bad manners (bad education).

  What are the positive or best qualities of life in your city/town/country?
Cultural events, The Danube.

Narratives:
Peer-Conflict Narrative:
The conflict occurred during the hectic period before the parliamentary elections. A couple of friends and I were a minority regarding political orientation. Apparently, our problem was that we were "too open minded" and "insufficiently conservative". We were challenged with no argumentative support, while we supported our responses with arguments. However, the major issue was the mentality which we have not been able to change so far.

Adult-Conflict Narrative:
The problem emerged when a neighbor appropriated half of the street – remnants of the last century's mentality. The neighbor is an ex-cop who still thinks that he has the power. There has been a lot of argument, but the status quo has prevailed.

Fictional Community Narrative/Conflict:
Administration and local community. . .
The building is wonderful, but taxes are high in this area, i.e. the building has been built in the wrong area – it does not meet the standards of the local community.

Letter to Public Official:
Curriculum should be reduced; modernization of educational resources and educational system; more influence of students on the development of education.

Group Participant in Conversations: Guided Review of Survey Results, Public Story Re-write-Debate, Small Group Creation of Original Youth Survey

FIGURE 6.5. Data for Pseudonumia, 17, male, Serbia.

in contrast, has an intensely cognitive approach, involving planning, intentions, deception, and irony; counterpoints are embedded.

For Ema, cognitive consciousness also dominates, although with relatively heavy intentional orientations. The little affect is negative, including the mention of "happy" referring to "happy for others' misfortune." Irony and contradiction applied to self ("I was intimidated.... If I was him I might attack the boy even though I am physically weaker"). Ema also situates consciousness in the milieu – "look for opportunity to argue... get used to it") and expands to a broader societal perspective ("The building remained unfinished and everyone was happy for at least others won't have it either"). Negative cognitions dominate Ema's conclusions, not only with the spiteful "... at least others won't have it either" but also with specific negative psychological expressions and sarcasm. Crosscurrents are evident in Ema's more positive, agentic approach in the advisory genre, as though she uses the letter to an official to snap out of negativity and sarcasm and to craft a more positive self-object.

SUMMARY: A DIFFERENT IMAGE OF THE INDIVIDUAL

This chapter turns on variation among individuals as they use cultural tools, specifically, self concept as an activity for transforming shared scripts from unique perspectives. In this way, self involves not only explicit self-referrals but also presentations. We can compare these mediation processes that emerge in cultural–historical developmental analyses to those in previous research, like those defining individuals in terms of traits (such as vulnerability or resilience) or the coherence of their life stories. The present sociobiographical approach focuses on the dynamics of discourse rather than representation by focusing on how young people *use* various genres to relate to their world rather than to report about themselves or to craft a coherent self-story. We see in the results of this multigenre design that if we understand discourse as social–relational, we observe within-country differences and thereby learn about complexities and contradictions enacted by individuals. Consistency of variation within national scripts is intriguing for future inquiry into developmental trajectories that may be more and less prevalent from specific national scripts. The variations on "moving beyond difficulties" in the relatively well-positioned Croatia, for example, include more and less individualistic self-foci, while variations on a similar script in the United States group have to do with whether the self position is more or less other-worldly. Longer-term developments of these orientations are important not only relative to understanding the effects of growing in political violence but also for developmental theory.

Previous accounts of war-affected children have offered compelling personal tales of damage (Apfel & Simon, 1996; Weine, 2004; 2006; 2006) and resilience (Beah, 2007; Filipovic, 2006). In addition to the undeniable harmful effects of political violence, such analyses have considered individual personalities and traits relative to the nature and duration of war-related trauma and developmental delays. This image of individuals as more or less vulnerable or resourceful to recover from any damage they may have suffered has value, especially in clinical practice. The developmental approach in this chapter proposes a complementary analysis, especially when considered for research, education, and certain types of clinical contexts.

The activity of story making is what young people do to manage societies whose consciousness they share but also must transform. In this process, contradictions are central because they motivate reflection and action to mediate taken-for-granted reality. After beginning broadly to characterize the political-violence system and then the national responses, we have considered individuals interacting with those environments via the details of everyday life. The focus is thus not so much on the nature of the particular child but on the child's uses of cultural tools to achieve desired ends. As we saw at the beginning of this chapter the symbolism of war is an unavoidable albeit location-specific object. Narea uses inquiry and advisory discourses, for example, to cope with various negative aspects of the place where she lives and a fictional one to share her sadness about the tragedy of war that she is so aware has changed her people's lives forever. This 16-year-old's superiority and sarcasm when she is exposed but poignant sense of pain when she is not is a complex communication with the apparently alienating place where she lives. This mediation maintains her rights (such as to give the president some pointers about peace), her truthfulness, and her strength. In similar ways, Amer-Ci, Anamaria, and Pseudonumia communicate crosscurrents they perceive, as do the other participants. Integrating cultural–historical and psychodynamic approaches, in this way we identify the common focus of human object, embodied and located in the world, transformed in social relations, and used by individuals with the intent to grow.

The significance of this analysis is that it offers theory and method for considering that development occurs through uses of cultural tools in meaningful activities (rather than as a reflection of identity and/or self). That is, individual development is a mediational process, not primarily an unfolding of the inevitable. In this way, we focus on developmental interactions in situations of political violence and the resulting sociopolitical transitions, identifying national scripts imprinted with the past but transformed in terms of everyday activities. These scripts do not have to reduce individuals but serve them when they have the opportunity to engage with them critically and creatively from their personal locations. With this analysis, we illustrate how individuals are social beings rather than collections of capacities or traits.

Individual variations show that, although children growing up in political violence develop understandings in direct relation to their environments, individuality also flourishes. Differences identified herein relate systematically around scripts, such as claiming more or less responsibility to address societal divisions among participants in Serbia, more or less individualistic orientations to moving beyond difficulties in Croatia, more or less practical and emotional orientations to tense circumstances in BiH, and more or less other-worldly solace to deal with exclusion among participants in the United

States. These options relate to shared scripts, so they are not completely open, but choice emerges as an option, especially when issues are open for examination. This inquiry, thus, suggests that many more responses than trauma or risk are available. Ongoing practice-based research can, moreover, promote complexity, diversity, development, and, ideally, choice.

FIGURE 7.1. Supporting youth development in political violence and transition.

7

Human Development in Conflict

Play is important in development, especially in contexts of political violence, instability, and limited resources (Hyder, 2005). One group of scholars pointed out that for adolescents, their "'toys' are world affairs" (Winnicott et al., 1989, p. 62). As though agreeing with this claim, participants in our study across the former Yugoslavia indicated in numerous ways that they were ready to play. These young people know that world affairs are serious and deadly, but with support they are ready to consider how life could be better. Youth across the former Yugoslavia use discourse critically and creatively to respond to political violence in the research workshop and maybe for their own purposes. As in the drawing in Figure 7.1, participants generated novel meanings in their activities. "Peace through education" is an intriguing idea related to the workshop, although the research purpose was to learn from participants rather than to teach them.

Analyses in this book show how young people use cultural tools to mediate their understandings of each challenging context and how they fit within it. Participants' uses of activities indicate the promise of a developmental approach that broadens from assuming trauma or deficits to one that invites imagination. We have seen how adolescents and young adults, play, for example, with literature, letters to public officials, and other challenging activities to take advantage of their psychosocial powers to play. Playing imposes a sense of order in chaotic environments. Even if writing a letter to a public official does not mean the official will act for the betterment of the generation subjected to war, the young letter writer has had to analyze a situation and imagine a solution, which exerts some control over the circumstances, if only for increased understanding. The play involved in advising a president is, moreover, important as "a leading factor in development" (Vygotsky, 1978, p. 101), in which young people across age groups can exert their "greatest self control" (*ibid.*, p. 99).

If play serves to address challenge, then children and youth growing up in violent contexts thrive on intellectually challenging activities rather than relatively easy drawing, drama, or multiple-choice tasks designed for those presumed to be vulnerable or aggressive. Inviting young people in challenging circumstances, like those across the political-violence system of the former Yugoslavia or even more extreme circumstances elsewhere, engages play in serious ways that create the possibility for critique of a violent world. Young people have the right and should have opportunities to imagine, suggest, and demand alternatives to violence and the aftereffects.

That adults do not take young people seriously was expressed by many of the participants, ranging from a high of 23 percent for youth in Serbia to a low of 5 percent for youth in the United States (as shown in Table 3.2). Also, as discussed in Chapter 5, approximately half of the participants in the DSTY research workshop claimed to be very active in community organizations, and those especially active participants reflected astutely on problems as well as on positive qualities in their societies. Other indications that young people are prepared to engage in the future development of their societies come from the kinds of questions they pose in an original survey titled "By and for Youth," advertisements for that survey, and letters to public officials (see Chapter 5). These and other results point to participation not only as a result but also as a means of development.

WHAT IS A DEVELOPMENT ANALYSIS OF THE EFFECTS OF POLITICAL VIOLENCE?

The developmental inquiry in this book highlights young people's perspectives in a variety of daily activities. This developmental approach, in brief, considers the normative nature of growing up in extremely challenging circumstances. Given the interactive focus of individual and societal development, the design sampled a political-violence system, focusing on a generation that has grown up across time and space defined by war. Because this developmental process requires interacting with physical and symbolic circumstances, children who have lived in danger from the beginning of their lives appear to be especially focused on threats and opportunities. Analyzing dangerous situations can be stressful, but children characteristically attend to what they perceive as salient to their elders, interact with those salient events, people, and meanings, and consider their own roles in those situations. In the context of a research workshop, we found that young people described circumstances that were frustrating more than debilitating and oriented to those circumstances in ways suggesting agency rather than despondency.

Analyses indicate that young people use a range of DSTY activities to indicate that they are informed, attuned, engaged, and committed to living in situations better than the ones they inherit. Their complex and diverse knowledge, experience, and intentions emerge in interaction with various audiences, including powerful political structures, from various positions including advisor as well as narrator. Young people in this study exploited the features of fictional and autobiographical narrating, for example, to express locally required and silenced views in clever ways. They used advisory genres, including writing letters to public officials, to imagine positive possibilities. They used inquiry activities like creating surveys for their wartime adversaries to ask critical questions about injustices and possible common bonds. In addition to such information about how young people growing up in situations where expressing desired narratives and silencing undesirable ones is more than preference, this inquiry offers insights about individual variations on national scripts and, thus, foundations for practice and research.

Diverse expressions of participants across countries in the study support the idea that context-specific developmental dilemmas (threats and opportunities) are especially salient to children as they grow. The intense reflections on the old-versus-new ideologies in Serbia, compared to the embodiment of tensions in BiH and the future-oriented possibilities of Croatia as well as the sense of isolation of their peers who relocated to the United States, speak of interdependent developments of generations and individual young people. This chapter discusses how development itself becomes the salient object organizing young people's psychosocial orientations, as indicated in their reflections on society and their role in it. As part of this analysis, we consider the relationship between young people's potentially debilitating *and* developmental responses.

INTERACTIVE DEVELOPMENT

In this book, I apply several theoretical innovations to consider child and youth development in dramatically changing contexts. The case-study design across the former Yugoslavia is based on the idea that development occurs in relation to "multiple interacting activity systems focused on a partially shared object" (Engestrom, 2009, p. 6) "aimed at the formation of the motivational-needs sphere" (Polivanova, 2006, p. 81) and sensitive to "the world of human relations" (*ibid.*).

Attempting to explain how children and youth respond to violence and its aftermath, we observe the interdependence of the personal and societal goals guiding perception in everyday events and interpretations of society as manifested in conversations about public stories, diverse narratives, letters, and youth inquiries. Context-sensitive scripts provide evidence of young people's developmental motivations relative to local threat–opportunity complexes. We then further explored how this process occurs, not through some amorphous internalization of ideas in the air but through participation in purposeful activities focused on contentious issues. This process is illustrated with participants' uses of cultural tools to mediate conflict, in particular the affordances of literary narratives, to negotiate tensions between what can and cannot be expressed. For example, given the national goals of Croatia to conform to standards of the EU, motivations for social inclusion are especially intense, yielding a prohibition on war-talk and ethnic-talk. Young people indicate the need, moreover, to address contemporary problems and obstacles to their progress as independent adults. Such dynamics are developed within specific plot structures, emotional valences, and functions of story-telling.

In Chapter 6, we shifted focus from national scripts to individuals' diverse and nuanced perspectives. Within the broader scripts, development is organized around the "formation of the motivational-needs sphere" (Polivanova, 2006, p. 81), which involves recognizing and exerting control over ongoing threats to and opportunities for development. Meeting these challenges requires youth sensitivity to "the world of human relations" (*ibid.*) and, given the dramatic changes since their birth, involves forging new strategies in the absence of clear role models, rules, or well-worn pathways.

This notion maintains that individuals are constantly interacting bodily and symbolically with their environments, motivating the unfolding of cognitive, social, and emotional capacities based on a child's chronological age. This view involves identifying principles and processes whereby those interactions become complex enough to explain how young people grow up or even thrive in some horrible situations. These context-dependent leading activities rely on normative strategies like attending to what others deem important in the environment, making generalizations about the myriad details of self–other–environment interactions, and integrating the crucial messages to guide future action. These activities are, moreover, enacted concretely in action and developed in discourse.

Strategies worthy of ongoing research and practice include interactive, purposeful activity with cultural tools for figuring out what is going on in the world, how one fits, and how one can change circumstances for the better. This discussion progresses by focusing on several major phenomena for developmental designs with young people in violent and other contexts across the world. These developmental processes, discussed below, include experience, mediation, balancing threat–opportunity dilemmas, and designing for developmental complexity and diversity.

A brief discussion about how two cohorts of young participants interacted with the wars in their homeland connects this analysis to traditional developmental approaches. Because scholars and practitioners typically define development in terms of chronological age, we consider whether and how content-sensitive uses of cultural tools to mediate threat–opportunity complexes differ by age, defined here in terms of exposure to acute violence.

EXPOSURE AND EXPRESSIVENESS

Age is typically the factor defining development for various reasons, including that it chronicles physical maturation and the related unfolding of cognitive, social, and emotional capacities. Relevant to inquiry with a generation growing up in political violence and transition, however, age interacts with experience in the violence system. As a way to address the issue of age, this case study focuses on exposure to political violence and expressiveness across two age-based cohorts. Exposure to different manifestations of political violence, such as acute phases of the war and the myriad consequences, is an important, albeit under-examined, phenomenon (Barber, 2009). Younger (ages 12 to 18) and older (ages 19 to 27) participants in this inquiry were exposed to acute phases of political violence in their local areas at different ages. Participants 18 and younger were likely to have been more protected from effects outside the home, while those 19 and older were more likely to have been outside playing, at school, with relatives, or serving functions such as getting water from an emergency source because they could navigate the streets relatively unnoticed. The study design did not allow for a conclusive distinction among these explanations (such as distinguishing age and nature of exposure to violence), but it offers compelling insights to warrant future research to disentangle these issues.

Measures of expressiveness provide information about cognitive capacity, psychosocial damage, and interaction with sociopolitical factors. Cognitive–developmental models of cognitive capacity (Piaget, 1968), information processing (Case, 1985), writing ability (Bereiter & Scardamalia, 1987), and narrating abilities (Berman & Slobin, 1994; Thorne, et al., 2004) all assess expressive abilities, indicating an increase beyond childhood and into early adulthood. Explanations of those increases include a focus on neurological pathways (Rutter, 1997), knowledge (Piaget, 1968), and communication strategies (Bereiter & Scardamalia, 1987). Young people facing the challenges of migration, for example, must learn multiple languages, suffer gaps in schooling, and master diverse cultural practices that result in expressive delays, albeit temporarily (Zentella, 2005).

Given such demands of changing environments along with the possibility of traumatic reactions during acute phases of violence, the older cohort of participants would likely be less expressive than the younger cohort. Lack of expressiveness or dysfluency could result from psychosocial problems, but a person's age during that experience is also relevant. Being younger when involved in or witnessing violence might offer more protection, because young children may not understand the import of the events, or might exacerbate vulnerability, because younger children may have fewer defenses and strategies to deal with aggression and loss. Having had a relatively longer time to think and talk about prior experiences as well as to learn that people survive could, alternatively, spark expressiveness among the older group, while the younger group may suffer from worries related to having only second hand knowledge of past events.

Assuming damage from acute or prolonged exposure to political violence and its aftermath, one would also predict differences across the contexts, especially among those in BiH, which experienced the largest number of onsite deaths and environmental destruction for the most prolonged period. Individuals who experienced trauma may need to express themselves as a means of release (Pennebaker, 1997), so if circumstances encourage such release or provide a societal narrative to explain what is going on, those youth in relatively dire circumstances may have a lot to say. Another factor that could contribute to cross-context and age differences in expressiveness is motivation, explored in the analysis of conflict scripts and prospects for thriving discussed in Chapter 3. Even if the older cohort suffered in ways that negatively affect expressiveness, becoming an adult in a society with relatively more employment potential, such as in Croatia, could also lead to positive outcomes.

The extensive database of oral and writing activities is a rich resource for applying various measures of expressiveness, including number of texts produced, number of words per text, expressions

TABLE 7.1. *Expressiveness in Narrative Genres by Younger and Older Cohorts*

Measures of narrating by	Younger (<18) and older (19+)	
Participants	71	66
Narratives	137	150
Narratives by genre		
# Peer conflict	57	52
# Adult conflict	52	49
# Fictional community	28	49
Expressive fluency		
Words/narrative		
Peer conflict	69.53	101.57
Adult conflict	61.21	78.61
Fictional community	83.07	79.22
Psychosocial states/words		
Peer conflict	6.67	12.6
Adult conflict	6.48	8.9
Fictional community	7.57	8.73
Affective valence		
Negative affect states		
Peer conflict	1.64	1.94
Adult conflict	1.44	2.02
Fictional community	1.76	1.9
Positive affect states		
Peer conflict	0.38	0.25
Adult conflict	0.31	0.39
Fictional community	1.2	1.13

of psychological states, and affective valence. Table 7.1 presents a sampling of expressiveness measures in narrative genres by younger and older cohorts across the political-violence system of the former Yugoslavia. As shown in Table 7.1, 71 participants were 18 and younger and 66 participants were 19 and older (Daiute, 2008).

Analyses indicate greater expressive fluency by the older cohort on some measures and greater expressive fluency by the younger cohort on others. Although requiring confirmation in future research, the pattern of differences indicates positive effect of communicative development through adolescence, even among the older cohort who experienced relatively acute phases of violence.

Participants were encouraged to be involved in all phases of the DSTY workshop, but it was their choice about whether to participate in any specific activity. Given this choice, the fact that fewer older participants contributed more narratives overall, 150 compared to 137 respectively, indicates a willingness to express, that is, to share their experiences. Because the narrative genres were varied systematically for narrator–focus–audience relationships, whether and how the cohorts chose to narrate across the genres is also a measure of expressiveness by context. The older cohort wrote more fictional community narratives than the younger cohort (49 by 66 older participants compared to 28 by 71 younger participants, respectively), but these groups wrote roughly equivalent numbers of peer- and adult-conflict narratives.

Also shown in Table 7.1, the older cohort wrote more words per autobiographical context (adult- and peer-conflict narratives), while the younger cohort wrote more words per fictional narrative, even though they wrote fewer of those. The older cohort expressed more psychological states per word than the younger cohort, except in the adult-conflict narratives.

Examining the valence in narrative expressions provided additional insight about the engagement of the younger and older cohorts with their environments. Another reasonable measure of possible damage is negativity, indicated as evaluative markers (Labov & Waletzky, 1997) including "no," contractions with "n't," negative adjectives, "hardly," and so forth. Although affective valence was generally negative, the older cohort included more negative markers per word than the younger group across genres. Detailed analysis indicates a balance of negative and positive in the fictional narrative, suggesting the use of the fictional genre to imagine positive orientations for both groups. In summary, however, it seems reasonable that the older cohort may be slightly savvier or even more jaded than the younger group, simply given their experience in the world. Because exposure to the war could, of course, also be a factor, these measures seem worthy of ongoing inquiry in such contexts and relatively easy to apply.

In addition to expressiveness as measured by number of narratives, words per narrative, and psychosocial state expressions, an analysis of script structures in narratives by the younger and older cohorts also reveals differences indicating ongoing development by the older group. The following narratives, first by a female in the younger cohort in BiH and then by a female in the older cohort in BiH, illustrate more narrative complexity among the older cohort.

This narrative by 16-year-old Narandjica organizes an account in public space in terms of a "moving beyond difficulties" script characteristic of younger cohorts across contexts. Although Narandjica recounts tensions on public transportation, the whole of this narrative is refigured in terms of the ending, in which a public official takes a stand to create order.

> *One of the conflicts occurred on the bus. I was going back home from school with some friends. The bus was crowded. On the second stop, the door opened and an elderly gentleman was trying to get off, but he couldn't because of the crowd and because in his way was standing another man who himself didn't know where to move! The man who was trying to get off swore at the man standing next to him, who just kept gazing confusedly, not knowing what to do. Then they started exchanging bad words, which was soon followed by hitting each other. The bus driver solved the conflict by pulling over and throwing them both out of the bus.*

The following narrative by Zejna, a college student in BiH, occurs in the same context of tensions on public transportation, but the structure and outcome are quite different:

> *There is not enough place in our public transportation, and to make it even worse our retired senior citizens are getting up at 8 am and*

going as if they have to be someplace, while some people **must** *go to school or work. Retired people are occupying most of our space in all public transportation . . . there is one old man that is really primitive. Whenever he enters the trolley he rudely tells someone to get up so that he can sit, as if that is someone's duty and not just a show of good manners. This is why the old man got into conflicts many times with others, and he always gets a "shorter end of the stick." The conflict is never resolved.*

Twenty-one-year-old Zejna, in contrast to her younger peers, does not present the conflict as one among individuals, nor does she resolve the conflict. Instead, this narrative embodies two scripts characteristic of the older cohort: "reflecting on societal divisions" and "tensions abound." The conflict is among workers and retirees regarding issues of space on the bus and affective implications of the conflict and outcome. This pattern of difference between a single and multiple scripts indicates a subtle but important difference in how younger and older, less and more war-affected young people interact with the same contemporary circumstances. That older participants weave multiple conflicts with multiple affective dimensions illustrates the cumulative integration of experiences of having grown up during the conflict (accentuating societal divisions) and after (accentuating resulting tensions in society, especially in BiH). That the younger participants construct a single conflict that they resolve indicates some control over the narrative, which may have to do with the relative simplicity of a single plot structure or their less direct and extended experience with a violence system.

These peer-conflict narratives by the same two participants also reveal differences in the narrator perspective, with the younger being more self-focused and the older more focused on social conventions:

One of the conflicts happened at school. Namely, I agreed with a friend to meet half an hour before classes started, so we could go to school together. However, she didn't show up, which made me extremely mad, for I was waiting for her for half an hour and I was late for school. When I came to school and saw her there, I said to her nicely that what she had done wasn't OK. She started to defend herself making excuses, which were fake and stupid!!! So, we had a bit of a disagreement, which soon developed into an argument. Naturally, most of our classmates took my side, although there were some who objected and thought that I was not in the right. I felt offended and betrayed and, of course, I lost trust in her.

As illustrated in these peer-conflict narratives, the younger Narjandjica is intensely focused on interpersonal conflict and her own role in it, whereas the peer-conflict narrative by Zejna recounts the event in terms of moral conventions of rudeness, purposeful, and mentality, which is described as "Neanderthal."

The conflict happened in the middle of the day when I went with my friend for a drink. I am non smoker but one guy was very rude and he was keeping his cigarette in front of my nose. I kindly asked him to move his cigarette to the side, he did not pay attention to me but instead purposely was blowing the smoke towards me. I was upset . . . and I told him he was a primitive Neanderthal. . . . I felt very upset.

Focusing on interpersonal relationships with a plethora of first-person references is the most common script, accounting for peer-conflict narratives by the younger group (36.8 percent) but only for 15.7 percent of narratives by the older group. Diversity in the range of scripts organizing narratives characterized the narratives by the older group more than those by the younger group. Although two scripts account for two-thirds of the narratives by the younger group, narratives by the older group introduce more diversity. Equal to the focus on interpersonal relationships foregrounding self is the "reflecting on societal divisions" script (also accounting for 23.5 percent of peer conflict narratives by the older group). The "moving beyond difficulties" and "denying conflict" scripts also describe greater percentages of narratives by the older than the younger groups, at 19.6 and 15.7 percent, compared with 7.1 and 8.8 percent, respectively.

The significance of these patterns is that among 57 youth aged 12 to 18 growing up across the former Yugoslavia, the peer-conflict narratives are relatively consistent, focusing on interpersonal issues and the self-role, as would be predicted in accordance with several theories emphasizing the salience of peer relationships. Among the older group, however, societal divisions are as common as interpersonal issues; moving beyond difficulties and denying conflict complicate the expressive repertoire by the older group. Relatively unique scripts by the older group include reflecting on societal divisions (19.6 percent compared to 8.8 percent by the younger group), which require broader analysis in their characterization of conflicts, not only in terms of individuals but also of individuals embedded in social categories, such as "gypsies," "Neonderthals," and "old-century mentality."

It makes sense that emergency workers focus on the acute phases of conflict, but their work can also be informed by developmental research to broaden the range of appropriate options for dealing with young people in crisis. With measures of narrative fluency, psychosocial intensity, communicative complexity, and affective valence (Daiute et al., 2001), this developmental analysis reveals intensely negative affect but not the flattened affect associated with trauma. The relatively expressive fluency and the organization of experience in terms of multiple co-occurring scripts indicate ongoing development among this older group, despite any increased exposure to violence and its aftermath. Also intriguing is the preliminary evidence that the multiple scripts in narratives by the older cohort indicate a cumulative integration of orientations over time (not only to immediate circumstances). That older youth would tend more than younger youth to organize conflict narratives in terms of societal divisions makes sense, given their exposure to warring factions integrated with the kinds of tensions characteristic of the postwar circumstances. Much more research with older youth in terms of their histories of interaction in diverse societies seems worthwhile, not only because such histories influence ongoing development but also because they offer insights

about complex effects of violence beyond trauma or any single ideological orientation.

PURPOSEFUL MEDIATION WITH CULTURAL TOOLS

Young people across the political-violence system of the former
Yugoslavia used cultural tools to mediate their challenging environments. Mediation in action is a major concept in cultural–historical
activity theory (Vygotsky, 1978). Given prior assumptions that people may be reduced to their most biological capacities and strategies
during conflict, it may follow that those considered most vulnerable
would be least likely to use their uniquely human symbolic capacities
(Vygotsky, 1978). This inquiry found, to the contrary, that participants aged 12 to 27 use complex cultural tools to organize their
experience, interpretation, and action in the context of purposeful
activity. Although those youth in the situations suffering the most
physical damage do emphasize ongoing tensions more than participants in the other contexts, those responses are also constructing
tension to mediate experience rather than merely being overcome by
tension, like the young man who made a joke about ptsd.

Mediation is not new in adolescence, but it may be a process
most deliberately functional when young people have highly motivating social goals. Scholars have found that interpersonal contact,
joint attention to environmental phenomena, and other activities that
constitute language development occur quite naturally across human
social groups, although not in other animal species (Nelson, 2003;
Tomasello, 2005). The nature and complexity of objects and participants in joint attention would, presumably, differ over developmental
time; however, we can build on theory of mediated mind to study uses
of joint attention among diverse groups across diverse circumstances,
including those of violence and instability, as we have discussed in
this book. An essentially social process, symbolic mediation may lag
developmentally among children who are isolated or mistreated. As

long as those conditions are not extreme, there is preliminary evidence that other kinds of very difficult circumstances, such as intergroup conflict or environmental destruction, elicit children's intense motivation to attend to community issues and employ mediation skills to understand those issues (Daiute et al., 2001; Sta. Maria, 2006).

In sociopolitically dangerous contexts, young people must read subtle symbols and manage them toward their own developmental goals. During interactions in highly contested political conflicts, like those in which neighbors are at war, children observe their parents as vulnerable or in pain, and entire families must flee their homes in impersonal caravans. Assuming that development stops because of trauma or hatreds in those situations discounts the potentially powerful mechanism of higher-order thinking. Young people's use of cultural symbols is not a leisurely pastime but a strategy for making sense of unpredictable and challenging situations. A childhood defined by political violence is one where means of survival are, at least in part, symbolically mediated because helpful symbols must be hidden from enemies and those who would exploit access to such resources.

Motivations and needs in situations of political violence and transition are related to dilemmas of threat and opportunity. Uses of cultural symbols such as war (see Chapter 6) can link present and past circumstances with psychosocial dilemmas, such as the need to make new alliances despite ongoing tensions from the past. These intersecting tensions of motivation-need and threat-opportunity are implied in Diana's advocacy "for all children in Sarajevo not only the Federation part," even though she lives in the Federation part. More than a focus on self-identity or peer relations, these young people are intensely focused on salient dilemmas about whether opportunities for some are threats to the other, whether acknowledgement of past atrocities requires maintaining hatred, while other circumstances require tolerance or compromise.

Because adolescents and young adults use the social–relational affordances of discourse (such as assumptions about themselves as speakers/authors and about their audiences), these activities become developmental genres. The array of engagements in the DSTY work-shop, including narrating conflicts from diverse narrator and charac-ter positions, writing letters to officials, evaluating society, working with peers to generate questions for international peers, discussing public stories, and evaluating the workshop, fosters diverse psy-chosocial engagements that lead new psychosocial, emotional, and intellectual experiences. With each activity, for example, individu-als and groups express new understandings and goals. Across each context, interactions that would be missing from inquiries assuming trauma, social reproduction, or universal stage theories stretch par-ticipants' abilities, which is evident in the diversity of any individual's expressions.

Multiple scripts mediate the tough stuff. An analysis of scripts organizing the adult- and peer-conflict narratives by youth across the two age cohorts can offer insights about the broader historical ways of knowing organizing the experience of each group. Analyses of script differences by age group and narrative genre also suggest fur-ther inquiry into whether and how any differing capacities for social analysis relate to different ways of organizing conflict. The analy-sis of peer-conflict narratives compared to adult-conflict narratives, moreover, relates the issue of youth positioning to the plight of dif-ferent generations, one similar to their own and the other the older generation that caused and fought the war. Narrating from different character perspectives not only elicits different information but also offers opportunities for participants to consider adults' perspectives, in particular via observations of them in public life, and in some cases, to find empathy, not only disdain, for their plights.

BALANCING THREAT–OPPORTUNITY DILEMMAS

The concepts "goals" and "leading activity" provide means for a context-sensitive notion of development, rather than assuming that ethnic, gender, national, or some other identity category organizes psychosocial life. While most prior research posits or assumes that identity is the primary conflict of adolescence and emerging adulthood, sociocultural-activity theory offers the concept of leading activity, allowing for conflicts that are more context dependent, that is, "the relation of the child to reality" (Vygotsky, 1978). In this view, identity is not a universal goal or process of adolescent development unless some aspect of identity becomes an obstacle to or opportunity for achieving goals. For this reason, we expand from identity to intention to account for circumstances like those in situations of conflict. Before focusing on the concept of leading activity, a brief review of other theoretical approaches indicates the need to consider societal relations in human development.

Development occurs not primarily within the individual organism as cognitive and other abilities unfold biologically but in "the social situation of development [which] is the starting point for all the dynamic changes that occur in development during the given age period" (Veresov, 2006, p. 14). The social situation fully determines how "the child successively acquires new properties of his personality, drawing them from social reality as the main source of development, that path along which the social situation becomes individual" (Vygotsky, cited in Veresov, 2006, p. 15). According to this view, we must broaden the notion of "evolving capacities of the child" beyond biological maturation to study mental development in activity because that "arises from the given, concrete situations of the child's life ... each stage of mental development is [thus] characterized by one dominant relationship of the child to his environment, by one dominant activity within that given stage" (Elkonin, 1971/2000).

Other theories have focused on the goal-oriented nature of development and the "moving relations" (Leont'ev, 1978) to resolve tensions and contradictions (Engestrom, 2009; Vygotsky, 1978). Consistent with this emphasis on goals is the idea of object, which could be a self-object. Developmental theories from psychosexual (Erikson,

1980; Freud, 1909) to maturational (Piaget, 1968) and sociomoral theories (Turiel, 2002) have identified mechanisms of conflict as catalysts of individual and human change over the life span. Proposed mechanisms include a child's assimilation to and accommodation of phenomena in the world (Piaget, 1968), issues of autonomy and connection relative to injustice (Turiel, 2002), and successive crises to resolve on the path to adult independence (Erikson, 1980).

Research on self-defining memories found moderate support between tension and meaning indicated in measures of "learning-lessons" and "insights" about a range of events highlighting relationships, mortality, leisure, and achievement narrated by late adolescents (Thorne et al., 2004). Researchers expected a stronger relationship between events that were likely to be more tension filled, such as mortality events, but used their alternative results to conclude that "stressful events are processed more thoroughly in an effort to promote adaptation" (Thorne et al., 2004, p. 536). Pointing to the value of adversity, they explain that "tension in events partially contributed to efforts toward meaning (Thorne et al, 2004, p.539). Offering advice for ongoing inquiry, they add that "a more refined coding category that integrated the presence of cognitive–emotional struggle may have been more discriminating" between the specific sample of youth or the artifact of "privileging retrieval over reflection" (*ibid.*).

Some processes emerge compellingly across these theories, such as the importance of complex thinking activities, including abilities to manipulate and use symbols, to engage in perspective shifting, self-monitoring, self-regulation, and to a lesser extent, to coordinate these processes. Recent international studies question the relevance of proposed universal categories emphasizing, instead, influences of religious beliefs, practices, and meaning systems on behavior and development (Barber, 2009; Brown & Larson, 2002). Moving away from defining *culture* in terms of identity, cultural–historical theory posits the need and strategies for situating oneself across a social milieu, beginning with monitoring one's physical, cognitive, emotional, and political (power) relations and advancing to interact purposefully with the environment via symbolic tools as mechanisms of human consciousness.

Research with youth in certain minority groups also explores the role of conflict in identity. Those studies considering development, rather than social injustice per se, tend to focus on identity in terms of threats posed by discrimination due to social-relational goals (Cross, 1991) or socialization (Cross & Fhagen-Smith, 2001). Processes like buffering are interesting as mechanisms for distancing from the identities of discriminators, referred to as outgroups in social psychology, during the process of consolidating one's own ethnic identity (Cross, 1991). It may be that identity clarification and assertion are salient for young people in acutely discriminatory contexts, perhaps like those discussed by Lee (2010). Because such identity focus emerges in relation to discrimination and injustice, we can apply this research to consider identity crises as context dependent rather than universally relevant to all adolescents.

Expanding the study of sociomoral development beyond maturation, one theory has considered issues of rights as a context for theory and research, as expressed in the following quote: "Placing rights into contexts invoking conflicts did make a difference in how people responded" (Turiel, 2002, p. 84); however, in some circumstances, "rights are subordinated to other moral and societal considerations" (Turiel, 2002, p. 87). Related research has identified different interpretations of rights by children at different ages (Helwig, Arnold, Tan, & Boyd, 2007; Peterson-Badali & Ruck, 2008); differences in societal abuses interact with age and thus qualify strictly age-based explanations, as suggested in the following quote: "It was found that older people were less likely than younger ones to subordinate rights to competing considerations. In other respects, with age there is more attunement to considerations of social processes and community. It was found that younger people judge in accord with psychological needs and older ones in accord with societal utility and processes of democracy" (Turiel, 2002, p. 85). That such results emerge in cross-cultural research underscores the need for considering interactions with diverse political–economic situations.

The research design with the political violence system discussed herein allows for within- and across-group diversity indicated similarities, including a focus on understanding relationships with peers and hope for a harmonious future in a community setting. Differences were notable as foundations for longer-term developmental trajectories among these groups of adolescents. The diverse psychosocial orientation patterns described above set the scene for examining the vitality of higher-order thinking among adolescents who have engaged in a range of cognitive, social, and emotional interactions in their society, in societies in flux. The analytic and executive cognitive skills enabling perspective taking, goal-directed thinking, analysis, and critique may or may not come into play across life circumstances, and certainly not in the same ways. Researchers identifying the extreme responsibilities of teenage parents with few financial or social resources have, for example, noted that an adolescent identity crisis in its traditional sense is a luxury (Burton, & Graham, 1998). Conversely, other researchers have found that adolescents and young adults in societies limiting women's rights may be more likely to question cultural and religious conventions than in societies with more equality or different issues of injustice (Wainryb & Turiel, 1994). Extending such insights about the context-dependent nature of adolescent thought, our analysis identifies psychosocial processes related to a broader range of circumstances defined by youth themselves as salient. Just as previous researchers have questioned the over-determination of cognitive development as defining adolescents' experiences and interpretations, results presented here suggest questioning the over-determination of cultural ways of knowing and rituals, in particular to account for a broader range of real-life political and economic circumstances facing millions of adolescents in the 21st-century world.

Goal making in response to threats, opportunities, and motivations becomes increasingly relevant and skilled during adolescence and emerging adulthood, especially when progression through those life phases as locally defined is at risk. We learn from examining different youth responses across positions in the war that motivations to address tensions between threats and opportunities emerge in relation to the local challenges, such as overcoming a legacy of being the aggressor in Serbia, overcoming intense discrimination in the United States, taking advantage of European opportunities while not selling out to them in Croatia, and overcoming ongoing tensions in BiH. Each of these situations requires considering the perspectives of others but in different ways, emerging as hypervigilance in Serbia, perhaps to demonstrate intense social sensitivity, causes of tensions in BiH, defensiveness to exclusion in the United States, and so forth. Leading activities among adolescents and young adults across those contexts are, thus, motivated to deal with the political-economic circumstances and to foster strategies for thriving in those circumstances.

DESIGNING FOR DEVELOPMENTAL COMPLEXITY AND DIVERSITY

Assuming that war history is dynamic, we see how it lives on in daily life; organizes perception, meaning, and action; and transforms those orientations when possible. From the perspective of cultural–historical theory, we interpret the past as a cultural tool, an affordance in the environment that young people use to make sense of, master, and transform their daily lives. Another benefit of this approach is that we must consider how contexts are embedded in social scripts. For example, the older generation who grew up with "the last-century mentality," as one participant in the study observed, may not be as knowledgeable about contemporary requirements of the global market economy as are children currently educated in relation to EU reforms. Youth exposed to news reports and blogs are equipped with terms like "privatization," "entrepreneurship," "social inclusion," "tolerance," and attendant requirements to assess the image of the nations where they live. Such 21st century concepts become part of the symbolic landscape, intermingling with references to the past to create living history.

Future research could apply this developmental model to political (violence) systems beyond the Western Balkans in other regions in conflict over sovereignty, turf, and resources. Conceptualizing the unit of analysis across such systems is an important step toward complexity and diversity in design of developmental studies of political change. Political scientists, sociologists, and anthropologists have studied protracted and shorter-term conflicts in the Middle East (Salomon, 2004), South Africa (Higson-Smith, 2006), Africa (Akinumi, 2006), Colombia (Botero et al., 2004–2007), and, unfortunately, many other regions of the world.

Research questions could begin inquiring into issues like How do young people positioned differently across a political (violence) system interact in and make sense of those systems and their positions in them? What threat–opportunity complexes emerge to motivate their goals and meanings? How do these results expose the power relations and figure of the child/youth in that system? How do these processes define development in this context? What activities can be highlighted to support developmental thriving? In addition to the broader design of the political-violence system, engagement with genre activities can bring these relations to life for the benefit of the participants and informed action by participants and researchers alike.

Basic features of the DSTY workshop and results of young people's uses of workshop activities highlight several features for further practical inquiry. For comparison, some researchers report that the motivation for children and youth who participate in violent activities relates to their having been orphans, poor, or caught in crossfires (Sta. Maria, 2006). Without glorifying those motivations, several researchers have identified the purposefulness that children involved on the front lines perceive. Even when they identify that what they did was morally wrong, they can also attest to the importance of being needed and a distorted feeling of being respected, although with age the realization is that they were manipulated because they were vulnerable (Beah, 2007). This sense of useful participation is in striking contrast to the numerous reports by youth who are attempting to serve positive nonviolent roles while also realizing that adults do not take them seriously.

Another aspect of purpose is clarity. The rallying cries recruiting young people into war are absolute and thus simple and clear. Reports indicate, moreover, that no particular religion can be blamed for overzealous youth but rather the exploitation of absolute statements and appeals to a higher power. Beyond clarity, the roles that people play in insurgency and other movements provide connections and power, albeit few instances for reflection.

Although I condemn young people's violent recruitment to participate in violence, I point out that the features identified in the DSTY design in Chapter 2 (see Table 2.1) involve young people along similar dimensions of purpose, clarity, and diverse positioning. Children and youth who feel a sense of purpose because they help their families survive during a war, like those who manage to escape the many sources trying to exploit them during conflicts and others who are spared because they are in the right place at the right time, still suffer in ways that can be addressed, if not remedied, with increased understanding about their participation.

EXTENDING TO A POLITICAL VIOLENCE SYSTEM IN SOUTH AMERICA

Even in acute phases, but certainly after them, young people can be involved in activities that engage their intellectual and communication capacities purposefully. The purpose should be applied to the context, as in the former Yugoslavia, where youth history was an issue to contrast to *no* history or histories divided by ethnic group. In other situations, like Colombia, where millions of children and youth have been displaced by internal conflicts, family histories could be beneficial to the millions of teenage mothers and their children caught in cycles of abandonment and abuse after displacement. Concerned for the millions of children orphaned and displaced by the now almost half-century of conflict in Colombia, we can apply the concept of a political-violence system. Teenage mothers at the center of our inquiry are interacting in broader systems, most intimately with their children. These young mothers, living in extremely difficult conditions in cities and towns across the country, must deal with the institutions of violence that exploit girl–mothers and provide some sustenance in the municipal systems where they live, often hidden from public life and the places and locales where they began their lives. Although this system cannot be defined perfectly, once the key relations impacting the lives of the young families is established, a context for purposeful activity can be designed for working with these families to support their interests and development as they contribute to knowledge beyond their personal plights. Within activities of a local theater company, for example, these young families could engage in purposeful narrating, inquiring, and advising.

Preliminary fieldwork would establish motivating purposes such as creating narratives of youth lives to acknowledge their journeys as more than displacement, stories for their children to provide a context for families' ongoing reflection and decision making, and stories that personify community activities and events. Of course, all of this must occur in ways that do not put the girls and their babies in further danger.

Finding out what is being provided to help young people in other parts of the country, city, or neighborhood could be interesting, not only for the information it would elicit but also because it could provide skills that could be useful to the girls if they ever have the

TABLE 7.2. *Dimensions of Designs for Complexity and Diversity: Draft Design for Workshop with Families of Displaced Teenage Girls in Colombia, South America*

Participant purpose	Genre	Diverse participant stances		
		Connection	Interpretation	Power
Antes *(Before)*	Narrative – Story of home and journey			
Mi Vida *(A Day in the Life)*	Narrative – Story of a day; making a new home			
Para Mi Hija/o *(For My Daughter/Son)*	Narrative – Story my child can remember about her/himself			
La Comunidad *(The Community)*	Inquiry – Geoprofile of the neighborhood; can be humorous, poetic			
Servicios *(Services)*	Inquiry – Newsletter about what is provided by the government			
Al Mayor/Educator *(To a Public Official)*	Advisory – Letter to an official stating a need as an expert (could be for a child)			

Note: Based on Table 2.1, *Discourse Genres by Youth in the Context of Political Violence and Transition.*

opportunity to work outside their homes. Given their poverty and lack of control over some aspects of their lives, many of these young mothers have used their skills well thus far so that supports would not only enrich research on human development in the context of chronic violence but would also provide a context for them to expand their futures. Using the critical tools the girls have already developed to survive in the absence of having achieved full literacy, these young mothers could, with support, dictate their stories and other projects, eventually increasing their literacy through these activities.

Collective purposes must also have concrete outcomes, like histories to be included in the library, contributions to newsletters, children's books, and so forth. Skills need not be advanced nor resources high-tech. In a related study in Colombia, for example, teenagers with minimal literacy skills dictated their narratives, which were not only heartbreaking but also structured (Botero et al., 2004–2007). Resources like computers add power for sharing a youth survey and viewing responses, but in a refugee camp or house populated by children parenting children, a newsletter or storybook can be made with minimal tools and distributed to create a sense of community, continuity, motivation, and power.

When understood as embedded in the Colombian conflict system, teenage moms can be catalysts for social change by writing contemporary history from their points of view, shifting their stance from storytellers to advisors, informing public officials of their needs and goals, assisting their peers, and perhaps most importantly, writing history for their children. Participating actively to create personal, family, community, and national histories is a developmental process as well as a method for assessing developmental capacities (Bruner, 1986; Daiute, 2010a & b; Gjerde, 2004; Hammack, 2008; Labov, & Waletzky, 1997). Few have, for example, examined such living histories by displaced youth systematically as they relate to participation in society, but, as we have summarized above, there is considerable theory and related research to suggest that narrating is a developmental process, especially relevant to dangerous situations where sociopolitical realities enforce certain narratives and silence others. Dynamic narrative methods such as fiction are a means for possible transformation of frozen narratives into thoughtful reflections and intentions, as we learned in research across the former Yugoslavia. Evidence from this study in the former Yugoslavia, for example, shows how a series of narratives, letters, and evaluations of society engaged young people to think critically about the specific circumstances of their postwar locale while also instilling a sense of their own potential to contribute, especially when active in community organizations.

Research with dynamic story-telling in Colombia could offer a unique contribution not only relevant to specific young teenage moms but also to expand models of research and practice with war-affected youth. This research design explores whether and how young people are integral to broader social and political developmental systems, not only as victims or potential perpetrators. In addition to contributing knowledge about those relatively understudied populations, we offer a practice-based research design uniquely foregrounding the potentially pivotal role of teenage moms. Although their role as victims and potential perpetrators in cycles of violence is a concern and, for some, a fact, teens who become moms in displacement could also become agents of change. Understanding such a role requires considering them as stakeholders for civic engagement.

A living history project with teen moms can contribute unique insights about how to break rigid scripts of violence that, unfortunately, research and practice reify when assuming that young people are passive victims subjected only negatively to extant conditions. By engaging in diverse stances, young people can concretely create new scripts when their histories are expressed and valued. Young Bosnian youth, for example, repeat the script of victims continuing to wait for relief from generous outsiders, but when given the opportunity, they also decry the sociopolitical paralysis and ongoing tension reinforced by a government organized around ethnic divisions. Especially important are the complexity and flexibility of scripts for organizing the past, present, and future by young moms, who are unlikely to have other supports for developing agency. If we see changes in the ways young moms narrate displacement journeys after narrating conflict from diverse points of view, advising public officials, and sharing their wisdom in newsletters for other teen moms, we will gain invaluable knowledge about the potential of such developmental genres. Publications and reports from such a study will offer insights about whether and how young people are capable of and can benefit from more intellectually challenging activities than are typically included when their primary response is assumed to be trauma. Drawing and playing parts can be enjoyable releases, but such activities underutilize young people's symbolic and developmental capacities.

With inspiration from a letter by Fadil and his peers in BiH, for example, such letters by young mothers could achieve some support:

> *My letter would address the demand to give rights to youth, so we do not make obstacles to their progress disagreeing with my claim. Youth should have equal rights in everything. Our "beautiful" country should be changed, so young people participate in politics in order to reduce corruption and bribery. Most importantly, we should provide for youth an opportunity to prove their capabilities. Otherwise, young people will continue to leave the country as long as this kind of situation is sustained.*

The spontaneous emergence of human rights as an issue in this letter by a 19-year-old living in BiH is not surprising because it is a focus of many community-development efforts in NGOs across post-war contexts. Fadil's letter, like many others, depicts challenges to youth rights, corruption, bribery, and youth fleeing because of "obstacles to their progress." Not passive in the face of these challenges, this young advisor voices a "demand to give rights to youth" because "our beautiful country should be changed." Fadil explains further that "we should provide for youth an opportunity to prove their capabilities" so that "young people participate in politics." Albeit not a complete analysis or a particularly literary expression, this letter identifies problems and solutions in the context of the broader issue of contemporary globalization: "young people will continue to leave the country as long as this kind of situation is sustained."

DEVELOPMENTAL PUNCH LINE

The following quote by 19-year-old Pero in Croatia is about the dilemma of development in the context of political transition. Interestingly, Pero relates environmental becoming, societal becoming, and child becoming. The message is one of stasis, yet given the theory of nonidentity of content and process, this exposé is the kind of breakthrough knowledge young people can have at the midst of major political change.

> *The Municipality representative arrived and said that the building would become a huge section of a textile factory where the children (for who the center was supposed to be built) would have an opportunity to become a part of the underpaid workers class. But it's not so bad; this is a great chance to learn some new social skills – a strict hierarchy on the job, becoming a part of a whole, subjection to the group. . . . This is how the children will become mature and ready for the world.*

Using a story as a developmental tool, Pero expresses a fear that development will stall across the systems influencing the life of his generation. Although the message of stasis is bleak indeed, the developmental process expressed here is "simultaneously a model of two objects – of a real phenomenon and of the artist's personality" (Polivanova, 2006, p. 82). That is, being able to express this bleak message also expresses the figured world of possibility and change (Holland et al., 1998). That the situation could be different during this time indicates knowledge of a new world, where children have a "chance to learn some new social skills," are "ready for the world," rather than being "part of the underpaid worker class," in a "strict hierarchy" in such mediational uses of cultural products are thus not only revealing for researchers but also for young people themselves, young people interacting in dynamic systems of social organization where causes and effects are not one-directional, from society to youth or environment to youth, but also reciprocal. Those antiquated systems that Pero recognizes are real, but he sees them as threats to an alternative. Engagements like creating a story, but certainly not limited to those, involve creating behavioral texts, like those that scholars have posited create action (Bruner, 1990).

Using irony in a narrating activity, Pero critiques the situation in a society where he and his peers are monitoring threats to the local maintenance of the society, which several reported is being bought by foreign companies, taking away supports that were supposed to be there for children only to see them transformed into something like the past. Not only does Pero mention a dilemma of becoming "mature and ready for the world," but he also expresses characteristics now associated with the past, "a strict hierarchy on the job, becoming part of a whole, and subjection to the group," which this young market-oriented generation has centrally in its sights.

When human development is the focus of research and practice in the context of political violence and transition, the focus can be on how progress through maturation may be delayed or damaged. When we zoom back to broader sociopolitical relations, however, as we have here, it becomes clear that defining "child" and "youth" in primarily biological terms offers a partial picture. Theories focusing on cultural differences also reveal the limits of biological explanations, in particular because child soldiers appear to heal after the same kinds of cleansing rituals that work for adults in their cultures (Honwana, 2006). Maturational theories that analyze children's cognitive, social, and emotional capacities in terms of physical features of sexual, neural, and other biological organs offer important and consistent insights about certain types of interactions in the world. Recent sociocognitive neuroscience has, moreover, shown that while neurological changes occur after puberty, effects on reasoning and/or behavior also appear to be context sensitive (Lerner, Freund and DeStefannis, 2001; Powell, 2006). Thus, without ignoring mood changes, the focus is most sensibly on individuals' interactions with their material and social environments.

Across the previous chapters in this book, we have focused on different aspects of this interaction with the environment of political violence and transition, yielding a range of related developmental processes. We now consider these engaged processes during adolescence and young adulthood in relation to maturation-based ones that have been applied to conflict, such as perspective taking and executive functioning. In particular, mediation is a process young people use to address threat–opportunity complexes. Young people's mediation of specific environmental factors via discursive activities involves development as a goal as well as a process. With this focus on activity in context, the figure of child–youth shifts from one who is a less-than, vulnerable, evolving being to one who is purposefully involved. Although specifics of this mediation process change in relation to biological maturation, limits to the process itself may occur primarily during infancy and early childhood. Such context-specific mediation relies on biological independence, neural complexity, and, perhaps, chemical energies of puberty, but correlates like identity that have been posited as universal obsessions of adolescence are likely to be much more context dependent than we have previously thought.

Although a major fear may be that societal violence interrupts or damages children and youth growing up in the midst, it may be the case that protecting children from knowing what happens is more damaging than knowledge. If development is the mediation of circumstances, then children who are aware have better chances than those who are protected. Broadening to the figure of violent societies, rather than the figure of violent and damaged children helps us generate new models for research and practice. We see from the analyses presented in this book that young people are sensitive to the explicit and implicit expectations of contexts where they interact. If nothing else, these analyses should indicate that human development is about the nature of those interactions and the cultural tools that we use to mediate those interactions. Practice-based research consistent with this new approach can, moreover, provide alternative activities in times of crisis as well as information to advance our understanding of human development. In situations where specific threats and opportunities define daily life, we learn more from considering how young people use cultural artifacts, including the symbol of war, to identify those threats and opportunities to the goals most salient to them. A major goal that has emerged by listening to youth in the study discussed herein is the goal of development itself. Pero, like many other youth, used irony to observe that society and children can regress when they should be developing together. Can those of us who listen to the stories of Pero and his peers take up his challenge to understand and promote child development, as well as our own?

Examples of Public Stories across Positions in the DSTY Research Workshop

SUMMARY OF THE PUBLIC STORY IN THE UNITED STATES

The public story for the workshop revolves around the contentious nature of policies and perspectives related to immigration, especially illegal immigration, to the United States after 9/11. The catalytic event for youth activism related to these issues was a game created, publicized, and enacted by the Young Republicans at New York University. Students who were opposed to the game and the views it represented at their university organized a demonstration and teach-in to expose the game. Organizers of the protest against the "Catch an Illegal Immigrant" game invited university officials, professors, and student leaders representing a range of perspectives on the issue. News sources used as resources for our public-story activity included comments by those participants in the demonstration, as well as by several people in the crowd. After reading the story, participants in the DSTY workshop were invited to discuss their views about the various participants in the demonstration.

SUMMARY OF THE PUBLIC STORY IN CROATIA

The public story for the workshop revolves around the contentious issue of tightening controls on the public media, especially electronic media, in the country, which is at odds with progress toward democracy and entrance to the EU (Goehring, 2007). The catalytic event for youth activism related to these issues was the expulsion of one of the first female members of the national board of media policy, which raised issues of social inclusion as well as renewed government control of the media. A public protest in the major square of the capital revolved around the central issues of government control and pressure for young people to be more directly involved in media policy and programming. Because this issue had emerged independently among young people in previous workshops as well as in some newspapers, it seemed appropriate for youth in rural as well as urban areas of the country. After reading the story, participants in the DST workshop were invited to discuss their views about the various participants in the demonstration.

SUMMARY OF THE PUBLIC STORY IN BIH

The public story for the workshop revolves around the contentious issue of the government being divided into two entities by ethnic groups (Bosnians and Serbs), which was a provision for settling the war in 1995. The catalytic event for youth activism related to these issues was a current proposal to organize the government structure into three entities to account for the third major ethnic group living in and returning to the country (Croatians). Political science students at the university organized a teach-in for young people to discuss relevant issues, specifically myths related to ethnic separatism in the country.

SUMMARY OF THE PUBLIC STORY IN SERBIA

The public story for the workshop revolves around the contentious issue of the former president, Slobodan Milosevic, regaining control in the height of the war. The catalytic event for youth activism related to those issues was election fraud and Milosevic's seizing control of the media. Students at the University of Belgrade organized a protest to demand free and unbiased elections; a reported one hundred thousand turned out in support of the demonstration. Public support was in favor of a peaceful movement toward democracy, but there was a range of positions expressed in reports of the event. After reading the story, participants in the DSTY workshop were invited to discuss their views about the various participants in the demonstration.

REFERENCES

Abraham, N., & Torok, M. (1994). *The shell and the kernel: Renewals of psychoanalysis.* Chicago: University of Chicago Press.

Akinwumi, O. (2006). Youth participation in violence in Nigeria since the 1980s. In C. Daiute, Z. Beykont, C. Higson-Smith, & L. Nucci (Eds.), *International perspectives on youth conflict and development* (pp. 73–85). New York: Oxford University Press.

Amnesty International (5-6-08). Available at thereport.amnesty.org/eng/ Regions/Europe-and-Central-Asia/Bosnia/Croatia/Serbia.

Amsterdam, A., & Bruner, J. *Minding the law: How courts rely on story-telling and how their stories change the way we understand the law and ourselves.* Cambridge, MA: Harvard University Press.

Apfel, R., & Simon, B. (1996). *Minefields in their hearts.* New Haven, CT: Yale University Press.

Arnett, J. J. (2004). *Emerging adulthood: The winding road from the late teens through the twenties.* New York: Oxford University Press.

Bajraktari, Y., & Serwer, D. (2006). Explaining the Yugoslav catastrophe: The quest for a common narrative. *USI Peace Briefing.* Washington, DC: Center for Postconflict Peace and Stability Operations at the U.S. Institute of Peace.

Bakhtin, M. M. (1935/1981). Discourse in the novel. In M. Holquist (Ed.); C. Emerson & M. Holquist (Translators), *The dialogic imagination: Four essays by M. M. Bakhtin* (pp. 259–422). Austin: University of Texas Press.

Bakhtin, M. M. (1986). The problem of speech genres. In C. Emerson, & M. Holquist (Eds.), *Speech genres and other late essays* (pp. 60–102). Austin: University of Texas Press.

Bamberg, M. (2004). Positioning with Davie Hogan. In C. Daiute & C. Lightfoot (Eds.), *Narrative analysis: Studying the development of individuals in society* (pp. 135–158). Thousand Oaks, CA: Sage Publications.

Bamberg, M. (2006). Stories: Big or small. Why do we care? *Narrative Inquiry*, 16:1, 139–147.

Barber, B. (Ed.) (2009). *Adolescents and war: How youth deal with political violence*. New York: Oxford University Press.

Beah, I. (2007). *A long way gone: Memoirs of a boy soldier*. New York: Farrar, Straus, Giroux.

Bereiter, C., & Scardamalia, M. (1987). *The psychology of written composition*. Hillsdale, NJ: Lawrence Erlbaum Associates.

Berman, L. (1999). Positioning in the formation of a 'national' identity. In R. Harre & L. van Langenhove (Eds.), *Positioning theory: Moral contexts of intentional action* (pp. 138–159). Malden, MA: Blackwell Publishers, Ltd.

Berman, R., & Slobin, D. I. (1994). *Relating events in narrative: A cross-linguistic developmental study*. Mahwah, NJ: Lawrence Erlbaum Associates.

Bieber, F., & Wieland, C. (Eds.) (2005). *Facing the past facing the future: Confronting ethnicity and conflict in Bosnia and former Yugoslavia*. Ravenna, IT: Longo Editore Ravenna.

Biesta, G. (2007). Education and the democratic person: Towards a political conception of democratic education. *Teachers College Record*, 109:3, 740–769.

Billig, M. (1995). *Banal nationalism*. Thousand Oaks, CA: Sage Publications.

Bloome, D., Shuart-Faris, N., Carter, S., Christian, B., Madrid, S., Otto, S. (2008). *On Discourse Analysis in Classrooms*. New York: Teachers College Press.

Bonanno, G. L. (2004). Loss, trauma, and human resilience. *American Psychologist*, 59, 20–28.

Botero, P.; Calle, A.; Daiute, C; Lugo, N. V.; Pinilla, V. E.; Ríos; D.; Col. (2004–2007). Narratives on the cultural and socio-political conflict from male and female youth in local Colombian contexts (University of Manizales, CINDE, FESCO, CUNY).

Boyden, J. (2003). The moral development of child soldiers: What do adults have to fear? *Pease and Conflict: Journal of Peace Psychology*, 9:4, 343–362).

Boyden, J. (2009). Why the current fascination with children and armed conflict? Public Debate with C. Daiute. *Children's lives and development during war and armed conflict*. Coventry, UK: University of Warwick.

Boyden, J., & Mann, G. (2005). *Children's risk, resilience, and coping in extreme situations*. In M. Ungar (Ed.), *Handbook for working with children and youth: Pathways to resilience across cultures and contexts* (pp. 3–26). Thousand Oaks, CA: Sage Publications.

Brown, B. B., & Larson, R. W. (2002). The kaleidoscope of adolescence: Experiences of the world's youth at the beginning of the 21st century. In B. B. Brown, R. W. Larson, & T. S. Saraswathi (Eds.), *The world's youth: Adolescence in eight regions of the world* (pp. 1–20). New York: Cambridge University Press.

Bruner, J. S. (1986). *Actual minds, possible worlds.* Cambrtidge, MA: Harvard University Press.

Bruner, J. S. (1990). *Acts of meaning.* Cambridge, MA: Harvard University Press.

Bruner, J. S. (2002). *Making stories: Law, literature, life.* New York: Farrar, Straus, & Giroux.

Burton, L. M., & Graham, J. E. (1998). Neighborhood rhythms and the social activities of adolescent mothers. In A. C. Crouter & R. Larson (Eds.), *Temporal rhythms in adolescence: Clocks, calendars, and the coordination of daily life.* (pp. 7–22) San Francisco, CA: Jossey–Bass.

Caruth, C. (1996). *Unclaimed experience: Trauma, narrative, and history.* Baltimore, MD: The Johns Hopkins Press.

Case, R. (1985). *Intellectual development: Birth to adulthood.* New York: Academic Press.

Cole, E. A., & Barasalou (2006). Unite or divide?: The challenges of teaching history in societies emerging from violent conflict. Special Report 163. Washington, D.C.: United States Institute of Peace.

Coles, R. (1986). *The political life of children.* New York: Atlantic Monthly Press.

Collier, P. (2003). *Breaking the conflict trap: Civil war and development policy.* Washington, DC: The International Bank for Reconstruction and Development/The World Bank.

Cross, W. E., Jr. (1991). *Shades of black.* Philadelphia, PA: Temple University Press.

Cross, W. E., Jr., & Fhagen-Smith, P. (2001). Patterns of African American identity development: A life space perspective. In C. L. Wijeyesinghe & B. W. Jackson (Eds.), *New perspectives on racial identity development* (pp. 243–270). New York: New York University Press.

Daiute, C. (2004). Creative uses of cultural genres. In C. Daiute & C. Lightfoot (Eds.), *Narrative analysis: Studying the development of individuals in society* (pp. 111–133). Thousand Oaks, CA: Sage Publications.

Daiute, C. (2006). Stories of conflict and development in U.S. public schools." In C. Daiute, Z. Beykont, C. Higson-Smith, & L. Nucci (Eds.), *International perspectives on youth conflict and development* (pp. 207–224). New York: Oxford University Press.

Daiute, C. (2007). *Dynamic story-telling by youth across the former Yugoslavia* (Guide to a research workshop curriculum). New York: The Graduate Center, CUNY.

Daiute, C. (2008). *Alternatives to trauma as adolescent responses to war.* Paper presented at the Annual Meeting of the Jean Piaget Society, Quebec City, June.

Daiute, C. (2009a). Young people and armed conflict. In A. Furlong (Ed.), *Handbook of youth and young adulthood.* London: Routledge.

Daiute, C. (2009b). Developmental understandings of the effects of war. Public debate with J. Boyden: *Children's lives and development during war and armed conflict.* Coventry, UK: University of Warwick.

Daiute, C. (2010a). Commentary: Adolescents' purposeful uses of culture. In C. Lightfoot & C. Milbrath (Eds.), *Art and human development* (pp. 167–182). New York: Taylor and Francis.

Daiute, C. (2010b). Critical narrating by adolescents growing up in war: Case study across the former Yugoslavia. In K. McLean, & Monisha Pasupathi (Eds), *Narrative development in adolescence* (pp. 207–230). New York: Springer.

Daiute, C., & Nelson, K. A. (1997). Making sense of the sense-making function of narrative evaluation. *Journal of Narrative and Life History,* 7:(1–4), 207–215.

Daiute, C., Buteau, E., & Rawlins, C. (2001). Social relational wisdom: Developmental diversity in children's written narratives about social conflict. *Narrative Inquiry,* 11:2, 1–30.

Daiute, C., Stern, R., & Lelutiu-Weinberger, C. (2003). Negotiating violence prevention. *Journal of Social Issues,* 59, 83–101.

Daiute, C., & Lucic, L. (2008). *A cultural-historical analysis of migration out of war.* Paper presented at the Convention of the International Society of Cultural Historical Activity Research, San Diego, CA.

Daiute, C., & Turniski, M. (2005). Young people's stories of conflict in post-war Croatia. *Narrative Inquiry,* 15:2, 217–239.

Daiute, C., Beykont, Z. Higson-Smith, C., & Nucci, L. (Eds.) (2006). *International Perspectives on Youth Conflict and Development.* New York: Oxford University Press.

Damon, W., Lerner, R., & Eisenberg, N. (Eds.) (2006). *Handbook of child psychology.* Vol. III. *Social, emotional, and personality development, 6th Edition.* New York: Wiley Blackwell.

Dewey, J. (1929). *Democracy and education: An introduction to the philosophy of education.* New York: The Free Press.

Dyson, A. H., & Genishi, C. (2005). *On the case.* New York: Teachers College Press.

Earls, A., & Carlson, M. (1999). Children at the margins of society. *New Directions in Child and Adolescent Development*, 85, 71–82.

Elkonin, D. B. (1971/2000). Toward the problem of stages in the mental development of children. *Psychology of Marxism Internet Archive (www. Marxists.org).*

Elliot, D. S., Hamburg, B. A., & Williams, K. R. (Eds.) (1998). *Violence in American schools.* New York: Cambridge University Press.

Engestrom, Y. (2009). The future of activity theory: A rough draft. In A. Sannino, H. Daniels, & K. Guitierrez (Eds.), *Learning and expanding with activity theory.* New York: Cambridge University Press.

Engestrom, Y., Miettinen, R., & Punamaki, R.-L. (1999). *Perspectives on activity theory.* New York: Cambridge University Press.

Erikson, E. H. (1980). *Identity and the life cycle.* New York: W.W. Norton & Company.

Filipovic, Z. (2006). *Zlata's diary: A child's life in wartime Sarajevo.* New York: Penguin.

Flanagan, C. A., Gallay, L. S., Sukhdeep, G., Gallay, E., & Nti, N. (2005). What does democracy mean? Correlates to adolescents' views. *Journal of Adolescent Research*, 20, 193–218.

Foucault, M. (2001). *The order of things: Archaeology of the human sciences.* New York: Routledge.

Freedman, S. W., & Abazovic, D. (2006). Growing up during the Balkan Wars of the 1990s. In C. Daiute, Z. Beykont, C. Higson-Smith, & L. Nucci (Eds.), *International perspectives on youth conflict and development* (pp. 57–72). New York: Oxford University Press.

Freud, S. (1909). *Five lectures on psychoanalysis.* New York: Norton.

Gagnon, V. P., Jr. (2004). *The myth of ethnic war: Serbia and Croatia in the 1990s.* Ithaca, NY: Cornell University Press.

Gilligan, C. (1993). *In a different voice: Psychological theory and women's development.* Cambridge, MA: Harvard University Press.

Goehring, J. (Ed). (2007). *Nations in transit: Democratization from Central Europe to Aurasia.* New York: Freedom House, Inc.

Gordy, E. D. (2005). What does it mean to break with the past? In F. Bieber & C. Wieland (Eds.), *Facing the past facing the future: Confronting ethnicity and conflict in Bosnia and former Yugoslavia* (pp. 85–101). Ravenna, IT: Longo Editore Ravenna.

Graves, D. H. (2003). *Writing: Teachers and children at work, 20th anniversary edition.* Portsmouth, NH: Heinemann.

Hammack, P. L. (2008). Narrative and the cultural psychology of identity. *Personality and Social Psychology Review*, 12, 222–245.

Harre, R., & van Langenhove, L. (Eds.) (1999). *Positioning theory: Moral contexts of intentional action.* Malden, MA: Blackwell Publishers, Ltd.

Hart, R. A. (1999). *Children's participation: The theory and practice of including young citizens in community development and environmental care.* New York: UNICEF.

Heft, H. (2007). The social constitution of perceiver-environment reciprocity. *Ecological Psychology,* 19:2, 85–105.

Helwig, C. C., Arnold, M. L., Tan, D., & Boyd, D. (2007). Mainland Chinese and Canadian adolescents' judgments and reasoning about the fairness of democratic and other forms of government. *Cognitive Development,* 22, 96–109.

Hermans, H. J. M., & Hermans-Jansen, E. (2001). *Self-narratives: The construction of meaning in psychotherapy.* New York: Guildford Press.

Higson-Smith, C. (2006). Youth violence in South Africa: The impact of political transition." In. C. Daiute, Z. Beykont, C. Higson-Smith, & L. Nucci (Eds.), *International perspectives on youth conflict and development* (pp. 177–193). New York: Oxford University Press.

Holland, D., Lachiotte, W., Skinner, D., & Cain, C. (1998). *Identity and agency in cultural worlds.* Cambridge, MA: Harvard University Press.

Honwana, A., & De Boeck, F. (Eds.) (2005). *Makers and Breakers: Children and Youth in Postcolonial Africa.* Oxford, UK: James Currey Publishers.

Honwana, A. (2006). Child soldiers: Community healing and rituals in Mozambique and Angola. In C. Daiute, Z. Beykont, C. Higson-Smith, & L. Nucci (Eds.), *International perspectives on youth conflict and development* (pp. 225–245). New York: Oxford University Press.

Hyder, T. (2005). *War, conflict, and play.* New York: Open University Press.

Inter-Agency Standing Committee (IASC) (2007). *IASC Guidelines on mental health and psychosocial support in emergency settings.* Geneva: IASC.

Johnstone, D. (2002). *Fools' crusade: Yugoslavia, NATO, and Western delusions.* New York: Monthly Review Press.

Knight-Abowitz, N., & Harnish, J. (2006). Contemporary discourses of citizenship. *Review of Educational Research,* 76:4, 653–690.

Kovac-Cerovic, T., Popadic, D., Knezevic, G., & Matkovic, G. (2006). *Analysis of conflicts in Serbia: Final report.* Belgrade: CAFOD, Just One World.

Labov, W., & Waletzky, J. (1997). Narrative analysis: Oral versions of personal experience. *Journal of Narrative and Life History,* 7, 3–38.

Lazic, M. (1999). *Protest in Belgrade: Winter of discontent.* Budapest: Central European University Press.

Lee, C. D., & Smagorinsky, P. (Eds.) (2000). *Vygotskian perspectives on literacy research: Constructing meaning through collaborative inquiry.* New York: Cambridge University Press.

Lee, C. D. (2010). Every shut eye ain't sleep: Modeling the "scientific" from the "everyday" as cultural practices. In C. Lightfoot & C. Milbrath (Eds.), *Arts and human development* (pp. 139–166). New York: Taylor & Francis.

Lelutiu-Weinberger, C. (2007). Transforming formal learning through educational permeability to student knowledge. Dissertation. New York: The Graduate Center, City University of New York.

Leont'ev, A. N. (1978). *Activity, consciousness, and personality.* Englewood Cliffs, NJ: Prentice-Hall.

Lerner, R. M., Freund, A. M., DeStefanis, I. (2001). Understanding developmental regulation in adolescence: the use of the selection, optimization, and compensation model. *Human Development,* 44:1, 29–50.

Lewin, K. (1951). *Field theory in social science: Selected theoretical papers.* D. Cartwright (Ed.). New York: Harper & Row.

MacDonald, D. B. (2002). *Balkan holocausts?: Serbian and Croatian victim-centered propaganda and the war in Yugoslavia.* Manchester, UK: Manchester University Press.

McLean, K. C., & Pratt, M. W. (2006). Life's little (and big) lessons: Identity statuses and meaning-making in the turning-point narratives of emerging adults. *Developmental Psychology,* 42:4, 714–722.

McMahon, P. (2009). *Much ado about nothing? Civil society and the NGO embrace in Bosnia.* Paper presented at the Association for the Study of Nationalities (ASN) 2009 World Convention. Available at www.nationalities.org.

Miller, P. J., Hoogstra, L., Mintz, J., Fung, H., & Williams, K. (1993). Troubles in the garden and how they get resolved: A young child's transformation of his favorite story. In C. A. Nelson (Ed.), *Memory and affect in development* (Vol. 26, pp. 87–114). Hillsdale, NJ: Lawrence Erlbaum Associates.

Nelson, K. (2003). Narrative and self, myth and memory: Emergence of the cultural self. In R. Fivush & C. Haden (Eds.), *The development of autobiographical memory: Memory and self-understanding* (pp. 3–28). Mahwah, NJ: Lawrence Erlbaum Associates.

Nelson, K. (2007). *Young minds in social worlds: Experience, meaning, and memory.* Cambridge, MA: Harvard University Press.

Nilan, P., & Feixa, C. (Eds.) (2006). *Global youth?: Hybrid identites, plural worlds.* New York: Routledge.

Pennebaker, J. W. (1997). *Opening up: The healing power of expressing emotions.* New York: Guilford Press.

Peterson-Badali, M., & Ruck, M. (2008). Studying children's perspectives on self-determination and nurturance rights: Methodological issues and challenges. *Journal of Social Issues,* 64:4, 749–769.

Piaget, J. (1968). *Six psychological studies.* New York: Random House.

Polivanova, K. N. (2006). On the problem of the leading activity in adolescence. *Journal of Russian and Eastern European Psychology,* 44:5, 78–84.

Polkinghorne, D. (1991). Narrative and self-concept. *Journal of Narrative and Life History,* 1, 135–153.

Popadic, D. (Ed.) (2000). *Introduction to peace studies.* Washington, DC: United States Institute of Peace.

Posada, R., & Wainryb, C. (2008). Moral development in a violent society: Colombian children's judgments in the context of survival and revenge. *Child Development,* 79:4, 882–898.

Powell, K. (2006). Neurodevelopment: How does the teenage brain work? *Nature,* 422, 865–867.

Ricoeur, P. (1984). *Time and narrative.* Vols. I and II. Chicago, IL: University of Chicago Press.

Ruck, M. D., Abramovitch, R., & Keating, D. P. (1998). Children's and adolescents' understanding of rights: Balancing nurturance and self-determination. *Child Development,* 64:2, 404–417.

Rutter, M. L. (1997). Nature-nurture integration: The example of antisocial behavior. *American Psychologist,* 52:4, 390–398.

Salomon, G. (2004). A narrative-based view of coexistence education. *Journal of Social Issues,* 60:2, 271–288.

Scott, J. C. (1990). *Behind the official story: Domination and the arts of resistance.* New Haven, CT: Yale University Press.

Searle, J. R. (1970). *Speech acts: Essays on the philosophy of language.* New York: Cambridge University Press.

Selman, R., Watts, C., & Schultz, L. H. (1997). *Fostering friendship: Pair therapy for treatment and prevention.* New York: Aldine.

Sherrod, L. (2003). Promoting the development of citizenship in diverse youth. *Political Science & Politics,* 36:2, 287–292.

Silber, L., & Little, A. (1995). *The death of Yugoslavia.* London: Penguin, BBC Books.

Smagorinsky, P. (Ed.) (2006). *Research on Composition: Multiple Perspectives on Two Decades of Change.* New York: Teachers College Press.

Solis, J. (2004). Narrating and counter-narrating illegality as an identity. In C. Daiute & C. Lightfoot (Eds.), *Narrative analysis: Studying the development of individuals in society* (pp. 181–200). Thousand Oaks, CA: Sage Publications.

Spajic-Vrkas, V. (2003a, July). *Project Education for Democratic Citizenship: From policy to effective practice through quality assurance. Stocktaking in*

Southeast Europe Country Report: Croatia. Zagreb: Research and Training Center for Human Rights and Democratic Citizenship, Faculty of Philosophy, University of Zagreb.

Spajic-Vrkas, V. (2003b, August). *All-European study on policies for Education for Democratic Citizenship (EDC): Croatia.* Council of Europe, doc. DGIV/EDU/CIT (2001) 45 Croatia.

Srna, J. (2005). Towards reconciling with ourselves and others. *Psihologija,* 38:2, 117–132.

Sta. Maria, M. A. (2006). Paths to Filipino youth involvement in violent conflict. In C. Daiute, Z. Beykont, C. Higson-Smith, & L. Nucci (Eds.), *International perspectives on youth conflict and development* (pp. 29–42). New York: Oxford University Press.

Stetsenko, A., & Arievitch, I. M. (2004). The self in cultural–historical activity theory: Reclaiming the unity of social and individual dimensions of human development. *Theory and Psychology,* 14:4, 475–503.

Suarez-Orozco, C., Suarez-Orozco, M., & Todorova, I. (2004). Wandering souls: The interpersonal concerns of adolescent immigrants. In G. A. DeVos & E. DeVos (Eds.), *Cross-cultural dimensions in conscious thought: Narrative themes in comparative context* (pp. 463–495). London, UK: Rowman & Littlefield Publishers, Inc.

Summerfield, D. (1999). A critique of seven assumptions behind psychological trauma programmes in war-affected areas. *Social Science and Medicine,* 48, 1449–1462.

Tanner, M. (1997). *Croatia: A nation forged in war.* New Haven, CT: Yale University Press.

Thorne, A., McLean, K. C., & Lawrence, A. M. (2004). When remembering is not enough: Reflecting on self-defining memories in late-adolescence. *Journal of Personality,* 72:3, 513–542.

Tomasello, M. (2005). *Constructing a language: A usage-based theory of language acquisition.* Cambridge, MA: Harvard University Press.

Torney-Purta, J., Schwille, J., & Amadeo, J.-A. (Eds.) (1999). *Civic education across countries: Twenty-four national case studies from the IEA Civic Education project.* Amsterdam: The International Association for the Evaluation of Educational Achievement.

Turiel, E. (2002). *The culture of morality.* New York: Cambridge University Press.

Ukeje, C. (2006). Youth movements and youth violence in Nigeria's delta region. In C. Daiute, Z. Beykont, C. Higson-Smith, & L. Nucci (Eds.), *International perspectives on youth conflict and development* (pp. 289–304). New York: Oxford University Press.

United Nations Convention on the Rights of the Child (1989). Available at www.crin.org and elsewhere.

United Nations High Commission of Refugees (2008). Available at www .unhcr.org/statistics.html.

Veresov, N. (2006). Leading activity in developmental psychology. *Journal of Russian and East European Psychology*, 44:5, 7–25.

Vygotsky, L. S. (1978). *Mind in society: The development of higher order thinking.* Cambridge, MA: Harvard University Press.

Vygotsky, L. S. (1998). Pedology of the adolescent. In R. W. Rieber (Ed.), *The collected works of L.S. Vygotsky.* Vol. 5. *Child psychology* (pp. 3–84). New York: Kluwer Academic/Plenum Publishers.

Wainryb, C., & Turiel, E. (1994). Dominance, subordination, and concepts of personal entitlements in cultural contexts. *Child Development*, 65, 1701–1722.

Walker, P. C. (1998). *Voices of love and freedom: A literacy-based ethics and prevention program.* Iowa City: Prescription Learning.

Ware, A. (2006). *Latina mothers' parenting and girls' anxiety and depression in an urban sample: Associations with ethnic identity and neighborhood.* Dissertation Abstracts. New York: The Graduate Center, City University of New York.

Weine, S. (2004). *When history is a nightmare.* New Haven, CT: Yale University Press.

Weine, S. (2006). *Testimony after catastrophe: Narrating the trauma of political violence.* Chicago, IL: Northwestern University Press.

Wertsch, J. (2002). *Voices of collective remembering.* New York: Cambridge University Press.

Widom, C. S. (1989). Does violence beget violence? A critical examination of the literature. *Psychological Bulletin*, 106:1, 3–28.

Winnicott, D. W. (1971). *Playing and reality.* New York: Basic Books.

Winnicott, C., Shepherd, R., & Davis, M. (Eds.) (1989). *Psychoanalytic explorations: D. W. Winnicott.* Cambridge, MA: Harvard University Press.

Woodward, S. L. (1995). *Balkan tragedy: Chaos and dissolution after the Cold War.* Washington, DC: Brookings Institute Press.

www.crin.org

www.un.org

www.unhcr.org

www.unhcr.org/basics.html, February 9, 2009

www.worldbank.org/website/external/state/statistics

www.worldhealth.org

www.state.gov

Youniss, J., Bales, S., Christmas-Best, V., Diversi, M., McLaughlin, M., & Silbereisen, R. (2003). Youth civic engagement in the 21st century. In R. Larson, B. Bradford Brown, & J. Mortimer (Eds.), *Adolescents' preparation for the future: Perils and promise.* (pp. 121–148). Ann Arbor, MI: The Society for Research on Adolescence.

Zentella, A. C. (2005). *Building on strengths: Language and literacy in Latino families and communities.* New York: Teachers College Press.

INDEX